New Directions in
Educational Evaluation

New Directions in Educational Evaluation

Edited and
Introduced by

Ernest R. House

The Falmer Press

(A member of the Taylor & Francis Group)
London and Philadelphia

UK   The Falmer Press, Falmer House, Barcombe, Lewes, East Sussex, BN8 5DL

USA   The Falmer Press, Taylor & Francis Inc., 242 Cherry Street, Philadelphia, PA 19106-1906

First published 1986

Library of Congress Cataloging in Publication Data

Main entry under title:

New directions in educational evaluation.

    1. Education—United States—Evaluation—Addresses, essays, lectures. 2. Education—Research—United States —Addresses, essays, lectures. 3. Curriculum planning— United States—Evaluation—Addresses, essays, lectures. I. House, Ernest R.
LA217.N48   1985   370′.973   85-6742
ISBN 0-85000-047-6 (pbk.)
ISBN 0-85000-048-4

Typeset in 10½/12 Plantin by
Imago Publishing Ltd, Thame, Oxon

Printed in Great Britain by Taylor & Francis (Printers) Ltd, Basingstoke

Contents

Contents

*For Tom Hastings
who saw the flaws and
pioneered a new beginning*

Acknowledgements

The Publishers are grateful to the following for permission to reproduce copyright material:

Review of Educational Research for Nevo, D. 'The conceptualization of educational evaluation', Vol. 53, No. 1, 1983; and Darling-Hammond, L., Wise, A. and Pease, S. 'Teacher evaluation in the organizational context: a review of the literature', Vol. 53, No. 3, 1983.

Jossey Bass for House, E. (1983) 'How we think about evaluation' from *New Directions for Program Evaluation*, No. 19; Weiss, C. (1983) 'The stakeholder approach to evaluation' from *New Directions for Program Evaluation*, No. 17; Farrar, E. and House, E. (1983) 'The evaluation of Push/Excel: a case study' from *New Directions in Program Evaluation*, No. 17; and Weiss, C. (1983) 'Toward the future of stakeholder approaches in evaluation' from *New Directions in Program Evaluations*, No. 17.

Australian Educational Research Association, publishers of Australian *Educational Research*, for 'Evaluation as a paradigm for educational research', Vol. 00, No. 00, 1983.

Taylor and Francis Ltd, publishers of the *Journal of Curriculum Studies*, for 'Three good reasons for not doing case studies in curriculum research', Vol. 15, No. 2, 1983; and 'Seven principles for programme evaluation in curriculum development and innovation', Vol. 14, No. 3, 1982.

General Editor's Preface

Measuring the outcomes of educational practices is a modern phenomenon. Valuing their worth is as old as philosophy itself. It is the singular
value of this collection of papers set in context and introduced by Ernest
House that it holds in dynamic equilibrium both the measurement and the
valuing sides of educational evaluation.

There are few more fitted by experience, cool-tempered intellect and
humane sensitivity than Ernest House to provide the conspectus of the
educational evaluation scene that this book offers. Within its covers the
student will find the theoretical analysis of educational evaluation in its
several meanings, suggested practices, cautionary tales and the new
frontier, nor is the controversial issue of the evaluation of teaching
avoided. The specialist will also find much, not least a critical and
challenging appreciation of educational evaluation theory and practice as
it faces the problems of the final decades of the twentieth century.

There can be little doubt that educational evaluation is here to stay. It
has not only entered the academic bloodstream, it has become a tool of
government policy and decision-making. It is these twin facts that make
this book a primer for all concerned with education. They could not be
better served.

Philip Taylor
Birmingham
July 1985

1
Introduction:
Evaluation and Legitimacy

Evaluation and Legitimacy

Ernest R. House

Over the past two decades or so, education evaluation has evolved as a field of intellectual endeavor complete with its own theorists, controversies, journals, and conferences. For example, at the 1984 annual meeting of the Evaluation Conference in San Francisco, 600 people attended, and this was only a fraction of the total number engaged in evaluating educational programs. Most of this activity has centered on the United States, but there is considerable interest in Britain, Canada, Australia, some northern European countries, and a nascent interest in Latin America and Asia.

There was, of course, formal evaluation of education prior to the 1960s, embodied primarily in the regional accreditation organizations in the United States and the Inspectorate in Britain. In the late 1950s and early 1960s, however, the development of the so-called new curricula, such as the new maths and new science, generated an interest in social science evaluation of these curricula. The Elementary and Secondary Education Act passed by the US Congress in 1965 required that all Title I (economically disadvantaged student) programs be evaluated. This requirement engendered a flood of evaluation activities.

Eventually, an evaluation mandate was placed upon most federal social programs in the United States. In other countries evaluation has not been mandated across the board but has been initiated for particular programs. As a result a sizable evaluation establishment has come into being with its own organizations, publications, institutions, and ways of behaving. The purpose of this book is to bring the reader up to date with some of the most pressing issues and controversies in this rapidly developing field, although no single book could possibly do justice to all the evaluation developments now underway.

As I have indicated, the overwhelming number of evaluation activities are in the United States, and the Reagan administration has had a strong influence on evaluation, indirectly by cutting back the funding of social programs. Since evaluations have been tied directly to social programs, this has meant a significant decline in the number of evaluations undertaken. The field of evaluation is no longer permeated by the boom town atmosphere that it once was, and this decline has led to a more sober and pessimistic view of the future, perhaps the inevitable outcome of all recessions. One can say unequivocally that evaluation is intimately tied to the initiatives of governments, and that shifts in government policies can result in significant changes in evaluation practices in a particular country or region. To put it another way, if evaluation is the watchdog of the public welfare, as some would have it, then it is a securely leashed watchdog.

A second significant development is in the social role that evaluation is expected to play. In the United States, at least, public education is being subjected to yet another round of industrialization. The immediate pressure stems from the harshly critical reports of several national commissions and the actions of state governors and legislators. American education is being transformed by so-called scientific management techniques, also called Tylorism. This trend is most clearly manifested in a massive employment of standardized tests — tests to promote students from one grade to another, to certify graduation from high school, to allow older students to enter teacher training, and to certify teachers when they finish training. In addition, experienced teachers are being evaluated to determine their competency and to assign them merit pay. In this social transformation evaluators are often designing, implementing, and monitoring the necessary evaluation machinery. This monitoring role is akin to the role of efficiency engineers in the scientific management movement, and I believe is a further extension of that movement. Of course, this shift in the role of what evaluators do also changes the content of evaluation.

I do not perceive this trend towards strong accountability policies in other countries at this time. In fact, in some parts of Australia there is movement in the opposite direction, towards action research and teachers controlling their own evaluation. Whether the industrialization of American education spreads to other countries or remains another manifestation of the American mania for technology, I do not know. It does seem to me that we may witness in the United States, at least, the industrial transformation of vast sectors of society, such as education and health care, that have never been fully rationalized in the industrial sense, and evaluation is playing an instrumental role in that transformation and is being transformed itself in the process.

Several of the chapters in this book reflect this social transformation. For example, in the first chapter Nevo tries to order the issues now current in the evaluation literature and finds that there is a lack of consensus among evaluation theorists concerning the social-political role of evaluation. In the second chapter I analyze the conceptual structure of one of the most widely-used evaluation textbooks and find it to be based extensively on deep-seated metaphors of industrial production so that the criteria for judging social programs are efficiency and effectiveness. In the last chapter in the book, which deals with teacher evaluation, the authors contend that the evaluation of teachers differs depending upon whether one sees teaching as labor, craft, profession, or art. If one sees teaching as labor, as a set of standard operating procedures planned and programmed by administrators, then evaluation becomes direct monitoring of teacher performance according to set standards. This is the direction American evaluation is currently taking.

The reader interested in evaluation would do well to keep this developing drama in mind since evaluation will be affected differently in countries where this trend is and is not occurring. Perhaps I should add that the industrialization of education is not a trend of which I approve nor a use of evaluation which I endorse. But my resistance to these events seems to have no bearing upon their realization.

An issue of long standing in the study of evaluation is the connection between fact and value. The traditional position of positive social science, of course, is that fact and value are quite separate and that it is the evaluator's job to ascertain the facts and the clients and the sponsors and the public will place value upon these facts. Hence, the evaluator is in a value-free or a value-neutral position. This value-neutral position is manifested in many different ways in the extant approaches to evaluation. The distinction between fact and value is one of the most fundamental to evaluation, and to social science, and it is now under serious attack.

At least two of the papers here directly reflect dissatisfaction with the traditional fact-value dichotomy and the consequent role for the evaluator. Scriven asserts that all social science is in fact value-based and that researchers had best adopt the evaluation paradigm for all educational research. According to Scriven, ascertaining the value of something is quite analogous to ascertaining a fact about something and can be accomplished just as objectively as the determination of fact. The determination of the worth of various approaches and teaching techniques is precisely what the educational researcher should be doing.

For her part Kirkup claims that she has tried various approaches to evaluation and has found them wanting, particularly when she deals with a controversial and value-laden area like women's studies. Her radical solution is to abandon the burden of objectivity altogether and to join with the program developers in a collaborative effort to determine the worth of what they are doing. The evaluator becomes in part an advocate rather than a judge or a neutral broker of information.

These are only a few of the possible positions along the fact-value line, and I expect considerable intellectual activity and controversy in the future as traditional evaluators try to defend their own objectivity, and hence legitimacy, by claiming their approaches are value-neutral, while other evaluators disengage from this position and attempt more radical approaches. Few issues are as fundamental to evaluation.

Several new evaluation approaches have been tried over the past two decades and we now have enough experience to see how some have turned out in practice. One of the hottest controversies has been the use of qualitative as opposed to quantitative evaluation techniques. Quantitative techniques have long been considered the *sine qua non* of modern social science, largely because their advocates believe that quantitative techniques ensure a degree of objectivity that any science must possess. This position has been assailed by advocates of qualitative studies, who have been successful in establishing qualitative approaches as more or less legitimate ways of evaluating. The more or less qualification is advisable because qualitative studies are still not considered quite up to par with proper quantitative techniques, the reason being, of course, that qualitative approaches are considered too subjective by many. Nonetheless, qualitative studies have been established as a legitimate minority approach and the warfare between the camps is diminishing in intensity, although skirmishing continues.

Some qualitative evaluators work under the banner of naturalistic evaluation and the two primary centers for naturalistic evaluation have been the Centre for Applied Research in Education (CARE) at the University of East Anglia and the Center for Instructional Research and Curriculum Evaluation (CIRCE) at the University of Illinois, the former founded by Lawrence Stenhouse and the latter by Tom Hastings. The ties between the two centers have been close ones since the early 1970s, although the ideas and context of each center are different. Although the boundaries of naturalistic evaluation extend far beyond East Anglia and Illinois, it seems appropriate that the chapters here are from personnel at those centers. Stake presents the fullest rationale he has yet attempted of the nature of naturalistic generalization, which he sees as the basis for naturalistic evaluation, while Walker struggles with the ethical problem of actually trying to employ naturalistic techniques. As his article demonstrates, these approaches are not panaceas but have formidable difficulties of their own. The final chapter in this section is by Kemmis, who was educated at CIRCE and employed at CARE for several years before returning to Australia. Kemmis proposes several principles for naturalistic studies, although there is some question whether he has not extended the principles to the point where his approach should be labeled a new one together. In any case, having achieved a measure of legitimacy for their approaches, the naturalistic evaluators now face the problem of refining and explicating naturalistic studies. One would expect to see differences emerge among them now that the common goal of legitimizing naturalistic studies has been reached.

Another effort in evaluation has been to encourage non-evaluators to participate in evaluations, in other words to democratize evaluations somewhat. This has not been very successful. As Weiss notes in her chapter, there have been several attempts, one of the most ambitious being to apply the stakeholder notion to two large, highly politicized programs.

What happened in one of them is documented here in detail. It is clear that evaluation is a highly political activity which can even affect politics at the national level. It is also clear that participatory approaches have a very long way to go and face an uphill struggle against evaluation conceived as a purely technical act conducted by experts. I expect renewed attempts at participatory evaluation and renewed controversy.

Finally, I would like to note a structural shift that has long-range implications for the practice of evaluation. This is the shift towards moving evaluators inside the organizational structures. That is, organizations such as state education agencies and local school authorities now have their own offices of evaluation. In earlier days evaluation studies were usually contracted out to other agencies, such as universities, and almost all the evaluation literature assumes that evaluation will be conducted by an outside agency on a contractual basis. Increasingly, however, evaluation has been moved inside the organization. This means that the evaluators are now subject to the internal administrative structure, and the authority relationships inside their own organizations. This has profound implications.

Evaluation has become so important a function that major government agencies cannot afford to be without their own experts. Hence, many organizations establish units inside to perform this task. In modern liberal society there are few deep-seated beliefs shared by everyone. Legitimating ones policies and decisions has become a major difficulty. One way of doing this is to appeal to formal evaluation studies, which presumably are premised upon scientific techniques. Evaluation seems to be a necessity for modern governments, and too important a function not to be brought under some government control.

2

New Analyses:
Issues and Metaphors

Introduction

The first two chapters in this book provide recent analyses as to the status and nature of the field of educational evaluation. Nevo's chapter assesses the current status of the field by defining the key issues. My own chapter investigates the internal workings of how we actually develop ideas about a field like evaluation. One chapter attempts to be comprehensive, the other in-depth.

Nevo's chapter orders the vast evaluation literature by focusing upon ten critical questions that he believes determine the shape of actual evaluations. These questions include who should do the evaluation, to whom the evaluation should be addressed, and how the evaluation should be done. On some of these questions he finds a considerable degree of consensus among evaluation theorists. On other questions there is little consensus.

For example, there is considerable consensus on the definition of evaluation, the objects of evaluation, who should do the evaluation, and on standards for judging an evaluation. On the other hand, there is not much consensus upon what the functions of evaluation are, who should be served by an evaluation, or what the criteria for judging an evaluation object should be. Nevo contends there is an emerging consensus upon the issues of what kinds of information should be collected and what methods of enquiry should be used, but no consensus as to the socio-political function of evaluation or the role that evaluation should play in society. Overall, Nevo's brief chapter provides a quick entry into the voluminous evaluation literature and his ten key questions provide an update on the current status of the field. Some of the questions he has posed will receive rather different answers from other authors in this book.

My own chapter provides a rather different kind of analysis. Rather than surveying the entire field of evaluation and seeing how different theorists address key questions, my chapter takes one prominent evaluation work and examines the conceptual structure of this work in detail. The purpose is to discover what fundamental ideas lie beneath a particularly elaborate and systematic theory of evaluation. I contend in this chapter that the conceptual base of one of the most widely used evaluation textbooks is in fact composed of several highly elaborated, overlapping metaphors. In particular, these are metaphors of industrial production and sporting contests. The industrial production metaphors include concrete images of the machine, the assembly line, and the pipeline. In other words, social and educational programs are *seen as* machines, assembly lines, and pipelines.

These metaphors are not merely casual, adventitious uses of imagery to enliven the narrative of the textbook occasionally, but are rigorously and systematically developed analogues for educational programs: in fact they comprise the fundamental cognitive structure of the work. Furthermore, the evaluation of the program is based upon these systemic metaphors. That is, the criteria for the program emerge directly from the metaphorical transformation of the program into industrial production and the other metaphors.

If my analysis is correct, it raises a number of questions about evaluations of educational programs. Are all evaluation approaches based upon implicit metaphors? How does this change the nature of evaluation? Where do these metaphors come from? Does this make evaluation arbitrary? Unscientific? Some of these issues are addressed in the chapter.

The Conceptualization of Educational Evaluation: An Analytical Review of the Literature

David Nevo
Tel-Aviv University

Many attempts have been made in recent years to clarify the meaning of evaluation and expose the distinction between evaluation and other related concepts such as measurement or research. The literature contains many approaches regarding the conceptualization of evaluation and the determination of its countenance in education. Many of those approaches have been unduly referred to as 'models' (for example, the CIPP Model, the Discrepancy Model, the Responsive Model, or the Goal-Free Model) in spite of the fact that none of them includes a sufficient degree of complexity and completeness that might be suggested by the term 'model'. Stake (1981) rightly suggested that they be referred to as persuasions rather than models.

For the benefit of those of us who lost their way among the various evaluation models, approaches, and persuasions, several attempts have been made to put some order into the growing evaluation literature through classifications of evaluation approaches. Such classifications (for example, Guba and Lincoln, 1981; House, 1980; Popham, 1975; Stake, 1976; Stufflebeam and Webster, 1980; Worthen and Sanders, 1973) made a significant contribution through their critical reviews of the evaluation literature denoting similarities and differences among the various approaches. Those classifications were based on a somewhat holistic approach by placing each evaluation model as a whole in one of the labeled categories with some other models. Trying to do justice to each evaluation model as a whole they sometimes ignored the major issues underlying the agreements and disagreements among the various evaluation approaches.

Stufflebeam (1974) suggested eight questions to be addressed in any attempt to conceptualize evaluation. Nevo (1980) revised Stufflebeam's list of questions and extended it to ten major dimensions in a conceptualization of evaluation. These ten dimensions represent the major issues addressed by the most prominent evaluation approaches in education. They will be used here as an organizer for an analytical review of the literature on educational evaluation.

The ten dimensions for our analysis are expressed by the following questions:

1   How is evaluation defined?
2   What are the functions of evaluation?
3   What are the objects of evaluation?
4   What kinds of information should be collected regarding each object?
5   What criteria should be used to judge the merit and worth of an evaluated object?
6   Who should be served by an evaluation?
7   What is the process of doing an evaluation?
8   What methods of enquiry should be used in evaluation?
9   Who should do evaluation?
10 By what standards should evaluation be judged?

We shall review the literature seeking the various answers to those questions provided by the various evaluation models, approaches, and persuasions. The significance of such a review for evaluation practitioners as well as evaluation theoreticians and researchers will be pointed out at the conclusion of the chapter.

1   How is evaluation defined?

Many definitions of evaluation can be found in the literature. The well-known definition originated by Ralph Tyler perceives evaluation as 'The process of determining to what extent the educational objectives are actually being realized' (Tyler, 1950, p. 69). Another widely accepted definition of evaluation has been that of providing information for decision making suggested by various leading evaluators such as Cronbach (1963), Stufflebeam (Stufflebeam *et al.*, 1971), and Alkin (1969). In recent years considerable consensus has been reached among evaluators regarding the definition of evaluation as the assessment of merit or worth (Eisner, 1979; Glass, 1969; House, 1980; Scriven, 1967; Stufflebeam, 1974), or as an activity comprised of both description and judgment (Guba and Lincoln, 1981; Stake, 1967). A joint committee on standards for evaluation, comprised of seventeen members representing twelve organizations associated with educational evaluation, recently published their definition of evaluation as 'the systematic investigation of the worth or merit of some object' (Joint Committee, 1981, p. 12).

A major exception to that consensus regarding the judgmental definition of evaluation is represented by the Stanford Evaluation Consortium group who defined evaluation as '[a] systematic examination of events occurring in and consequent of a contemporary program — an examination conducted to assist in improving this program and other programs having the same general purpose' (Cronbach *et al.*, 1980, p. 14). Cronbach and his associates (1980) clearly reject the judgmental nature of evaluation advocating an approach that perceives the evaluator as 'an educator [whose] success is to be judged by what others learn' (p. 11) rather than a 'referee [for] a basketball game' (p. 18) who is hired to decide who is 'right' or 'wrong'.

A definition that points to the judgmental character of evaluation might create considerable anxiety among potential evaluees and raise resistance among opponents of evaluation. Obviously, a non-judgmental definition of evaluation, such as 'providing information for decision-making,' might be accepted more favorably by evaluees and clients. However, it may be unrealistic to create positive attitudes toward evaluation by ignoring one of its major features. Another approach intended to develop positive attitudes toward evaluation might be to demonstrate its constructive functions within the various domains of education.

2 *What are the functions of evaluation?*

Scriven (1967) was the first to suggest the distinction between 'formative evaluation' and 'summative evaluation,' referring to two major roles or functions of evaluation, although he was not the first to realize the importance of such a distinction. Later, referring to the same two functions, Stufflebeam (1972) suggested the distinction between proactive evaluation intended to serve decision-making and retroactive evaluation to serve accountability. Thus, evaluation can serve two functions, the 'formative' and the 'summative.' In its formative function evaluation is used for the improvement and development of an ongoing activity (or program, person, product, etc.). In its summative function evaluation is used for accountability, certification, or selection.

A third function of evaluation, the psychological or socio-political function, which has been less often treated by evaluation literature (Cronbach *et al.*, 1980; House 1974; Patton, 1978), should also be considered. In many cases it is apparent that evaluation is not serving any formative purposes nor is it being used for accountability or other summative purposes. However, it is being used to increase awareness of special activities, motivate desired behavior of evaluees, or promote public relations. Regardless of our personal feelings about the use (or misuse) of evaluation for this purpose, we cannot ignore it.

Another somewhat 'unpopular' function of evaluation is its use for the exercise of authority (Dornbusch and Scott, 1975). In formal organizations it is the privilege of the superior to evaluate his or her subordinates and not vice versa. In many cases a person in a management position might evaluate someone to demonstrate his authority over that person. We may refer to this as the 'administrative' function of evaluation.

To summarize, evaluation can serve many functions: (a) the formative function for improvement; (b) the summative function for selection, for certification, for accountability; (c) the psychological or socio-political function for motivation and to increase awareness; and (d) the administrative function to exercise authority.

Some evaluators (Alkin, Daillak, and White, 1979; Cronbach *et al.*, 1980) express a clear preference for the formative function of evaluation, but the general perception seems to be that there are no 'right' or 'wrong' roles of evaluation, and that it can serve deliberately more than one function. However, different functions can be served in various ways and by different evaluation methods. It is therefore important to realize the existence of the various evaluation functions and to determine the specific function(s) of a concrete evaluation at an early stage of its planning.

3   What are the objects of evaluation?

Students and teachers have always been popular objects of evaluation in education. Almost all the measurement and evaluation literature in education up to the mid-sixties dealt with the evaluation of students' learning. Up to that time one could hardly find in the educational literature any substantial guidance regarding the evaluation of other objects such as educational projects or programs, curricular materials, or educational institutions. Various developments in the educational system of the United States (for example, the Elementary and Secondary Education Act of 1965) led to a significant shift of focus regarding the objects of educational evaluation from students to projects, programs, and instructional materials, which have been since then most common in the writings of the major authors in the evaluation literature in education (Alkin, 1969; Provus, 1971; Scriven, 1967; Stake, 1967; Stufflebeam, 1969; Stufflebeam *et al.*, 1971).

Two major conclusions can be drawn from the review of contemporary evaluation literature: (a) almost everything can be an object of evaluation, and evaluation should not be limited to the evaluation of students or school personnel; and (b) the clear identification of the evaluation object is an important part of the development of any evaluation design.

In planning an evaluation it seems to be important to determine what is 'the thing' (or 'the evaluand,' to use Scriven's, 1980, term) that has to be evaluated. It helps to determine what kind of information should be collected and how it should be analyzed. A clear object identification helps keep an evaluation focused. It also helps to clarify and resolve value conflicts and potential threat among stakeholders and others likely to be affected by the evaluation (Guba and Lincoln, 1981).

4 *What kinds of information should be collected regarding each object?*

After an evaluation object has been chosen, a decision must be made regarding the various aspects and dimensions of the object that should be evaluated. Information pertinent to such aspects must be collected. Earlier approaches to evaluation focused mainly on results or outcomes. Thus, to evaluate an educational object (for example, a new curriculum) would mean to evaluate the quality of the results of its functioning (for example, students' achievements). In recent years some interesting attempts have been made to extend the scope of evaluation variables is various evaluation models (Alkin, 1969; Provus, 1971; Stake, 1967; Stufflebeam, 1969 and 1974; Stufflebeam *et al.*, 1971). Stufflebeam's CIPP Model suggests that evaluation focus on four variables for each evaluation object; (a) its goals; (b) its design; (c) its process of implementation; and (d) its outcomes. According to this approach an evaluation of an educational project, for example, would be an assessment of (a) the merit of its goals; (b) the quality of its plans; (c) the extent to which those plans are being carried out; and (d) the worth of its outcomes.

Stake (1967) in his Countenance Model suggested that two sets of information be collected regarding the evaluated object: descriptive and judgmental. The descriptive set should focus on intents and observations regarding antecedents (prior conditions that may affect outcomes), transactions (the process of implementation), and outcomes. The judgmental set of information is comprised of standards and judgments regarding the same antecedents, transactions and outcomes.

Guba and Lincoln (1981), expanding Stake's Responsive Education Model (Stake, 1975) and applying the naturalistic paradigm, suggest that the evaluator generate five kinds of information: (a) descriptive information regarding the evaluation object, its setting, and its surrounding conditions; (b) information responsive to concerns of relevant audiences; (c) information about relevant issues; (d) information about values; and (e) information about standards relevant to worth and merit assessments.

Thus, the evaluation literature seems to suggest that a wide range of information should be collected by evaluation regarding the evaluated object. It should not limit itself to the narrow scope of evaluation regarding outcomes or results. This does not mean that each single evaluation must always collect all possible kinds of information; it may focus on some of them according to identified evaluation priorities or practical constraints.

5   *What criteria should be used to judge the merit and worth of an evaluation object?*

To choose the criteria to be used to judge the merit of an evaluation object is one of the most difficult tasks in educational evaluation. Those who think that evaluation should attempt to determine whether goals have been achieved (Provus, 1971; Tyler, 1950) make this task easy for themselves by partially ignoring the issue of evaluation criteria. What they actually do is use 'goal achievement' as the evaluation criterion without having justified its being an appropriate criterion. What about trivial goals or all kinds of 'stated objectives' that aren't worth achieving? Should they be used as evaluation criteria?

Another way to avoid the issue of evaluation criteria is to ignore the judgmental nature of evaluation. Those who defined evaluation as an information collection activity to serve decision-making or other purposes (Alkin, 1969; Cronbach, 1963; Stufflebeam, 1969) did not have to deal with the problem of choosing evaluation criteria.

Apparently, the achievement of (important) goals is one possible basis for evaluation criteria. Alternative bases for evaluation criteria suggested by the literature might be: identified needs of actual and potential clients (Joint Committee, 1981; Patton, 1978; Scriven, 1972b), ideals or social values (Guba and Lincoln, 1981; House, 1980), known standards set by experts or other relevant groups (Eisner, 1979; Guba and Lincoln, 1981; Stake, 1967), or the quality of alternative objects (House, 1980; Scriven, 1967).

Most evaluation experts seem to agree that the criterion (or criteria) to be used for the assessment of a specific object must be determined within the specific context of the object and the function of its evaluation. While in many cases the evaluator does not have the authority to choose among the various alternative criteria, it is the evaluator's responsibility that such a choice be made and that he be able to provide a sound justification for the choice, whether it is made by him or by somebody else.

6   *Who should be served by an evaluation?*

Those who define evaluation as providing information for decision-making (Alkin, 1969; Cronbach, 1963; Stufflebeam *et al.*, 1971) seem to have a clear opinion as to who has to be served by evaluation. They identify the relevant decisionmakers and attempt to determine their information needs. Others (Cronbach *et al.*, 1980; House, 1980) reject the notion of serving 'decision-makers' because of the threat of co-optation or oversimplification of social and organizational processes. Cronbach and his associates (1980) are inclined to serve the 'policy-shaping community' rather than some kind of managerial decisionmaker. Many authors refer to 'evaluation clients' or 'evaluation audiences' as those who have to be served by evaluation. Guba and Lincoln (1981) suggested the term 'stakeholders' or 'stakeholding audience' for the whole group of persons having some stake in the performance of the evaluand and therefore should be served by the evaluation.

If evaluation is to be useful at all, it has to be useful to some specific client or audience. The evaluation literature does not suggest which is the 'most appropriate' audience for evaluation, but three important propositions can be found in writings regarding this issue. They are: (a) an evaluation can have more than one client or audience; (b) different evaluation audiences might have different evaluation needs; and (c) the specific audiences for an evaluation and their evaluation needs must be clearly identified at the early stages of planning an evaluation.

Differences in evaluation needs might be reflected in many ways: for example, the kind of information to be collected, the level of data analysis to be used, or the form of reporting the evaluation results. Sometimes it is impossible to serve all identified evaluation needs at the same time, and some priorities have to be set regarding the specific evaluation needs to which the evaluation will respond.

7   What is the process of doing an evaluation?

The process of doing an evaluation might differ according to the theoretical perception guiding the evaluation. A theoretical approach perceiving evaluation as an activity intended to determine whether goals have been achieved (Tyler, 1950) might recommend the following evaluation process: (a) stating goals in behavioral terms; (b) developing measurement instruments; (c) collecting data; (d) interpreting findings; and (e) making recommendations.

According to Stake's Countenance Model (Stake, 1967) the evaluation process should include (a) describing a program; (b) reporting the description to relevant audiences; (c) obtaining and analyzing their judgments; and (d) reporting the analyzed judgments back to the audiences. Later on, in his Responsive Evaluation Model Stake (1975) suggested a continuing 'conversation' between the evaluator and all other parties associated with the evaluand. He specified 12 steps of dynamic interaction between the evaluator and his audiences in the process of conducting an evaluation.

Provus (1971) proposed a five step evaluation process including (a) clarification of the program design; (b) assessing the implementation of the program; (c) assessing its in-term results; (d) assessing its long-term results; and (e) assessing its costs and benefits.

The Phi Delta Kappa Study Committee on evaluation (Stufflebeam *et al.*, 1971) presented a three-step evaluation process. It included (a) delineating information requirements through interaction with the decision-making audiences; (b) obtaining the needed information through formal data collection and analysis procedures; and (c) providing the information to decision-makers in a communicable format.

Scriven (1972a) has suggested nine steps in his Pathway Comparison Model. Guba and Lincoln (1981) suggest in their recently published book that a naturalistic-responsive evaluation be implemented through a process including the following four stages: (a) initiating and organizing the evaluation; (b) indentifying key issues and concerns; (c) gathering useful information; and (d) reporting results and making recommendations.

While there seems to be no agreement among evaluation experts regarding the 'best' process to follow when conducting an evaluation, most of them would agree that all evaluations should include a certain amount of interaction between evaluators and their audiences at the outset of the evaluation to identify evaluation needs, and at its conclusion to communicate its findings. Evaluation cannot be limited to the technical activities of data collection and analysis.

8   What methods of enquiry should be used in evaluation?

While challenging the usefulness of various research methods for evaluation studies (Guba, 1969; Stufflebeam *et al.*, 1971),recent years have also introduced various methods of enquiry into the field of educational evaluation. In addition to traditional experimental and quasi-experimental designs (Campbell, 1969; Stanley, 1972; Cook and Campbell,1976), naturalistic methods (Guba and Lincoln, 1981; Patton, 1980), jury trials (Wolf, 1979), case studies (Stake, 1978), art criticism (Eisner, 1977 and 1979), journalistic methods (Guba, 1978), the modus operandi method (Scriven, 1974), and many others became legitimate methods for the conduct of evaluation. Some methodologists still advocate the superiority of certain methods such as experimental design (Boruch and Cordray, 1980; Rossi, Freeman and Wright, 1979) at one extreme, or naturalistic methods (Guba and Lincoln, 1981; House, 1980; Patton, 1980) on the other extreme, but overall there seems to be more support for a more eclectic approach to evaluation methodology. At the present state of the art in evaluation it looks like 'the evaluator will be wise not to declare allegiance to either a quantitative-scientific-summative methodology or a qualitative-naturalistic-descriptive methodology' (Cronbach *et al.*, 1980, p. 7). It might be also true that for a complicated task such as the conduct of evaluation an approach is needed that seeks the best method or set of methods for answering a particular evaluation question, rather than assuming that one method is best for all purposes.

9 *Who should do evaluation?*

Becoming a professional group, evaluators devoted much attention to identifying the characteristics of 'good' evaluators and appropriate ways to train them (Boruch and Cordray, 1980; Cronbach *et al.*, 1980; Guba and Lincoln, 1981; Stufflebeam *et al.*, 1971; Worthen, 1975). To be a competent and trustworthy evaluator one needs to have a combination of a wide variety of characteristics. These include technical competence in the area of measurement and research methods, understanding the social context and the substance of the evaluation object, human relations skills, personal integrity, and objectivity, as well as characteristics related to organizational authority and responsibility. Because it is difficult to find one person possessing all these qualifications, it often becomes necessary to have a team conduct an evaluation or to choose the person with the most appropriate characteristics for a specific evaluation task.

The evaluation literature also suggests two important distinctions that should be taken into account when deciding who should do an evaluation. The first is the distinction between an internal evaluator and an external evaluator (Scriven 1967 and 1975; Stake and Gjerde, 1974; Stufflebeam *et al.*, 1971). An internal evaluator of a project is usually one who is employed by the project and reports directly to its management. Obviously, the internal evaluator's objectivity as well as external credibility might be lower than those of an external evaluator, who is not directly employed by the project and/or enjoys a higher degree of independence.

The second distinction is between a professional evaluator and an amateur evaluator. This distinction, suggested by Scriven (1967), refers to two different foci of training and expertise rather than to a value judgment regarding the quality of an evaluation. An amateur evaluator is usually one whose major professional training is not in evaluation, and involvement in evaluation represents only part of his or her job description (for example, the associate director of a new maths curriculum development project conducting the formative evaluation of the project, who has an MA in maths education and some on-the-job training in evaluation). A professional evaluator is one with extensive training in evaluation and whose major (or even only) responsibility is conducting evaluation (for example, the internal evaluator of a special education project, who has an MA in measurement and evaluation and five years' experience evaluating special education projects). While the amateur evaluator's technical evaluation skills might be lower than those of a professional evaluator, he or she might have a better understanding of the project's unique evaluation needs and be able to develop better rapport with the members of the evaluated project.

These two distinctions are independent; there may be an internal-amateur evaluator, an external-amateur evaluator, an internal-professional evaluator, and so forth.

10 *By what standards should evaluation be judged?*

Several attempts have been made in recent years to develop standards for evaluations of educational and social programs (Evaluation Research Society, 1980; Joint Committee, 1981; Stufflebeam *et al.*, 1971; Tallmadge, 1977; US General Accounting Office, 1978). In spite of the fact that some writers (Cronbach *et al.*, 1980; Stake, 1981) have criticized the rationale for the whole standard-setting effort as being premature at the present state of the art in evaluation, there seems to be a great deal of agreement regarding their scope and content.

Boruch and Cordray (1980) analyzed six sets of such standards and reached the conclusion that there has been a large degree of overlap and similarity among them. The most elaborate and comprehensive set, and the one based on the largest amount of consensus, is probably the set developed and published by the Joint Committee on Standards for Educational Evaluation (1981). These standards have been developed by a committee of seventeen members, chaired by Dr. Daniel Stufflebeam, which represented twelve professional organizations associated with educational evaluation. The committee suggested thirty standards, which are divided into four major groups: utility standards (to ensure that evaluation serves practical information needs), feasibility standards (to ensure that evaluation is realistic and prudent), propriety standards (to ensure that evaluation is conducted legally and ethically), and accuracy standards (to ensure that evaluation reveals and conveys technically adequate information).

Summary

Risking oversimplification, one could summarize the review of the literature with the following most common answers to our ten questions. This could be one way to describe briefly the state of the art in the conceptualization of educational evaluation.

1 *How is evaluation defined?*

Educational evaluation is a systematic description of educational objects and/or an assessment of their merit or worth.

2 *What are the functions of evaluation?*

Educational evaluation can serve four different functions: (a) formative ('for improvement'); (b) summative (for selection and accountability); (c) sociopolitical (to motivate and gain public support); and (d) administrative (to exercise authority).

3 *What are the objects of evaluation?*

Any entity can be an evaluation object. Typical evaluation objects in education are students, educational and administrative personnel, curricula, instructional materials, programs, projects, and institutions.

4 *What kinds of information should be collected regarding each object?*

Four groups of variables should be considered regarding each object. They focus on (a) the goals of the object; (b) its strategies and plans; (c) its process of implementation; and (d) its outcomes and impacts.

5 *What criteria should be used to judge the merit of an object?*

The following criteria should be considered in judging the merit or worth of an educational object: (a) responding to identified needs of actual and potential clients; (b) achieving national goals, ideals, or social values; (c) meeting agreed-upon standards and norms; (d) outdoing alternative objects; and (e) achieving (important) stated goals of the objects. Multiple criteria should be used for any object.

6 *Who should be served by an evaluation?*

Evaluation should serve the information needs of all actual and potential parties interested in the evaluation object ('stakeholders'). It is the responsibility of the evaluator(s) to delineate the stakeholders of an evaluation and to identify or project their information needs.

7 *What is the process of doing an evaluation?*

Regardless of its method of enquiry, an evaluation process should include the following three activities: (a) focusing the evaluation problem; (b) collecting and analyzing empirical data; and (c) communicating findings to evaluation audiences. There is more than one appropriate sequence for implementing these activities, and any such sequence can (and sometimes should) be repeated serveral times during the life span of an evaluation study.

8   *What methods of enquiry should be used in evaluation?*

Being a complex task, evaluation needs to mobilize many alternative methods of enquiry from the behavioral sciences and related fields of study and utilize them according to the nature of a specific evaluation problem. At the present state of the art, an a priori preference for any specific method of enquiry is not warranted.

9   *Who should do evaluation?*

Evaluation should be conducted by individuals or teams possessing (a) extensive competencies in research methodology and other data analysis techniques; (b) understanding of the social context and the unique substance of the evaluation object; (c) the ability to maintain correct human relations and to develop rapport with individuals and groups involved in the evaluation; and (d) a conceptual framework to integrate the above-mentioned capabilities.

10   *By what standards should evaluation be judged?*

Evaluation should strike for an optimal balance in meeting standards of (a) utility (to be useful and practical); (b) accuracy (to be technically adequate); (c) feasibility (to be realistic and prudent); and (d) propriety (to be conducted legally and ethically).

Conclusion

As stated at the beginning of this chapter, a critical analysis of the various theoretical approaches to educational evaluation might have important implications for practitioners of evaluation as well as for theoreticians and researchers who are concerned with developing new concepts and better methods. All of them could benefit from the analytical scheme of the ten questions, which guided our analysis, as well as from the review of the answers contained in the evaluation literature.

Evaluators could use the ten questions to organize their own perceptions of evaluation using the evaluation literature to develop their own sets of coherent answers of the ten questions rahter than adopting piously one evaluation model or another. Understanding what others mean when they refer to evaluation could be another use of the ten question. Evaluators may encounter considerable difficulties if their perceptions of a concrete evaluation differ from those of their clients and audiences. It is appropriate before one starts planning an evaluation or even decides to do it all to find out what is meant by evaluation by the various parties involved in the evaluation, what purpose it is intended to serve, what is to be evaluated, what are some feasible alternatives for doing it, and by what standards the evaluation is to be judged if it is to be conducted at all. In other words, addressing the ten questions discussed in this chapter might help evaluation problems before they get themselves into all kinds of dubious evaluation adventures.

Discussions among theoreticians of evaluation can be a fruitful contribution to the advancement of evaluation theory and practice. It could be even more so if those discussions focused on issues in disagreement rather than on competing models and paradigms. The contribution would be even more robust if the various theoretical propositions were substantiated by some research findings. The ten questions reviewed here could provide a framework to delineate research variables for an empirical study of evaluation. Data on the actual relationships among those variables as well as their relationships with other variables (for example, evaluation utilization or variables reflecting the context of evaluation) would be very much appreciated by the evaluation profession.

References

ALKIN, M.C. (1969) 'Evaluation theory development', *Evaluation Comment*, 2, pp. 2–7.

ALKIN, M.C., DAILLAK, R. and White, P. (1979) *Using Evaluations: Does Evaluation Make a Difference?*, Beverly Hills, Calif., Sage.

BORUCH, F.R. and CORDRAY, D.S. (1980 *An Appraisal of Educational Program Evaluations: Federal, State, and Local Agencies*, Evanston, Ill, Northwestern University.

CAMPBELL, D.T. (1969) 'Reforms as experiments', *American Psychologist*, 24, pp. 409–29.

COOK, T.D. and CAMPBELL, D.T. (1976) 'The design and conduct of quasi-experiments and true experiments in field settings' in DUNNETTE, M.D. (Ed.) *Handbook of Industrial and Organizational Psychology*, Chicago, Rand NcNally.

CRONBACH, L.J. (1963) 'Course improvement through evaluation', *Teachers College Record*, 64, pp. 672–83.

CRONBACH, L.J., AMBRON, S.R., DORNBUSCH, S.M., HESS, R.D., HORNIK, R.C., PHILLIPS, D.C., WALKER, D.E. and WEINER, S.S. (1980) *Toward Reform of Program Evaluation*, San Franciscio, Jossey-Bass.

DORNBUSCH, S.M. and SCOTT, W.R. (1975) *Evaluation and the Exercise of Authority*, San Francisco, Jossey-Bass.

EISNER, E.W. (1977) 'On the uses of educational connoisseurship and educational criticism for evaluating classroom life', *Teachers College Record*, 78, pp. 345–58

EISNER, E.W. (1979) *The Educational Imagination*, New York, Macmillan.

Evaluation Research Society (1980) *Standards for Program Evaluation*, Evaluation Research Society.

GLASS G.V. (1969) *The Growth of Evaluation Methodology*, research paper No. 27, Boulder, Laboratory of Educational Research, University of Colorado, mimeo.

GUBA, E.G. (1969) 'The failure of educational evaluation', *Educational Technology*, 9, pp. 29–38.

GUBA, E.G. (1978) *Metaphor Adaptation Report: Investigative Journalism*, Research on Evaluation Project, Portland, Ore, Northwest Regional Educational Laboratory, monograph.

GUBA, E.G. and LINCOLN, Y.S. (1981) *Effective Evaluation*, San Francisco, Jossey-Bass.

HOUSE, E.R. (1974) *The Politics of Educational Innovation*, Berkeley, Calif., McCutchan.

HOUSE, E.R. (1980) *Evaluating With Validity*, Beverly Hills, Calif., Sage.

Joint Committee on Standards for Educational Evaluation (1981) *Standards for Evaluations of Educational Programs, Projects, and Materials*, New York, McGraw-Hill.

NEVO, D. (1981) 'The evaluation of a multi-dimensional project' in LEWY, A., KUGELMASS, S., BEN-SHAKAR, G., BLASS, N., BORUCH, R.F., DAVIS, D.J., NEVO, B., NEVO, D., TAMIR, P. and ZAK, I. *Decision Oriented Evaluation in Education: The Case of Israel*, Philadelphia, International Science Services.

PATTON, M.Q. (1978) *Utilization Focused Evaluation*, Beverly Hills, Calif., Sage.

PATTON, M.Q. (1980) *Qualitative Evaluation Methods*, Beverly Hills, Calif., Sage.

POPHAM, W.J. (1975) *Educational Evaluation*, Englewood Cliffs, NJ, Prentice Hall.

PROVUS, M.M. (1971) *Discrepancy Evaluation*, Berkeley, Calif., McCutchan.

ROSSI, P.H., FREEMAN, H.E. and WRIGHT, S.R. (1979) *Evaluation: A Systematic Approach*, Beverly Hills, Calif., Sage.

SCRIVEN, M. (1967) 'The methodology of evaluation' in STAKE, R.E. (Ed.), *AERA Monograph Series on Curriculum Evaluation*, No. 1, Chicago, Rand McNally.

SCRIVEN, M. (1972a) *The Pathway Comparison Model of Evaluation*, Berkeley, University of California, January, mimeo.

SCRIVEN, M. (1972b) 'Pros and cons about goal-free evaluation', *Evaluation Comment*, 3, 4.

SCRIVEN, M. (1974) 'Maximizing the power of causal investigations: The modus operandi method' in POPHAM, W.J. (Ed.) *Evaluation in Education*, Berkeley Calif., McCutchan..

SCRIVEN, M. (1975) *Evaluation Bias and its Control*, occasional paper No. 4, Kalamazoo, Western Michigan University.

SCRIVEN, M. (1980) *Evaluation Thesaurus* (2nd edn) Inverness, Calif, Edgepress.

STAKE, R.E. (Ed.) (1967) 'The countenance of educational evaluation', *Teachers College Record*, 68, pp. 523–40.

STAKE, R.E. (1975) *Evaluating the Arts in Education: A Responsiveness Approach*, Columbus, Ohio, Merrill.

STAKE, R.E. (1976) *Evaluation Educational Programmes: The Need and the Response*, Washington, DC, OECD Publications Center.

STAKE, R.E. (1978) 'The case study method in social inquiry', *Educational Researcher*, 7, pp. 5–8.

STAKE, R.E. (1981) 'Setting standards for educational evaluators', *Evaluation News*, 2, 2, pp. 148–52.

STAKE, R.E. and GJERDE, C. (1974) 'An evaluation of TCITY, the Twin City Institute for Talented Youth' in KERLINGER, F.N. (Ed.) *AERA Monograph Series in Curriculum Evaluation*, No. 7, Chicago, Rand McNally.

STANLEY, J.C. (1972) 'Controlled field experiments as a model for evaluation', in ROSSI, P.H. and WILLIAMS, W. (Eds) *Evaluating Social Programs*, New York, Seminar Press.

STUFFLEBEAM, D.L. (1969) 'Evaluation as enlightenment for decision making' in BEATTY, W.H. (Ed.) *Improving Educational Assessment and an Inventory for Measures of Affective Behavior*, Washington, DC, National Education Association.

STUFFLEBEAM, D.L. (1972) 'The relevance of the CIPP evaluation model for educational accountability', *SRIS Quarterly*, 5, pp. 3–6.

STUFFLEBEAM, D.L. (1974) *Meta-evaluation*, occasional paper No. 3, Kalamazoo, Western Michigan University.

STUFFLEBEAM, D.L., FOLEY, W.J., GEPHART, W.J., GUBA, E.G., HAMMON, R.L., MERRIMAN, H.O. and PROVUS, M.M. (1971) *Educational Evaluation and Decision-making*, Itasca, Ill., Peacock.

STUFFLEBEAM, D.L. and WEBSTER, W.J. (1980) 'An analysis of alternative approaches to education', *Educational Evaluation and Policy Analysis*, 2, 3, pp. 5–20.

TALLMADGE, G.K. (1977) *Joint Dissemination Review Panel Ideabook*, Washington, DC, US Government Printing Office.

TYLER, R.W. (1950) *Basic Principles of Curriculum and Instruction*, Chicago, Ill., University of Chicago Press.

US General Accounting Office (1978) *Assessing Social Program Impact Evaluations: A Checklist Approach*, Washington, DC, US General Accounting Office.

WOLF, R.L. (1979) 'The use of judicial evaluation methods in the formation of educational policy', *Educational Evaluation and Policy Analysis*, 1, pp. 19–28.

WORTHEN, B.R. (1975) 'Competencies for educational research and evaluation', *Educational Researcher*, 4, 1, pp. 13–16.

WORTHEN, B.R. and SANDERS, J.R. (1973) *Educational Evaluation: Theory and practice*, Belmont, Calif., Wadsworth.

How We Think
about Evaluation

Ernest R. House
University of Illinois

Much of our everyday thinking is metaphorical in nature. That is, we experience one thing in terms of another, according to such theorists as Lakoff and Johnson (1980). They present the following metaphor about argument as an example:

Arguments Are Wars

- Your claims are *indefensible*
- He *attacked every weak point* in my argument
- His criticisms were *right on target*
- I *demolished* his argument (p. 4).

Underlying these separate metaphoric statements is a deep-seated metaphor: *Arguments Are Wars*. This generative metaphor is the basis for a number of expressions, and these expressions constitute a systematic, recognizable pattern. Based primarily upon such evidence, some linguists and philosophers contend that such extended metaphors, which occur in our ordinary thinking, are not haphazard or idiosyncratic: All of us employ them in a systematic fashion to structure the way we think about the world. Thus, these metaphoric concepts are extended, conventional, and intersubjective — much like language itself. Moreover, in structuring our thinking about argument in terms of concepts about war, we do more than just express ourselves colorfully We actually win or lose arguments, attack and defend positions, and gain or lose ground. We live and experience arguments in these terms. The metaphor — *Arguments Are Wars* — shapes our actual behavior.

Until recently, the employment of metaphor was thought to be merely ornamental. Metaphor was used to make an expression more poetic or to emphasize a point rhetorically. However, novel experiences usually are structured in terms of more familiar ones, abstract concepts in terms of more concrete ones, and cultural notions in terms of physical ones. Metaphor is essential to our most complicated thought processes and a vital intellectual tool that we use to understand the world. For example, argument as war reflects aspects of our concept of *argument*. The metaphor highlights how participants in an argument relate to each other, how they treat one another, and how the argument might progress. However, argument as dance would indicate quite a different set of relationships between participants — that is, opponents would be partners. Therefore, *Arguments Are Dances* is not a common metaphor in our culture.

Complex concepts also can be structured by more than one metaphor. For example, the concept of argument is shaped not only by *Arguments Are Wars* but also by other metaphors:

Arguments Are Buildings

- The argument is *shaky*
- *We need to construct a strong* argument
- The argument *collapsed*
- Is that the *foundation* of your argument? (p. 46)

Arguments as building indicates other aspects of our concept of argument that we consider to be important. *Arguments Are Buildings* highlights how arguments are put together, based, and constructed — quite different aspects than those conveyed by *Arguments Are Wars*. We might refer to how arguments proceed in waves, are calm or stormy, and appear on the surface as opposed to what is beneath the surface — that is, *Arguments Are Oceans*. But we do not.

The images of wars and buildings are quite different. But neither are they incompatible with one another. In emphasizing two distinct aspects of our notion of arguments, the two metaphors do not present a single, consistent image but they are coherent. This fundamental coherence is demonstrated by the fact that we mix *Arguments Are Wars* and *Arguments Are Buildings* in our thinking:

- When I *attacked* his argument, it *collapsed*
- The *foundation* of his argument is the *weak point*
- We need to *construct* an argument that is *defensible*
- Your *defense* is a *shaky* one

As the last statement indicates, even a strange mix of metaphors makes sense to us, since these two aspects of argument are used and associated with one another so commonly. Coherent metaphors often fit together by being sub-categories of a major category and sharing a common entailment. For example:

Love Is a Journey

- It's been a long, bumpy road
- We're just spinning our wheels

- We've gotten off the track
- Our marriage is on the rocks (p. 44)

Although all of these statements concern journeys, they are based on different kinds of journeys: a car trip, a train trip, and a sea voyage. The concrete images in each sentence define a more general category and, in that sense, are coherent rather than consistent. They fit together but do not compose a single image.

Quite a number of other metaphors also shape our conception or argument, usually in terms of familiar, concrete, and physical experiences like wars and buildings. Abstract, complex concepts are usually shaped by a number of metaphors that are coherent because the ideas themselves are too complex to be conveyed by one single, consistent image. Whether argument commonly is seen as a war or a dance is culturally determined, and the user of the concept ordinarily is not aware of the underlying metaphor that shapes his or her experience of the actual phenomenon. The user believes that arguments naturally happen that way. Thus, arguments follow certain social patterns because of the common conception that the participants have (Turner, 1974). These fundamental metaphoric concepts are essential to our understanding of the world because they form coherent systems of thought that we use extensively in everyday life (Lakoff and Johnson, 1980).

Metaphors Underlying Social Policy

Schön (1979) contends that social problem-setting is mediated by the stories people tell about troublesome situations. The framing of the social problem depends on the metaphors underlying the stories, and how the problems are framed is critical to the solutions that emerge. For example, a pervasive description of the social services is that they are 'fragmented,' and the implicit solution to this problem is that they be 'coordinated.' But services seen as 'fragmented' could also be seen more benignly as 'autonomous.' Therefore, the underlying metaphor gives shape and direction to the problem solution.

Schön maintains that we are guided in our thinking about social policy by pervasive, tacit images that he calls *generative metaphors*, in which one frame of reference is carried over to another situation. These metaphors generally are used because the user is immersed in the experience of the phenomenon. Thus, these guiding images are necessary to his or her thinking. For example, urban renewal can be viewed in different ways. The slum can be seen as a once healthy community that has become diseased. A social planner with such an image envisions wholesale redesign and reconstruction as the cure to urban blight. However, the slum can also be viewed as a viable, low-income community, which offers its residents important social benefits. The second view obviously implies strikingly different prescriptions for improving the community.

The predominant image of the slum in the 1950s was that of a blighted community. However, in the 1960s the slum as a natural community arose as a countermetaphor that vied for public and expert attention in social planning. Each image features certain themes — taken from a reality that is ambiguous and indeterminate — that define the phenomenon of the slum (Schön, 1979). In the first vision, terms like *blight, health, renewal, cycle of decay*, and *integrated plan* are highlighted in descriptions of social planning. In the second vision, *home, patterns of interaction, informal networks*, and *dislocation* represent key ideas about what should be done with slums. Each overall image presents a view of social reality by selecting, naming, and relating elements within the chosen framework. According to Schön, *naming* and *framing* are the key processes in such conceptualization. By selecting certain elements and coherently organizing them, those processes explain what is wrong in a particular situation and suggest a transformation. Data are converted to recommendations.

Naming and framing proceed by generative metaphor. The researcher sees the slum as a blight or as a natural community. In seeing A as B, the evaluation implicit in B is carried over to A. The first metaphor is that of disease and cure. The second is that of natural community versus artificial community. The transferred evaluations are based on images deeply ingrained within our culture, and once we define a complex situation as either health and disease or nature and artifice we know in which direction to move. Seeing A as B greatly facilitates our ability to diagnose and prescribe. On the other hand, it may lead us to overlook other important features in the situation that the metaphor does not capture. Since generative metaphors usually are implied rather than expressed openly, important features may pass undetected. Schön argues that we should be more aware of our generative metaphors, and that this is best done by analyzing the problem-setting stories we tell. The 'deep' metaphor accounts for why some elements are included in the story while others are not, some assumptions are taken to be true in spite of disconfirming evidence, and some recommendations seem obvious. It is the metaphor of the slum as diseased — or as a natural community — that gives shape to the study and direction of a social planner's actions.

Industrial Production as a Metaphor for Social Programs

Evaluation concepts are often derived from fundamental, generative, and deep-seated metaphors that remain hidden. These metaphors guide one's thinking in certain directions. In this sense, evaluative thinking is no different from the metaphoric thinking in other areas. To illustrate this point, I turn to an examination of the ideas presented in Rossi and others' book, *Evaluation: A Systematic Approach* (1979). This book is one of the most widely used textbooks in the teaching of evaluation, and the authors' work is exemplary of thinking in the field of evaluation — and pervasively metaphoric.

The most fundamental metaphor that the authors use is that of the delivery of social services as industrial production. In their conceptualization, social services are utilities or commodities that are required by the public, and it is the duty of a social program to supply these services. The notion that services are produced by social programs and that they are to be delivered to a clientele manifests the production metaphor. For example, related ideas taken from the book include:

Social Service Delivery Is Industrial Production

- Program elements are defined in terms of *time, costs, procedures,* or a *product*
- A delivery system consists of organizational arrangements that provide program services
- These services are delivered to a target population
- Program development is equivalent to designing the system
- There are production runs
- Services can be calculated in terms of service units delivered
- One should monitor the delivery of these services
- There are operational indicators of success
- A *monitoring evaluation* is an assessment of whether the program conforms to the design and reaches the target.

Even more specifically, social programs as conceived in the preceding examples not only as industrial production in general but as a particular kind of industrial production — that is, an assembly line. At other times within the book, social programs are viewed as machines:

Social Programs Are Machines

- A program consists of elements
- Program elements are discrete intervention activities
- Programs may be broad, complex, but also have component parts
- They are implemented
- They operate according to a design
- They produce benefits, effects, and outcomes
- They can be replicated and replaced
- They can be tested
- They can be fine-tuned
- Accountability means conformity to program specifications
- A major failure is unstandardized treatment
- Variables can be manipulated to achieve results

Rossi and others employ yet a third specific metaphor of industrial production — that of a pipeline or conduit:

Social Delivery Systems Are Conduits

- A delivery system is a combination of pathways that allow access to services
- A major failure in systems is dilution of the treatment to an insufficient amount
- Outcomes always represent changes in the level of measurable variables
- Contaminants may either enhance or mask true changes
- Assessing net intervention effects requires purification of outcomes by purging contaminating elements
- The point of assessing the magnitude of effects is to rule out causal links between inputs and outcomes
- The unreliability of measuring instruments may dilute the difference in outcomes

Social programs as machines, assembly lines, and conduits all fit the overall metaphor of social programs as industrial production. But each metaphor emphasizes a slightly different aspect of the nature of social programs. That is, in thinking about social programs, one may emphasize the way social programs are put together and operate to produce benefits. Or the inputs and outputs, the raw material, and labor that go into programs may be emphasized — or the way benefits or services are delivered to the program recipients. Therefore, social programs can be conceived as involving all of these aspects, and the various separate metaphors are used to emphasize different ones.

Different conceptions of what evaluation entails follow from these different metaphors of social programs: conformity to program design, monitoring of production processes, and measuring of purified outcomes. The evaluation of the program corresponds to the perceived nature of social programs. Sometimes the emphasis is on design specifications and the parts of the program; sometimes it is on the inputs and outputs, and other times the emphasis is placed on the outcomes — the latter metaphor being that of a pipeline with certain substances that issue from it and the corresponding evaluation resembling a chemical analysis from which the evaluator seeks to ascertain the results, purified of possible contamination. Of course, the overall metaphor is that of industrial production but there is no single, consistent image for all of the metaphors. Taken together, the three images present a coherent picture of social programs as industrial production (see Figure 1). The internal coherence among these metaphors is demonstrated in the mixed metaphors that make sense within this conceptual structure and used throughout the book. For example, delivery systems are said to deliver programs or program elements or treatments.

Programs may produce benefits or outcomes or outputs. These terms are used interchangeably.

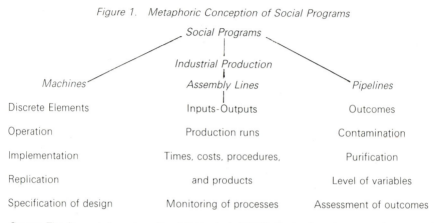

Figure 1. Metaphoric Conception of Social Programs

Source: The figure is based on Rossi P.H. *et al.* (1979) *Evaluation: A systematic approach,* Beverley Hills. Calif, Sage.

The internal coherence of these metaphors is derived from their shared entailments. That is, the better the discrete elements of the program fit together, the more efficiently the time, costs, and procedures are converted into products, and the more outcomes the program delivers. Hence, the design of the programs, the inputs of the program, and the delivery of outcomes are linked together, though by no means synonymous with one another. There is a sequentiality that underlies all three: a sense in which a social program must be created, made, or produced, and in which it must reach the people for whom it is intended. The concept of industrial production is not the only way in which this process can be conceived and made coherent, but it is one way of doing so. Of course, such an overall metaphor entails certain types of evaluations.

The ubiquitous metaphoric nature of these concepts is illustrated further by a detailed examination of the concrete images. For example, the assembly line is a fundamental image in our culture, and it is not surprising that Rossi and others apply this notion to social programs. Raw materials come in one end of the assembly line, labor is performed in stages, and products come out the other end. Underlying the assembly line concept are deeper metaphors that define both labor and time as material resources. A material resource is a kind of substance that can be used in a manufacturing process, quantified precisely, assigned a monetary value per unit of quantity, serve a purposeful end, and used up progressively as it serves its purpose. If time and labor are material resources, they also can be quantified, assigned a value per unit, serve a purposeful end, and be used up (Lakoff and Johnson, 1980). In addition, in our society labor is seen as an activity — and an activity is defined as a substance. Hence, labor can be treated as a substance and a material resource; likewise, time commonly is viewed as a substance — defined in units. Conceiving of labor and time as substances and material resources permits them to be measured, used up, assigned monetary value, and used for various ends. Thus, in conceiving of social programs as assembly lines, Rossi and others can state '*Program elements* may be defined in terms of *time, costs, procedures,* and *products*' (p. 137). Doing a cost-benefit analysis of how time and labor are used in social programs is a logical next step and an important part of the authors' ultimate thinking.

In such a metaphoric framework, efficiency quite naturally looms large as a criterion for successful social programs. Social programs are expected to be efficient just as industrial production is expected to be. In the Rossi and others' conceptualization a comprehensive evaluation must include monitoring, impact assessment, and cost-benefit or cost-effective analysis, and one chapter is entitled 'Measuring Efficiency.' Production functions and econometrics are an extension of this type of analysis, although these authors do not go so far, choosing instead to emphasize both the desirability and difficulty of measuring the benefits and costs of social programs. However, other theorists have been less reticent in setting up equations for social programs that model the production processes, and the discovery of such production functions has at times been the object of considerable federal effort such as the evaluations of Title I of the Elementary and Secondary Education Act of 1965 (McLaughlin, 1975).

Rossi and others also repeatedly speak about social programs as being *effective, efficient, adequate,* and *useful.* This language suggests that there is a job to be done and that the program must accomplish this job. The notion of particular job or task to be performed is congruent with the entire industrial production metaphor. Within the world defined by the fundamental metaphor, these terms become major evaluative terms. They indicate that the program is good if one can apply these terms and also suggest where to look to see if the program is good. They become major criteria of evaluation, criteria that are entailed by the general metaphors.

Targets and Goals as Metaphors

Although the industrial production metaphors dominate Rossi and others' view of evaluation, other metaphors also play a key role in their thinking. These are the metaphors of *target* and *goal*. The target metaphor is used extensively in the book in reference to *target problems, target populations,* and *impact.* The social program has impact on the targets. Presumably, the targets are social problems that social planners attack or alleviate.

Social Problems Are Targets

- Programs and projects are *aimed* at the target problems
- The program can be *misguided*
- The problems are located *in* the target population
- Problems are distributed and have location, extent, type, scope, and depth
- A needs assessment determines the nature, extent, and location of social problems
- Targets have boundaries and rules of inclusion and exclusion
- Programs have *impact* on the targets
- Impacts vary in magnitude
- An *impact evaluation* assesses the extent to which the program causes changes in the desired direction in the target population (Rossi *et al.*, 1979, p. 16).

The underlying metaphoric conception is that social problems are targets, and that the social program is aimed at the target. Hitting the target results in the impact, and the magnitude of the impact is an indicator of how effective the program has been. The evaluator must measure the impact of the program on the target. The target population must be defined, and social services are directed not *to* the target population but *at* the target problems. The targeting metaphor entails quite a different image than the industrial production metaphors but one coherent with these. The target metaphor is employed when the authors discuss the ultimate effects of the program, and the industrial production metaphors are used in discussing the monitoring of the program itself. They use the pipeline or conduit image when discussing outcomes and the target image when discussing impact, which is the ultimate result.

Once again, the metaphors can be mixed to a certain degree. Interventions can be delivered to the target or directed to the target population. *Coverage* is defined as the extent to which the program reaches the target population, combining the notions of both delivery systems and targets. The targeting metaphor maps out a particular aspect of social programs and their evaluation. And, according to Rossi and others, a comprehensive evaluation includes monitoring, impact assessment, and cost-benefit analysis.

A third possible metaphor employed extensively in the book is that of the *goal*. However, there is some question as to whether it should still be called metaphor. That is, goal is used literally to mean *purpose*. The notion of goals appears to be derived originally from sports or games, but it has lost much of its metaphoric connotation. Concepts can be derived from metaphors and gradually transformed into literal meanings, thus losing their metaphoric meanings. The more the concepts are used, the more they take on the meaning of their new application. For example, the *foot* of the mountain is clearly metaphorical in origin but is close to meaning literally the bottom of the mountain. On the other hand, most of the terms and concepts of industrial production applied to social programs are clearly metaphorical, though some are more so than others. A term like *outcomes* is well on its way to literal usage in the evaluation community. Thus, there seem to be degrees of metaphoric meaning for particular concepts, and these meanings change over time. In a few years we may see literal dictionary definitions for terms that we now consider metaphoric. Their metaphoric nature will then reside only in their etymology. With that caveat I will proceed to a metaphoric analysis of *goal* and its connection to the other concepts, bearing in mind that these notions may have passed into literal usage.

The original definition of goal seems to be that of a physical distance, in which a goal is set along a course — such as a race course, a game, or a sport. In the course of the race, game, or sport, the player is supposed to reach or attain that goal.

Program Activities Are Goal-Directed Movements

- Goals are unattained standards
- Goals and objective can be *set* and measured
- There are *gaps* between the goals and reality, between *where* one wants to be and where one is
- The intervention *closes* the *gap* between the two
- One seeks *convergence* between the program design and its implementation; there is *distance* between them
- Evaluations can *direct* the *course* of social life
- Evaluation can be a firm *guide*
- Surveys assess whether the target has been *reached*.

The latter statement is derived from a mixing of the goal and target metaphors and indicates the coherence between the dominant metaphors. This mixing of metaphors can be seen clearly in Rossi and others' definition of impact evaluation: 'impact evaluation-assessment is the extent to which the program causes change in the desired direction in the target population' (p. 16). Although the basic metaphor is that of impact and target, impact is defined in terms of direction and physical distance, which is essentially goal language. Often in the assessment of goals and objectives, a land surveying metaphor of marking off the landscape, triangulating, and measuring distance is used. So again, even though these various metaphors do not present a single consistent image of evaluation, they form a coherent conception. Rossi and other's conceptualization of evaluation is so complex that several metaphors are necessary to highlight different aspects. No single metaphor will do, but both the target and the goal metaphors highlight the aim, direction, and purpose of the program.

Target is ultimately derived from war and sport. Originally a target was a light round shield used in combat, and this came to be the object one aimed at in target practice. The etymology of *goal* is less clear. Apparently, the term was derived form an ancient rustic sport *(Oxford English*

Dictionary). In Old English it meant an obstacle, boundary, or limit. Eventually goal came to mean the terminal point of a race or the posts between which a ball is driven in a game or sport, as in football or soccer. And in archery the goal is the mark aimed at — that is, the target. But the notion that a game is non-serious, or just for fun, has not carried over from goal's original meaning. The goal metaphor has been stripped of its non-serious side and is used to mean a serious striving for achievement, or an earnest contest that is perhaps akin to war. Even though sports language is employed, social program evaluation is at least as serious as a game in the National Football League, which is serious indeed. Within this context, the player attains a goal in a sport or a game by scoring. Originally a score was a cut or a mark on something to keep count and eventually came to mean a line drawn for runners or marksmen to stand at. Ultimately, to *score* as a verb came to mean to make points in a game or contest (*Oxford English Dictionary*). Score also means one's performance on a test, as in a test score. Scores on outcome measures are very important in Rossi and others' framework: For example, net effects are measured in differences in scores on outcome measures. Apparently, both the target and goal metaphors, which are so pervasive in social program language, are derived from equating social programs with sports or games, or, more generally, contests (see Figure 2). Yet many of the metaphoric meanings are now lost, especially for goals.

In general, there is a strong directionality within all of these diverse yet coherent metaphors. Industrial production, such as in an assembly line or conduit, moves from one point to another, as does the trajectory traced by a missile as in archery, by a runner in a race, or the throwing of a ball through the goal as in a sport. Implicit in these metaphors is the movement of a physical object from one place to another. As more services are produced by the assembly line, more are delivered to the target population. As more services hit the target, there is more impact from the program. The more goals that are attained, the higher the scores and the more successful the program. Beneath these fundamental metaphors are the rather abstract notions of linearity and directionality — movement from one point to another. All of the basic metaphors share this abstract property and serve the purpose of indicating a certain kind of movement that is correlated with program success. Greater production, stronger impact, and more goals attained are all correlates of program success. Underlying the coherent metaphors, then, is a shared topological concept, a concept that remains invariant across metaphors.

The Building Metaphor in Program Evaluation

Yet another set of terms is applied directly to the evaluation itself rather than to the program. The evaluation must be a *firm assessment*, be a *firm guide,* produce *firm estimates of effects* and *solid information,* and not result in *faulty conclusions.* The construction terminology in evaluation is derived from such conventional metaphors as *Arguments Are Buildings* (Lakoff and Johnson, 1980) Evaluations, like arguments and theories, are conceptualized as physical structures, quite possibly because evaluations are recognized tacitly as arguments themselves. The building and construction metaphor is quite commonly applied to evaluations, regardless of the particular metaphors applied to social programs. Evaluations are expected to be firm, solid, well-constructed, and so on. They share the same basic societal metaphors as arguments, and these terms are applied not only in Rossi and others but in much of the evaluation literature.

Figure 2. An Extended Metaphoric Conception of Social Programs

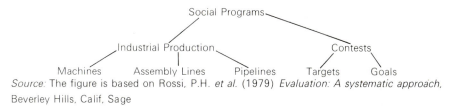

Source: The figure is based on Rossi, P.H. *et al.* (1979) *Evaluation: A systematic approach,* Beverley Hills, Calif, Sage

Thus, some aspects of evaluation are derived from particular metaphors about what social programs are. In conceiving of social programs as industrial production, the evaluation takes shape from the nature of the object evaluated. However, other aspects of evaluation are rendered by more general metaphors, such as *Arguments Are Buildings.* These aspects of evaluation seem to be independent of notions of what social programs are supposed to be. And there are even more fundamental metaphors employed in the articulation of programs and evaluation. These include metaphoric structurings of time and labor as material resources, events as objects, and activities as substances. Although these ideas fit well into the overall conceptual scheme, they are not dependent upon it. They are readily available in everyday thought. Hence, the metaphors employed in evaluations of social programs are both special ones drawn specifically for this purpose and common ones used in many other settings.

Even this does not exhaust the metaphoric structure of the book by Rossi and others. The discussion of cost-benefit analysis draws upon the economic and accounting literature, which has its own metaphoric structure. But, although the metaphoric structure is pervasive and extremely important in shaping the ideas in the book, it is difficult to discover and make explicit. We share so much of the common experience of assembly lines, goals, and targets that the discussion seems literal rather than metaphoric. In this sense, the metaphoric structure is nearly invisible.

The Metaphoric Nature of Evaluation

The realization that a great deal of evaluative thought is metaphoric in nature will no doubt surprise and disturb many evaluators. Many see evaluation of social programs as applied social science and may wonder how metaphors could be so crucial to their thinking. The metaphoric analysis raises a number of questions: To what degree does metaphor characterize all evaluative thinking? How does it work? Where do these metaphors come from? Are there conflicts between different schemes, depending upon one's underlying metaphors? Are all metaphors equally good? What is the scientific status of evaluation if this analysis is correct? Does such an analysis lead to relativism? Unfortunately, discussion of these issues is beyond the scope of this chapter. And, in general, the role of metaphor in thought is not well understood. (For further philosophical discussions of metaphor, see Sacks, 1978; Ortony, 1979; Johnson, 1981). This section briefly touches upon the origins of these metaphors, the values they embody, the purposes they serve, their scientific status, and their appropriateness.

Industrial production and sporting contests are often used as metaphors in evaluation because they are pervasive experiences in our society, and production and competition are primary values. Taken together, they entail winning. It is not surprising that we should evaluate our social programs from frameworks derived from such central experiences, and that these structural metaphors embody core values of American society. In employing these metaphors to evaluate social programs, we bring those values to bear upon social programs, sometimes explicitly but often tacitly.

Faced with the new task of evaluating social programs in the past two decades, evaluation theorists have turned to areas of their own experience that seem better defined. Evaluations therefore have been conceived and structured through concepts derived from other domains of experience. Differences in conceptions of evaluation often reflect differences in underlying metaphors, which are in turn derived from certain cultural experiences. The ultimate purpose of this metaphoric structuring is to tell us how to act as evaluators. In spite of the often expressed skepticism about the role of evaluation theory, without such conceptions to guide us we would not know how to act as evaluators. 'In all aspects of life, not just in politics or in love, we define our reality in terms of metaphors and then proceed to act on the basis of the metaphors' (Lakoff and Johnson, 1980, p. 158).

The metaphors discussed to this point substantially define the reality of the evaluator's world. Once an evaluator has accepted the basic metaphors, certain entailments follow. Of course, our thinking is not entirely determined by the metaphors we use, and we are not enslaved by our own concepts. The relationship between metaphors and thinking is more one of likelihood — of probability — than one of determination. For example, it is very likely that an evaluator will be led to certain types of evaluations if he or she sees social programs as industrial production. Furthermore, evaluators are taught certain metaphors as part of their training; it is part of their enculturation. Although they might conceivably overcome a particular way of viewing the world, as defined by certain metaphors, the pressure to be consistent is more likely to make them follow through with particular types of evaluations — to elaborate the metaphor, as it were. Such metaphoric structuring enables us to do a number of things in our evaluations and prevents us from doing others. Every way of viewing the world eliminates alternative possibilities. Metaphors highlight some things and shadow others, and the predominant views we have are necessarily partial and particular. Furthermore, metaphoric structures are derived from domains of our experience that are seldom logically consistent and fully coherent. This lack of consistency and coherence often carries over into our conceptions of evaluation.

Many evaluators and social planners see social programs as industrial production, targeting, and goal attainment and cannot see programs in any other way. Other theorists employ similar metaphors in their articulation of what evaluation is. In fact, these metaphors underlie one of the dominant views of social programs among professional evaluators in the United States, not because people adopt Rossi and others' point of view but because theorists draw upon common experiences and a common intellectual framework. However, as common as this point of view is, there are yet other evaluation theorists and planners who adopt different views of social programs and evaluations. They employ different metaphors — with different results in their conceptualization of evaluation. For example, responsive, illuminative, and stakeholder-based evaluation suggest different metaphors at work.

Not just any metaphor will do in structuring the concept of an evaluation. A former student of mine once wrote a paper in which she developed an evaluation system based upon the beliefs of a tribe of Plains Indians. Such a scheme is intriguing but unlikely to have much application in contemporary America, just as metaphors of industrial production would not have much appeal to the Plains Indians. Appropriate metaphors must be rooted in the experiences of the culture to be applicable. Metaphors used to evaluate social programs necessarily will be close to our core social values, although some theorists have attempted to create new evaluation approaches by deliberately developing different metaphors (Smith, 1981).

Embracing a particular set of metaphors not only expresses certain values but also promotes them. It is in the nature of metaphor that certain things are emphasized and others de-emphasized. Efficiency, effectiveness, goal seeking, and values of industrial production are promoted in the Rossi and others framework. The authors explicitly advocate these values which are embodied in their conceptual apparatus. Conceptions of evaluation are not value-neutral, and much of this inherent evaluation is embedded within the metaphoric structure. Different conceptions emphasize different values or weight the same values differently. Also the more common the metaphors employed to structure evaluation, the more persuasive and invisible the metaphors will be. Unusual metaphors are creative, but conventional metaphors shape most of our thinking and therefore seem natural.

Employing certain metaphors allows us not only to promulgate certain values but to do a number of other things as well, such as to refer and identify causes. For example, the employment of ontological metaphors, such as defining labor and time as substances, allows us to quantify things (Lakoff and Johnson, 1980). Defining a territory or putting a boundary around something is an act of quantification. Bounded objects, like social programs and social problems, have scope, dimension, and size. Within such a framework; an evaluator can locate social problems and measure them. This is usually accomplished through a *survey*, the original purpose of which was to determine the form, extent, and situation of parts of a tract of ground by linear and angular measurement *(Oxford English Dictionary)*.

Other entities can be thought of as containers. For example, the participants are *in* the program, but they cannot be *in* the problem, although they can be *part* of the problem. Containers define a limited space, with a bounded surface, a center, and periphery, and can be seen as holding a substance, which may vary in amount. If one sees the program as a container object, it can be measured.

Programs Are Containers

- That is *not much* of a program.
- The program *does not have any content.*
- The program *lacks substance.*
- That is the *core* of the program.

Machines, assembly lines, and pipelines can all be viewed as container objects. Things can be located in them or be part of them. The notion of a container object is abstract and deeply embedded in our thinking. In addition, one can conceive of the outcomes of a program as substances — which issue from the program container. The program has outcomes (a substance). For example, when discussing the outcomes of programs, Rossi and others often switch to their *Social Programs Are Conduits* metaphor. Contamination and purification are of primary concern, so that one can measure the net outcomes: 'An outcome is always a change in the level of a measurable variable' (Rossi and others, p. 164). The *gross* outcome effects are the measures of overall impact but the *net* outcome effects are those left after confounding effects have been removed (a mixing here of the conduit metaphor and an accounting metaphor, which they also use).

Both social programs and program outcomes can be quantified and measured via their metaphorical conversion into objects and substances, but the nature of their measurement differs. As metaphorical objects, programs have size, scope, and dimension, and require different methods of measurement than does the metaphorical substance of the outcomes. Objects may be described, and program description has received much attention. But, measurements of programs themselves have been limited compared to measurement of outcomes. Therefore, social programs normally must be converted into other categories, such as the time, costs, and procedures of the assembly line, before measurements become possible. In contrast, outcomes lend themselves more easily to direct measurement. An object may be dissimilar in its different parts but any quantity of a substance is like any other part of the substance. Hence, conceiving of outcomes as substances permits *cardinal* measurement — that is, the use of an interval scale. To be measurable in this way means that every instance of a commodity is a sum of perfectly identical parts or units. This is not literally true of the outcomes of social programs, but they often are treated that way in order to be quantifiable. In any case, quantification of programs and their outcomes is greatly facilitated by their metaphorical conversion into concrete objects and substances.

If outcomes are quantifiable we can define them as members of a particular statistical distribution, such as a normal curve. We might infer from the degree of overlap between the pre- and post-measured distributions the likelihood of the post-measure coming from a different statistical population. Hence, we begin employing statistical models, in which one treats the outcome scores as member of particular populations. A statistical treatment of impact data is a logical next step for Rossi and others to take, but the preliminary conceptual apparatus for doing this resides in the fundamental metaphors that they employ. For certain purposes, programs and activities are treated as if they were objects and substances. Obviously such conversions are useful.

The statistical model might be called a metaphor, but there is a significant difference between it and the overall metaphoric framework of Rossi and others. The statistical model is internally consistent: There is a single representation from which one can draw logical inferences that do not contradict each other. This is more similar to a scientific or mathematic model than the overall evaluation conceptualization of Rossi and others. But, there is no question that metaphoric thinking plays an important role in scientific thinking. For example, Kurt Lewin's theories draw heavily on analogies with physical theories in the use of certain concepts, such as *field, sector, force,* and *fluidity* (Black, 1962). More recently, cognitive psychology has conceived of the human mind as a computer, employing such concepts as *information processing, feedback, encoding*, and *memory storage* (Boyd, 1979). Metaphors play a constitutive role in scientific theories, although exactly how this role is performed is a matter of dispute (Kuhn, 1979). Of course, the use of metaphors does not mean that a conception is nonscientific. The traditional view of science as a clear, unambiguous, testable rendering of external reality in literal language has given way to a view of knowledge as based upon mental constructions (Ortony, 1979). Perhaps the significant difference between scientific theories and conceptions of evaluation is their internal consistency. Formal scientific theories can be seen as attempts to extend a set of metaphors consistently, whereas metaphors underlying evaluation are rarely consistent (Lakoff and Johnson, 1980).

However, there is another important difference between conceptions of evaluation and scientific theories — a difference of purpose. One might imagine that *minds are computers* and investigate the way in which information processing is done by the mind. According to Boyd (1979), a term like this provides 'espistemic access' to the phenomenon being investigated. Other investigators may extend the concept until it becomes descriptive of how the mind functions — and eventually far removed from what the term means in the study of computers. But metaphors in conceptions of evaluation are not quite like this. The purpose of *Social Programs Are Conduits* is not to arrive at a finer definition of social programs (though one may do so). The researchers in the field do not investigate the extent to which social programs really resemble conduits. Rather, the main purpose is to impose the metaphor so that one knows how to act — that is, how to evaluate. Given the fundamental metaphors, certain investigations and judgments become possible. The judgments are about whether the social programs are any good, not about whether the metaphors fit and not even about finer descriptions of the programs themselves. The difference is between describing and evaluating: these are fundamentally different acts. In both cases metaphors are employed but to different ends.

Perhaps this difference can be seen more clearly if the roles are reversed. Suppose that the *Minds Are Computers* metaphor is used for evaluation purposes. One can imagine trying to assess the information processing capacity, the memory storage, and the encoding processes of the mind — even comparing different minds on these dimensions. No doubt various criteria for evaluating would emerge from our experience with computers, and no doubt one could develop reliable procedures for assessment. One might end up saying that the information processing of a particular mind was very strong but the feedback mechanisms were poor. One would use concepts similar to those in cognitive psychology, but the purpose would be quite different than that of trying to describe the mind by computer analogies or judging the goodness of it. In the act of evaluating, the metaphor is used to generate criteria for making judgments of worth. Conversely, if one used the metaphor *Social Programs Are*

Assembly Lines in a descriptive investigation, one would investigate the degree to which social programs actually resemble assembly lines, modifying one's notions of industrial production to fit the operation of social programs. This is not what evaluation theorists or evaluators do.

In general, these underlying metaphors provide some of the basic concepts that instruct us on how to proceed. If one sees arguments as wars, one will argue in a certain fashion. If one sees social programs as industrial production, then one will evaluate in a certain fashion. Once one is committed to a particular metaphor, certain entailments arise for both thought and action. Thus, the dominant metaphors shape our actions. But not all metaphors are equally good for the purposes they are supposed to serve. There can be good and bad and appropriate and inappropriate metaphors, just as there can be good and bad social programs (Binkley, 1981; Booth, 1978; Loewenberg, 1981). The sense in which a metaphor is true, correct, or appropriate is beyond the limits of this chapter, but what can be said briefly is that the underlying metaphors must be considered within the context of the overall conception of evaluation. That is, one must judge the consequences of the overall conception. These judgments must be based upon criteria broader than being simply true or false as the notion is commonly understood. Evaluators of social programs must embrace comprehensive notions of correctness, including rightness and wrongness. The obligation of the evaluator is broader than that of the describer.

In retrospect, perhaps it is not so surprising that metaphoric thinking is important in evaluation. Black (1962) has explored the similarity between scientific models and metaphors and concludes that both models and metaphors play an indispensable role in scientific thinking. In fact, all intellectual pursuits rely upon such 'exercises of the imagination .... Perhaps every science must start with metaphor and end with algebra; and perhaps without the metaphor there would never have been any algebra' (Black, 1962, p. 242).

Acknowledgements

I would like to thank Lee Cronbach, Robert Ennis, Don Hogben, Mark Johnson, Sandra Mathison, James Pearson, and Paul Silver for providing helpful comments.

References

BINKLEY, T. (1981) 'On the truth and probity of metaphor' in JOHNSON, M. (Ed.) *Philosophical Perspectives on Metaphor*, Minneapolis, University of Minnesota Press.
BLACK, M. (1962) *Models and Metaphors*, Ithaca, NY, Cornell University Press.

BOOTH, W.C. (1978) 'Metaphor as rhetoric: the problem of evaluation' in SACKS, S. (Ed.) *On Metaphor*, Chicago, University of Chicago Press.

BOYD, R. (1979) 'Metaphor and theory change: What is "metaphor" a metaphor for?' in ORTONY, A. (Ed.) *Metaphor and Thought*, Cambridge, England, Cambridge University Press.

JOHNSON M. (Ed.) (1981) *Philosophical Perspectives on Metaphor*, Minneapolis, University of Minnesota Press.

KUHN, T.S. (1979) 'Metaphor in science' in ORTONY, A. (Ed.) *Metaphor and Thought*, Cambridge, England, Cambridge University Press.

LAKOFF, G. and JOHNSON, M. (1980) *Metaphors We Live By*, Chicago, University of Chicago Press.

LOEWENBERG, I. (1981) 'Identifying metaphors' in JOHNSON, M. (Ed.) *Philosophical Perspectives on Metaphor*, Minneapolis, University of Minnestoa Press.

McLAUGHLIN, M.W. (1975) *Evaluation and Reform*, Cambridge, Mass, Ballinger.

ORTONY, A. (Ed.) (1979) *Metaphor and Thought*, Cambridge, England, Cambridge University Press.

ROSSI, P.H., FREEMAN, H.E. and WRIGHT, S.R. (1979) *Evaluation: A Systematic Approach*, Beverly Hills, Calif., Sage.

SACKS, S. (Ed.) (1978) *On Metaphor*, Chicago, University of Chicago Press.

SCHÖN, D.A. (1979) 'Generative metaphor: a perspective on problem-setting in social policy' in ORTONY, A. (Ed.) *Metaphor and Thought*, Cambridge, England, Cambridge University Press.

SMITH, N.L. (Ed.) (1981) *Metaphors for Evaluation*, Beverly Hills, Calif., Sage Publications.

TURNER, V. (1974) *Dramas, Fields, and Metaphors*, Ithaca, NY, Cornell University Press.

3
Radical Propositions:
Fusing Fact and Value

Introduction

Michael Scriven has long been one of the most provocative thinkers in evaluation. He has produced some of the classic papers of this still-young field of endeavor and has taken some of the most unusual and controversial positions on various issues. This chapter follows in that tradition.

Scriven contends that most educational research is virtually worthless since it does not address the practical problems of the field faced by practitioners. The reason for this is that educational researchers have adopted the basic research paradigms of social sciences like psychology, which leads them to produce knowledge of little relevance. Rather than addressing problems of how children process knowledge, educational researchers should determine what teaching approaches work best in teaching children to read, a practical problem. Such problems are best addressed by studying successful teachers not by developing theories. Hence, evaluation is a better model for educational research than are the models of the basic sciences.

Evaluation very much involves values, according to Scriven. The value-free stance adopted by many researchers and evaluators — such as merely collecting information and letting administrators value it as they will — is completely wrong. The making of value judgments can be as objectively accomplished as the determination of fact, and in truth scientific investigations cannot proceed without evaluative judgments. As a result of these considerations, Scriven calls for a far-reaching reform of how research is conducted and of how educational researchers are trained. In Scriven's mind the separation of fact and value, a heritage of the logical positivist tradition, was ruinous for the practice of educational research and predicated upon the false dogma of value-free science.

Almost as an illustration of the inadequacy of value-free research, Kirkup begins her chapter by lamenting the inadequacy of 'straight' research to help her in her job of evaluating the women's studies courses at the Open University — she simply could not account for the critical interpersonal relationships and institutional politics that counted for so much. Faced with practical problems she has evolved her own theoretical position on evaluation, drawing upon both the feminist and evaluation literature to do so.

Kirkup claims that the experience of individuals and groups must be respected so much that one should not evaluate another's work unless one is thoroughly familiar, even sympathetic, to the other's experiences. This raises the question of whether men have any business evaluating women's studies at all, since men are too far removed from women's experiences and too biased.

Kirkup's solution was to adopt a collaborative research strategy in which she would rely heavily upon the students' experiences and in which she would also share responsibility for the evaluation with the students and staff. She then tried out her approach in an actual evaluation and found her strategy partially blunted by the institutional framework in which she worked. Although she was not satisfied with the results, all duly reported in the chapter here, her chapter and Scriven's demonstrate the dissatisfaction and questioning of the split between fact and value in the traditional educational research paradigm.

Evaluation as a Paradigm for Educational Research

Michael Scriven
University of Western Australia

Education is a field like medicine in that its name simultaneously refers to a practice and to a field of disciplined enquiry. In fact, both fields of enquiry have a number of very different sub-fields — there is the history of medicine or education; the area of medical ethics corresponding to one part of the philosophy of education; medical jurisprudence corresponding to the law of education, and so on. The paradigm of research in the area of the philosophy of education, to take one example, is surely the paradigm of philosophical research in any area — and the same for the history of education (or medicine) and for the law of education or medicine.

But that leaves open the area of research that we normally think of as the domain of scientific research in medicine or education. Traditionally, and I think rather carelessly, we have tended to suppose that in this area of medical or educational research the correct model is that of the related sciences. That is, for example, educational research has modelled itself on social science research. Now in medical research that approach has brought us some problems because it seems to lead to results that conflict with the practical wisdom of physicians and the economic realities of patients. The search for ever-more-perfect diagnoses (surely the correct model of scientific research) leads us to the CAT scanner 'race' and the latest magnetic resonance scanner, possibly costing more than a million dollars a year to maintain. The heart-lung machines, in vitro fertilization, artificial joints and hearts, and amniocentesis have all plunged us into raging controversies to which the scientific model of research provides no answer and no methodology for finding an answer. The same can be seen in education with the refined development of IQ tests, norm-referenced testing, teaching machines and token economies for classroom management. The conventional 'scientific paradigm' way of dealing with all this is to refuse to deal with it, that is, to say that these problems are not the business of science — they are values issues, and must be sorted out by the citizenry.

Most readers will probably feel a good deal of sympathy — perhaps complete agreement with this answer. But I think this answer is one we have been conditioned to accept by the wide acceptance of a certain paradigm of scientific research, a paradigm which crucially misrepresents the relation between pure science and practical science. In my view, the very idea that the problem of what to do with the internal combustion engine is a social problem, whereas the problem of how it works (or how to make it work better) is a scientific one, is a sign of three undesirable conditions:

- Social irresponsibility by scientists, due to the use of a wrong paradigm, and insensitivity to that fact.
- Laboratory science dominating field science instead of vice versa.
- A model of practical scientific research which excludes several crucial elements that the practitioner sees as defining the problem.

While it's clear that the traditional paradigm of scientific research in the social sciences does apply to many of the special problems that the academic scientist addresses, it's equally clear that it's a very poor model for most of what I'll call practical scientific research, by contrast with basic research. Of course, practical research is often done in the laboratory and in the academy, so I don't want to persist with the terms 'laboratory science' or 'academic science' as the antonyms to 'practical science' but the ease with which those terms come to mind for the task reminds us that the usual model, which after all emanates from the prestigious labs and academies, has ignored or misrepresented the practitioner. And the widespread use of the term *'applied science'* as a synonym for *'practical science'* nicely epitomizes this set of implicit values, because it presupposes that practical problems are to be handled by applying some more general or abstract principles uncovered by 'pure' or 'basic' science. The simple truth is quite different; practical problems are defined by reference to several parameters concerning which the basic scientist gathers no data and rarely has any competence. These include the not-entirely-independent parameters of cost, ethicality, political feasibility, the set of practicable alternatives, system lability, and overall practical significance. What I am proposing here is simply a model or paradigm for practical research — and hence for the central core of educational (and medical) research — that includes these parameters and regards them as absolutely crucial, while acknowledging the frequent but not universal importance of finding general laws, determining statistical significance, modelling deep structure, and hypothesis-testing — the processes that characterize various aspects of the traditional scientific model and comprise a fine model for basic research. To suggest that the basic research model is appropriate as a model for scientific research is either to suggest that the practical is unimportant, a self-contradiction, or to suggest that science is necessarily incapable of dealing with the dimensions of the practical, an allegation without evidence though attractive to many academics. The true situation is simply that the traditional scientific paradigm represents an extremely narrow conception of science, a conception that includes maths and physics and lab psychology but excludes half the subjects that we have been painstakingly raising to the status of science in more recent years, such as ergonomics and cost-analysis, policy studies, methodology and needs assessment. My general thesis is that practical science involves all of these (and more), and is dominated by a paradigm that integrates them all in a way analogous to the way in which experimental design integrates the other — the paradigm is the most general paradigm for scientific research so that pure science should be seen as a special case of limited interest.

The consequences of this proposal may be so serious as to force people to treat it as a joke. Let me illustrate two of its consequences briefly.

1   Consequences for training of educational researchers competent to handle practical problems. Given a relatively fixed amount of time for doing this, the two necessary consequences are first that a good deal of the time currently spent on statistics and traditional experimental design will have to be put into cost analysis, side-effect search techniques, external validity analysis, and generalizability analysis. Second, the existing sections of the associated curriculum, for example on philosophy of education, will have to cover the conceptual analysis of practical choices, and their presuppositions, the ethics of testing, affirmative action, etc., while the unit on sociology of education will have to develop political feasibility and systems analysis, the history unit will have to teach the use of history to develop projections, lability estimates and overall perspectives, the educational psychology component will have to teach needs assessment — and so on. Only a co-ordinated and massive effort from every faculty member in a department of education, combined with massive retraining of that faculty, can turn out professional educational researchers competent to handle practical problems in education.

That's a radical prescription, but the alternative to it is worse — and, I believe inevitable if we do not adopt the prescription. The alternative is the continued dismissal of the educational researcher and his or her work as irrelevant, an extravagance, not responsive, not reliable. This will mean the continued loss of necessary funding, social respect and influence. And, in my view, much though not all of that loss to date has been fully deserved. Which brings us to the second consequence of taking the new paradigm seriously — consequence for the content of research itself.

2   The first research consequence of the evaluation paradigm is that it is self-referent. One might say 'Evaluation begins at home'; evaluators have to be evaluated. To put it in other terms, practical research is itself an allegedly useful practical activity and hence must be subject to the same scrutiny for cost-effectiveness, ethicality, etc. that it will apply to the things that it studies. I invite you to apply these standards to the dissertation proposals and professional journal articles that you see. Are they economically justified expenditures of the author's time, and yours — and the taxpayer's money? Is there any way, by minor change or completely new choice of topic — that they could be more valuable? If so, why not make that change? Exactly what has research contributed to today's educational practice? It is not easy to say. Is that because the problems are so intransigent — or is it because the paradigm was pure research, not practical investigation? The research on classroom teaching, on school management, on discipline, on audiovisual, on special education, on computer-assisted education — in all these cases, and many more, much of the research, often nearly all of it, has been designed on the *'quest for knowledge'* model rather than the *'improvement of practice'* model. And has been wasted, trivial, unremembered as a result; as a result of not looking at itself as an activity to be ruthlessly evaluated.

Notice that this is in no way an attack on basic research. We need some basic research in order to solve practical problems, and some because of the great intellectual payoffs it promises — 'pure' research. And pure research often has unintended practical payoffs. It is nevertheless true that much and probably most education research has no possible justification within a practical field, which is what education is. All too often, people think that pure research is justified within education because it's part of the traditional package of scientific research — some pure and some applied. That's a non-sequitur. If you want to do pure research on learning, you get into psychology not education, and not educational psychology. Educational research is not, I am suggesting, to be defined as 'all research that in any way involves concepts related to education', because that's too broad (it includes learning theory), but as *'research that contributes to the facilitation of education'*, just as medical research should not be defined as 'all research that involves concepts related to medicine', since that brings in all physiological and haematological research, but simply as research contributing to health. The fact that pure research in related fields often surprises us by paying off for practical problems provides no justification for educational researchers to do it, since such results are accidental side effects and less frequent than payoffs from well-designed research aimed at problem-solving. (At least this is true as far as we know, when done by researchers of comparable talent. Certainly it has to be the operative assumption until disproved.)

Whether or not we tidy up the definition of the field of educational research in this way, however, is much less important than the need to tidy up our efforts to select and solve problems that really pay off for practitioners, rather than those that catch the interest of a researcher who was trained only to look at the narrowly conceived 'scientific' component of practical problems. We have to change our vision of ourselves, I believe, into service-researchers rather than pure-scientific-researchers — though what we should serve is not the whims of the Australian Federation of Teachers or of the Minister, but the needs of the student and the professional needs of those others who help students.

In case you think this is coming too close to platitudes, let's pick up a couple of the more striking consequences of this aspect of the position.

First, it relegates the search for explanations, i.e. for the theoretical understanding, to a secondary position by comparison with the search for improvements. It is policy-oriented rather than theory-oriented. It is part of the traditional mythology of ivory tower research that you can't improve something without understanding it, though the most naive student of the history of serendipity or folk medicine or pharmacy or the crafts knows of a dozen famous fixes whose mechanism was and often still is unknown, from aspirin and the boomerang up and down. (And others where an explanation is trivial.) The correct view is that the search for understanding sometimes yields solutions to practical problems; and it's sometimes worth a try because the alternatives seem unpromising and the prospect of either practical or intellectual payoff justifies the effort and cost. Without careful thought about that justification, however, we spend far too much of our time mimicking what we think pure scientists do instead of doing something worthwhile; searching for deep causes when fixes will do. Additionally, we often think that 'understanding' requires a theory: but understanding why a child is upset today, or struggling to cope with easy material, may only require knowledge of a simple fact about the home situation and the usual trivia about human nature known to our palaeolithic forbears.

So the first search for understanding, as for fixes, should eschew theory. The model to keep in mind is the Toll Bridge Model. You can save millions a year on the three San Francisco Bay toll bridges by collecting twice the toll in one direction; more, if you realize that before building the toll plazas. But that suggestion, though widely publicized, was ignored for nearly twenty years, apparently because it didn't come from the staff of the Bridge Authorities or traffic engineers in their consultancies. Even the beauty of solutions to practical problems is in the eye of the beholder and may be ignored if that eye has been conditioned to look only towards the heights for insights.

Consider another practical consequence of the evaluation paradigm's self-reference. In my view, the time for public defense of a dissertation is when the proposal has been formulated, not when the research has been completed. Some huge though unknown proportion of doctoral — let alone lower-level dissertations — simply lack justification of the effort involved, either because of design errors or because of failures to take account of the factors that matter in practice, such as cost or support requirements. And I do not mean to suggest — as one might suppose from what I've just said — that we need more complex or sophisticated studies, something for which we may well lack the time and talent. Not at all. Valuable studies of practical problems are often far simpler than the ones usually proposed. The practitioners, like psychological patients, need fixes not 'deep understanding — or at least they need to know when a supposed and popular fix is not a fix. How often in the literature does one find a distinguished educational researcher saying something like 'without an adequate theory of learning, it's impossible to evaluate teaching'! What nonsense! One might as well say that if you don't have an adequate theory of the operation of automobile engines, you can't tell whether your car is running well; or that without understanding the causes of illness one can't identify its presence. Here we have the confusion of theoretical under-standing with the very identification of a problem, let alone with its solution.

Evaluation is sometimes just as instant and certain as any observation or measurement; it is, for example, part of the database, not the set of conclusions of a study that a particular student composition is badly organized though it makes a good point. Only an idealogical block makes us think that evaluation must be arbitrary, capricious, subjective, idiosyn-cratic, unscientific; those who thunder to their introductory educational psychology courses about the empiricist paradigm of value-free research in the social sciences do not even notice the schizophrenia with which they grade — that is, evaluate — those same students, using tests designed and marked with all the considerable sophistication that educational psy-chology can contribute. Evaluation is not an add-on to true scientific research, it is part of all serious scientific activities. We'll come back to that point in a moment. First, let me pursue one step further the effects on educational research of what I am now saying.

Let us consider for a moment the difference between the ivory-tower research approach to particular problem and the practical research approach. The problem, or family of problems, is of unparalleled im-portance to education. It is the problem of how to improve the teaching of handicapped children; or of normal children; or the problem of how to maintain order in an unruly classroom or school. I have frequently posed this problem to groups of educational researchers or post-grad social scientists in education or even to educational administrators. In all cases, the results are about the same. What one must do, they suggest, is find out — from the literature or by developing a theory — which variables control the outcomes in question and then modify those variables. I ask: Is there any way to find that out besides the ways that researchers have been trying for decades? Well, basically, No, they say; except to do it better; the literature search, the design, the run, the data crunch. But there is a much better way, and the fact they do not think of it immediately shows how far we have come from commonsense. You must begin by identifying a number of practitioners who are outstandingly successful at the task in question; you must then use all the tricks in the book to identify the distinctive features of their approach (possibly but not necessarily by discrepancy comparisons with unsuccessful practitioners); you then teach new or unsuccessful practitioners to use the winning ways and retest until you get an exportable formula. If we'd done that 30 or 50 years ago with teachers, we could have saved most of the wasted efforts between then and the 'refined time on task' approach which we in fact reached by macro-analysis of relative success data. And in the administrative area we would almost certainly have a fix for many of the discipline problems that we still lack. It goes contrary to the very spirit of the traditional model to think that the practitioner knows more than the researcher about teaching or discipline; but the simple distinction between *knowing how* and *knowing that* could save one's self-respect and facilitate getting on with the job. You don't disregard successful prospectors because you can't understand how diamonds could possibly be found in the Pilbara, you rush out and start finding out where exactly to find them.

So the effects on training researchers and on selecting research problems and on research designs and on administering research, of the move to the evaluation model are substantial. It's time to summarize what's been said so far and perhaps say a little more about the model.

Evaluation research can be a far more complex business than hypothesis-testing, which is only part of some evaluations. Many evaluations involve no traditional experimental design and no quantitative analysis at all; but even those that do, involve many more dimensions such as cost and ethics. Yet it is completely wrong to conclude from this design complexity that evaluation is of its nature epistemologically or inferentially complex. The same mistake was made about causation — because it often takes a complex study to determine causation it was thought that causation was a logically complex notion. It is not: 'He moved the block across the table' reports an observation, not infallible but highly reliable, just like an evaluation of an answer in a maths test as wrong, or an evaluation of the organization of a presentation like this one. The traditional analysis of evaluation, then, like that of causation, was based on fear of the unknown rather than the common-sense uses of the terms. Reading the efforts by Bertrand Russell fifty years ago, and by recent writers in the *Educational Researcher* to dispense with the notion of causation in scientific research is just as clear an indication of contempt for the practitioner as the attempts to rule evaluation out of bounds. Those are the two key concepts of practice, in science and outside it, and it takes only moments of looking through the most austere writings of paradigm mathematicians or physicists, let alone social scientists, to find hard-core, rock-solid straight forward uses of *causation* and *evaluation*.

Our ideology misleads us more than we know. Description, classification, explanation, generalization, causation, prediction, evaluation — these are the key basic notions of scientific research, and they are highly independent; for example, prediction is just as independent of explanation as evaluation is, a fact still denied by many in the grip of an oversimplified philosophy of science. One might like to have a simpler world, and keep evaluation out of the scientific bed, but then of course you wouldn't have science itself, not because evaluation is too important to exclude, but because the difference between good and bad hypotheses, predictions, classifications, observations and so on is itself evaluative. Science needs methodology, and methodology is a normative subject. Economists often wish to dump welfare economics because it's such a tiresome subject, just as many political scientists would like to dump policy studies or political theory and statisticians would like to cut off evaluation — but when they get to the surgery, they find it is their own heart that they have condemned. It is often true that we detest part of ourselves, but it is no basis for surgery, only for therapy.

Let me finish this study of our defences against recognizing the importance of evaluation with a reference to the 'apples and oranges' argument.

One very often hears it said, by someone objecting to an attempt at a 'bottom-line' evaluative conclusion about the comparative merit of two rather disparate entities such as programs or products, that such an attempted comparison is 'like comparing apples and oranges'. And so it is. And so, of course, we can do it, in just the sensible ways that everyone does when shopping for fruit. That is, we use some of the cross-cutting criteria of quality, cost and consumer needs or preferences to help us pick a winner. The irony is that the very simile that the academic uses to justify eschewal of comparative evaluation needs only a little closer examination to be seen as containing the opposite message. It is of the essence of evaluation to compare what is different and, in particular, things that are different in more than one dimension. Differences along one dimension are completely handled by mere measurement. That measurement may comprise evaluation as when we evaluate runners by timing them over a fixed distance, or weightlifters and high jumpers analogously. But differences in more than one dimension, although they can be described by measurement, require a further process of weighting and combining those measurements in order to reach an evaluative conclusion. That further process is quite complex even in decathlon, where the events are equally weighted, because the intervals between the performances of competitors on each event (and not just their ranking) are converted to a common metric. In the yachting equivalent, the Admiral's Cup, by contrast, the events are differentially weighted but only the rankings in each count, and the ranking provides an easy common currency. But in gymnastics or diving, each individual performance is evaluated by considering it as a multi-dimensional achievement with certain pre-determined weights for the dimensions. How can one possibly compare a three-and-a-half forward somersault with a reverse gainer including a double twist, one might say — surely that is like comparing apples and oranges? Indeed it is — which means it's easy enough — and in fact we can do it quantitatively and with high reliability.

Thus evaluation of the simpler kinds can be thought of as a generalization of measurement; yet, at the other extreme, it extends far into the non-quantitative domain without losing its objectivity and reliability. Even the simpler kinds, however, are different from most measurements in that they involve an immensely important pair of decisions as to what performances are relevant and how they should be weighted. Those decisions require detailed justification, although they are rarely accorded it. No better example could be given than the evaluation of intelligence; but there are other good examples such as the evaluation of candidates for a teaching job or for college admission; of essays in an English examination or of whole exam papers; or of patients for sanity in court certification procedures or of prisoners for rehabilitation at parole board hearings. In each case a good deal is at stake and quite sophisticated methodology is involved. Yet little scholarly literature is devoted to the detailed procedure — by contrast with the semi-popular literature about IQ which merely reacts to certain overall features of the test and its results. And by contrast with the literature on the finer points of statistical analysis. And we find a similar backwardness in discussing the evaluative applications of statistics for example in assessing the significance of a hypothesis or the difference between statistical significance and educational significance. Few statistics texts even today contain a halfway decent discussion of either issue, and yet virtually no use of statistics in education can avoid them.

It is hard to avoid the impression that there is a reluctance to confront the practical issues. Indeed, as we look closer at, for example, the primitive state of the evaluation of teaching or research or applications for research funds, we begin to see the influence of a deeper reluctance, indeed a fear, of evaluation in particular. 'Judge not that ye be not judged' is a great approach to anxiety reduction but incompatible with the scientific mission — which requires that one judge, critically and constantly, the hypotheses, designs, experiments and analyses of oneself and others.

I do not believe one can reconcile the widespread support for the doctrine of value-free social science with the continued, indeed inescapable, practice of evaluation by social scientists — of the work and worth of students, subordinates, peers and selves — except by invoking a kind of phobia which made them blind to the contradiction between their doctrine and their practice. This phobia, which I call valuephobia, blocked us for nearly a century from addressing explicitly the methodology of evaluation and the systematic evaluation of our own practices in social science research. For educational research this was particularly unfortunate because these were years when vast resources were available for research, when vast new systems of education were developed, and when at last our supporters gave up on us. Opportunities on that scale may never come again. Certainly they will not be justified until we show that we understand, better than we have so far, ourselves and what we are doing and how to make it useful to others. The key to that understanding is understanding first, that science is essentially an evaluative process and hence that the value-free doctrine is nonsense; second, that very little educational reasearch that is not evaluative is justifiable, and whatever evaluative research is done must itself be evaluated; third, that the two previous points mean that our track record to date is appalling and we almost have to start justifying our existence from scratch, not because we lacked tools or talent, not because the problems were overwhelmingly difficult but principally because we worshipped false gods in order to disguise the truth from ourselves.

This is a terrible indictment, and it oversimplifies matters a little. A small part of recent research on teaching, for example, has been serious practical research. In Rosenshine's words: 'In the past five years our knowledge of successful teaching has increased considerably. There have been numerous successful experimental studies in which teachers have been trained to increase the academic achievement of their students.' ('Teaching Functions in Instructional Programs', *The Elementary School Journal*, March 1983, p. 335) The significance of this remark lies chiefly in the implied contrast, which is with the years prior to 1978. But the continued emphasis on the trivia of interaction analysis, for example, makes clear that no wholesale reform has occurred.

Perhaps the simplest demonstration of the still-desperate state of educational research is the lack of critical analysis or evaluation studies of computer assisted instruction. Here we have all the earmarks of social mania — vast amounts of money being spent on hardware without software, demands that a new subject be incorporated in a hard-pressed curriculum without needs assessment or with absurd suggestions about the need for it (to train programers, an essentially non-existent job market), with the added spice of pronouncements by heads of state or surgeons-general about the wickedness of arcade games. In this maelstrom, which has been raging for several years, can one detect the steadying influence of the educational researchers and their findings? Scarcely. One's fingers are not all needed to count the valid studies of CAI plus the press releases of our professional associations. Are such matters beneath contempt? Are our other research projects so much more important? The track record suggests otherwise. There was a time when the medical profession and associations thought it beneath their dignity to make announcements about the evils of smoking or the ineffectiveness of laetrile. Fortunately, they have changed and it is time for us to follow suit.

Unpacking the Evaluation Paradigm

When social scientists, apparently contrary to their religion, started accepting evaluation contracts in the late 1960s, the rationalization was embodied in what we can call the Naive Social Science Model of evaluation. On this approach, it was possible to do evaluations without actually making any judgments of value. One simply had the clients tell you what facts they lacked, for example, about program outcomes, you provided these facts and they then attached whatever values they liked to these facts. Ergo — evaluations without valuing!

You could even begin by finding out what they valued, investigate to see if any such things had emerged, score these results against the clients' values profile and report back. This variation would give a conditional evaluative result; 'If one values X more than Y, the program was a good one.' The scientists could still avoid any commitment to specific values.

A third variation exploited the marginally evaluative part of language which refers to 'success' and 'achievement' rather than 'good' and 'valuable'. If the program's goals are achieved, it is successful — and that, presumably, was what the client wanted to know.

These moves, which preserved the value-virginity of the investigator, ran afoul of several problems of which perhaps the leading ones were:

1   What to do about side effects; since nobody expects these, the evaluator hasn't been given any standards by which to judge them. Should they be disregarded; referred back to the client for evaluation; sought for; not sought for too assiduously; regarded as of potentially greater importance than the intended effects, and hence their discovery regarded as possibly the most important — and normally the most difficult — part of the investigation?

2   What to do about a number of obviously important issues like cost or extremely promising decision-alternatives if they happen not to have been included in the goals (the problem of missing factors) although it is obvious that they should have been taken into account by any rational decision-maker

3   What to do about a variety of possible errors in the values or goals of the client, such as inconsistency or factually false presuppositions or the failure to have detected serious ambiguities

4   What to do with clients who can't combine the results of a multidimensional report in a way that is consistent with their ends

5   What to do about ethics, an issue not always independent of the precending[1]

The tough-minded value-free disciple tried to treat as many as possible of these problems as not part of the job, but this obviously showed a lack of concern with professional ethics (which seemed immune to the value free prohibition), and a lack of concern for the client's needs which was rather more worrying than the ethics for someone interested in further contracts.

The next move is to try to handle these problems by referring them back to the client for answers. But evaluators' clients are not the only people with a stake in education; should not the stakeholders be consulted too? It's not good professional ethics to assume that just because someone wants another person or group investigated, one is entitled to undertake the investigation without consulting with the other group (one of the key differences between product and program evaluation). In deciding whether to go ahead, and also in deciding what to weigh to what extent, it seems appropriate to be at least consulting with and influenced by even if not controlled by the service providers (teachers, school administrators etc.), the parents, the taxpayers, the local authority or school board, and the students — rather than just with the funding or supervisory agency that is the usual client. Even if you ignore ethics, considerations of politics and of mere efficiency require more than a cosy client-consultant treatment of these problems.

But bringing everyone in on the act does not generate a solution in itself — though there are one or two evaluators who sometimes sound as if they think so — it merely makes the problem more complicated.

One way to think of evaluation as a discipline is to see it as the accumulation of ways to handle these and a number of related problems. What is characteristic about it is not the area of common ground that it shares with traditional social science research, much of which it frequently needs, but the differentiae. Amongst these one would have to list the intrusion of ethics, cost analysis and problem redefinition, especially the way in which the nature of whatever is being evaluated and the nature of a sound evaluation of it depends on very complicated social interactions.

Another way to see evaluation is simply as the effort to answer questions that require you to find out what the merit, worth or value of things are, rather than their size, weight or number. It is obvious to anyone who has ever read serious product evaluations that there is no difficulty of principle in applying scientific research to find out such answers. It's equally obvious to anyone who has done a few program evaluations, that product evaluation isn't all there is to evaluation; but its existence is an existence proof of the feasibility of the general type of enterprise since there are many cases of program evaluation that principally consist of product evaluation. For example, there are reading programs that cannot be justified for any school; there are others that are live options in some types of school and not in others; there are some that should be considered in almost any school. We don't have all the data and syntheses of the data that we need in order to list every current reading program under one or the other of those headings, but it isn't particularly hard to do the research that makes that listing possible. It's just that nearly all of our research on reading, all those millions of hours of work, has gone into studies that do not tell us the answer — or even moves us far towards an answer — to the basic question of what materials to use in teaching it. It's easy to find research-oriented rationalizations of this fact; but no excuse that should cut any ice with parents or teachers or taxpayers. They want consumer reports on the products they pay for, and there is no reason why they shouldn't get them. Of course, there will remain questions about how best to use the materials, train the teachers, group the pupils and so on, just as there are similar questions about every drug that comes on the market. But that doesn't mean we shouldn't be doing drug outcome studies, in which we standardize the environment of treatment for the sake of getting one answer at a time.

I would be inclined to say that it is now pretty obvious how to deal with the above problems, from the point of view of someone who accepts evaluation as one if not the most important type of research. It is even more obvious that one can hardly ignore such problems. Yet current texts in educational research more often than not produce a version of the Naive Social Science model that cannot deal with these problems at all; it usually reads something like this ...

'In order to evaluate a program, you
1 Identify the goals of the program
2 Convert them into behavioural objectives
3 Identify tests (or construct them) that will measure these objectives
4 Run these tests on the target population
5 Crunch the data
6 Report whether or not, or to what degree, the goals have been met.'

It will be obvious that this approach runs into all the problems listed above. It is also of some interest that the same problems apply to a slightly reworded version of the above that is sometimes called the Managerial Model of evaluation that is to be found in most texts on program and personnel management.

This is not the place to set out in detail how one goes about handling all these problems and many others; a concise treatment will be found in the entry 'Key Evaluation Checklist' and the cross-references from it, in the present author's *Evaluation Thesaurus* (3rd Edition, Edgepress, 1981). There is a standard set of about fourteen questions that need to be investigated in most evaluations, of which only one is the traditional investigation of alleged or hypothesized effects so familiar in social science research. The only points that need to be made are that these questions, be they concerned with cost or alternatives or ethics or unexpected effects or historical background, cannot be ignored; and that a systematic approach to them is possible, with about the same chances of getting an answer as we can expect in the usual scientific or criminological hunt for explanations and theories. The search is sometimes easy, sometimes close to impossible but still possible in principle and frequently, though not always successful, in practice with the help of searches for new information, more computing power, fresh minds, new models from other areas and so on.

In the end, then, the correct evaluation of some thing or person is just as objective a matter as the correct explanation of the behaviour of some thing or person, no more and no less. The latter is our standard of scientific objectivity, and evaluation can meet it, obviously in product evaluation but equally well in the evaluation of personnel and programs, plans and projections, schools and students. This is one place where we feared to follow the physicists, but partly because we believed the physicists who said that the path they trod led to no value judgments; while the same week they stood in front of their classes evaluating historical and contemporary physical theories and theoreticians, designs and instruments.

The attempt to do what the physicists said they were doing rather than what they did, has done us much harm in education. The other great harm besides the denial of the legitimacy of the evaluative heart of science (and history and literature was to take us away from the practitioners in a field where, unlike physics, they define the important problems and usually have better solutions than the scientists.

The fact that the practitioners define the problems that should be dealt with is unlikely to change in education; certainly not until the researchers have re-established credibility. The fact that the best — not the average or most — practitioners have much better solutions than the researchers will also only change when the researchers change and begin to work on problems whose importance is clear to someone besides themselves. There was a time when engineers thought that designing cars with reduced emissions was nothing to do with real automobile engineering, but an irritation interruption to the progress of engineering science forced on them by a political intrusion. On the contrary, it is the real problem, just as the real problems with atomic energy are the disposal of wastes and the safety factor. The fates have even been kind enough to arrange that solutions to the emissions problem have in fact improved the specific power production of all engines, regardless of emissions controls. Whether we get that lucky in education remains to be seen. First we have to accept a redefinition of the problems for educational research; not how do children process information nor how do their intellectual capabilities develop with age, but what books — or other materials or teaching approaches — work best in teaching what children in what school circumstances to read. Psychologists as such can address the first problem; educational psychologists have other and more practical agendas, from diagnosis to test analysis to determination of the variables that explain the success of great teachers or administrators by analysis of the performance of those people not by developing a general theory.

Traditional social science/educational research is sometimes important. But even to determine that is to do an evaluation. Evaluation is what distinguishes science from random bottletop-collecting, and to deny its legitimacy or primacy is to deny science its essence. We should not further delay our recognition of that fact and its implications for educational research.

Note

1 Ethics has an irritating way of coming into evaluations — irritating for the value-free protagonist, at least. For example, it is a little implausible to suppose that one can evaluate a program without any consideration of the way in which the staff of the program are treated; and one can hardly do that without checking for the absence of improper discrimination; and one can hardly determine what is improper discrimination without having worked out a legally and morally sound position on affirmative action; and not too many social scientists who do program evaluation can pass a serious examination on that.

The Feminist Evaluator
Gill Kirkup Open University

Introduction Educational Evaluation

Evaluation plays an increasingly important role in the development of educational projects and courses, and it is, therefore, important to examine evaluation models to see how they may be refined to make them appropriate to a particular educational situation. My own problem has been to carry out an evaluation of an undergraduate women's studies course, at a distance teaching university: the Open University of Britain. The aims of the course and its content material are grounded in value-based theories of sexual equality and liberation, values which I share. In a most obvious way this evaluation was one where attempts at value 'neutral' evaluation would have at worst been dishonest, and at best simply incapable of exploring some of the more problematic issues faced both by students and staff on the course. However, this is not an unusual situation in the context of educational evaluation, because education is not a value free activity, and those of us involved in it: professional educationalists and educators, researchers and evaluators, subscribe to its values. I believe, therefore, that the evaluation model I describe here has applications outside the area of women's studies, in situations where the evaluator has a commitment to the values of the educational programme, and where the purpose of the evaluation is to explicate these and to contribute to the success of the programme based on them.

Adelman and Alexander (1982) give the following general definition of educational evaluation:

> the making of judgments about the worth and effectiveness of educational intentions, processes and outcomes; about the relationship between these; and about the resource, planning and implementation frameworks for such ventures. (p. 5)

In terms of this definition we, at the Open University, have, in the past, concentrated mostly on processes and outcomes. Evaluation is a major activity of members of the Institute of Educational Technology at the University: evaluation of the effectiveness of course materials and teaching strategies, and more recently of the appropriateness of materials to community needs and potential markets. However, we are beginning to question whether our evaluations are really getting close to understanding the students' experience of the course and also how successful we are at measuring the produced course against its original intention.

In any evaluation project the role of an evaluator is often a complicated and confused one. Many of us come to evaluation from 'straight' research, and it takes some time before we appreciate that we can't operate in the same way in the new context. During the time that I have worked as an evaluator I have become less concerned about fulfilling the criteria for objective research and more concerned to negotiate methodological criteria to take account of interpersonal relationships and institutional politics. I had one experience of working on a project where problems over role definition, status of evaluation findings and even disagreements over the purpose of the evaluation after the event, caused enough controversy to swamp the findings (Kirkup, 1981). Since then I have begun to redevelop my role and to do so I have re-examined evaluation literature and criticism of research. I have been especially interested in the new feminist critique of research methodology, which is presenting a consistent and constructive criticism of research practice in both the arts and social sciences (see various collections, for example, Gamarnikow, *et al.* (Eds) 1983; Spender 1981; and articles in journals such as *Feminist Review*). Since evaluation is a branch of research practice, ethical and methodological issues that are of concern to social researchers in general are also of concern to evaluators.

Suchman (1967) argues that evaluation is better described as 'evaluative research' with the major emphasis

> upon the noun 'research' and evaluative research refers to those procedures for collecting and analyzing data which increase the possibility for 'proving' rather than 'asserting' the worth of some social activity. (p. 7)

However, in practice I have not found this a useful model. There are many points of difference between evaluation and 'pure' social research and the major ones have been summarized by Fife (1980) as being about

> the intent and type of criteria against which judgments are made. The intent of research is to know something in a generalizable way, while the intent of evaluation is to make a choice between options in a given situation. While both research and evaluation must have internal validity (measure what they are supposed to measure), external validity is much more important for research than evaluation. However, the data collected for evaluation must be considered believable by its users. (p. 1)

I have found that a flexible Illuminative Evaluation model has been more useful. I have taken this model as my base and redeveloped it to give a more expressive and value-bound role to the evaluator. I have called that role 'feminist' to identify the ideological context of my ideas and to acknowledge my debt to feminist theory.

Illuminative Evaluation has been a successful strategy in use in higher education for some years now (Parlett and Dearden, 1977) and is only one of a family of 'naturalistic' enquiry models (Guba, 1978). With these models it is possible to study both the process the evaluator is interested in, as well as the process of the evaluation and how it is used. They free the evaluator to be responsive to both the subjects and the clients of the evaluation. However, naturalistic enquiry is a very broad concept and as it stands a rather vague term, which serves mainly as a useful umbrella for a number of different evaluative models. The two most influential of these models have probably been Responsive Evaluation (Stake, 1967) and Illuminative Evaluation (Parlett and Hamilton, 1977). Responsive evaluation is an iterative process by which the evaluator presents and represents her findings to the various clients, each time attempting to increase their understanding of the issue and her understanding of their needs. It is a model which stresses the relationship between evaluator and clients. It also recognizes that clients' needs sometimes change, or are sometimes not clearly understood at the beginning of a project, and provides for ways in which an evaluation can take account of this and still provide useful results. Illuminative Evaluation begins with a general anthropological sort of data gathering and progressive focusing in upon general principles and special incidents. It is a type of responsive evaluation, in which the evaluator is most responsive to the setting and the activity occurring there.

> The research worker contributes to decision making by providing information, comments, and analysis to increase relevant knowledge and understanding. Illuminative Evaluation is characterized by a flexible methodology that capitalizes on available resources and opportunities, and draws upon different techniques to fit the total circumstances of each study. (Parlett, in press)

However, both models can be criticized in the ambiguous role they assign to the evaluator. The evaluator is to be committed to producing a clear and 'fair' report but is *not* to be committed to the process or product she is evaluating. I suspect that this is impossible in educational evaluation, as well as undesirable. House (1977), whose model of evaluation is that of evaluation as argument rather than evaluation as proof, comments on the notion of the objective evaluator:

> People being evaluated do not want a neutral evaluator, one who is unconcerned about the issues. A person on trial would not choose a judge totally removed from his own social system.
>
> Being disinterested does not give one the right to participate in a decision that determines someone's fate to a considerable

degree. Knowledge of techniques for arriving at objective findings is inadequate. Rather the evaluator must be seen as a member of, or bound to the group being judged, just as a defendant is judged by his peer. The evaluator must be seen as caring, as interested, as responsive to the relevant arguments. He must be impartial rather than simply objective. (p. 8)

New Models For Evaluators

The role of the researcher in the research process has concerned feminist and humanist social scientists greatly over the last few years. I believe that there are two major reasons why the role of researcher has concerned feminists so much. One of these is to do with the fact that as women in a society which privileges men and their view of the world, women have been able to demonstrate bias in research that was claimed as objective, and bias at all sorts of different levels: the choice of topic, the choice of method and the interpretation of results. Many, therefore, no longer believe in the possibility of unbiased enquiry and they are instead concerned that bias should be recognized and acknowledged because that way it becomes accessible to scrutiny.

The other major theme of feminism is signalled by the slogan: 'The personal is the political'. This is a philosophy which denies any separation between individual experience and intellectual theorizing and has much in common with phenomonological theory (for example, Schutz 1967), although its origins do not lie there. One advantage of feminist theory is that its language is simpler and more grounded in ordinary speech than the more abstract social theories it has much in common with. Like phenomenology it claims that the basis for all understanding is one's own personal experience of life and that all experiences have validity. Alongside it there has been a rejection of the scientific method and positivistic forms of theory building (Arditti, 1979) and attempts have been made to build theory through group activity, sharing and validating experience (Evans, 1982). Recognition is also given to the fact that theories so built will have limited generalizability that is, that because the black experience is different from the white, male from female, middle class from working class, it is impossible for one group of people to produce theories which adequately describe the experience of others. General descriptions and theories need to be produced collectively, if they can be produced at all, and the researcher or scholar has no particular monopoly of knowledge.

There are connections between this position and that of Habermas and the critical social theorists. He argues that social enquiry cannot use the same method as enquiry in the natural sciences. Social action depends on the individual's understanding of her situation, an understanding which is not idiosyncratic, but has intersubjective meanings which are part of the social context in which she operates, and these meanings embody value. The whole purpose in pursuing knowledge in this area is to emancipate (Habermas, 1972).

Two British feminists, Stanley and Wise (1981), make strong assertions about the implications such a position has for the researcher and her methods:

> Feminism either directly states or implies that the personal is the political; that the personal the everyday are important and interesting and must be the subject of feminist enquiry; that other people's realities mustn't be downgraded, sneered at or otherwise patronized; that feminists must attempt to reject the scientist/person dichotomy and, in doing so, must endeavour to dismantle the power relationships which exist between the researchers and researched ...
>
> ... But of course in order to examine 'the Personal' in this way it's necessary to locate not only the researched but also the researcher thus making her extremely vulnerable in ways usually avoided by researchers like the plague. (pp. 101 and 103)

In their later writing (1983), they have developed an ethnomethodological model of research where the researcher is the pivot of the enquiry. In common with many researchers who want to either humanize or politicize research practice they find scope for doing this if they adopt qualitative rather than quantitative research techniques, although such methods are not inherently less sexist than 'hard' methods.

The researcher's experience, argue Stanley and Wise, should be the core of the research. They go so far as to suggest that the researcher should not attempt to explain other people's views of the world because she risks misunderstanding them or presenting them as deficient. Instead she should present only her own understanding.

> ... researchers should present analytic accounts of how and why we think we know what we do about research situations and the people in them. The only way we can avoid overriding other people's understandings as 'deficient' in some way is not to attempt to present these within research. Instead, we should be much more concerned with presenting *ourselves* and *our* understandings of what is going on, by examining these in their context. We must make ourselves vulnerable, not hide behind what 'they' are supposed to think and feel, say and do. (p. 168)

Reinharz, an American sociologist, has developed a similar model which she calls 'experiential analysis' (Reinharz, 1979 and 1981). Her model is also an ethnographic one but it lays stress on the commitment and involvement of the researcher. Before beginning research, she writes, it is necessary that:

The research question be of sincere concern to the *researcher* and
that it be of sincere concern to the subject(s) (Reinharz, 1981,
p. 80)

Next the trustworthiness of the researcher has to be established. A
new model of the relationship between researcher and subjects has to be
built based on collaboration at all points during the project:

It begins with shared topic formation — the participants acting as
partners or consultants in shaping the research focus, selecting
research procedures and their implementations; collaborating in
data analysis and publication, or at least monitoring publications
before their distribution. (Reinharz, 1981, p. 86)

This collaboration and value-based planning is the core of her model,
she's less worried about methods of data collection and analysis except
'that the analysis draw heavily on the language of the persons studied i.e.
that it is grounded.' She claims, along with some writers on evaluation
(Guba) that there is never a final correct conclusion: 'there is no final
interpretation which is endowed by participants, conjured by readers and
cognitively satisfying the researcher.' (Reinharz, 1981, p. 87)

Such models are not restricted to feminist research. For example, a
humanistic psychologist Heron (1981) also uses the term experiential
research to describe a similar relationship. He describes how he sees the
basic difference between experiential research (cooperative enquiry) and
the usual social science research method:

But there are two quite different ways of interacting with persons
in research. One way is to interact with them so that they make no
direct contribution to formulating the propositions that purport to
be about them or to be based on their sayings and doings. This, of
course, is the traditional social science experiment or study in
which the subjects are kept naive about the research propositions
and make no contribution at all to formulation at the stage of
hypothesis — making, at the stage of final conclusions, or
anywhere in between. In the extreme, and still popular form of
this approach, the enquiry is all on the side of the researcher, and
the action being enquired into is all on the side of the subject.

The other way — the way of cooperative enquiry — is for the
researcher to interact with the subjects so that they do contribute
directly both to hypothesis-making, to formulating the final
conclusions, and to what goes on in between. This contribution
may be strong, in the sense that the subject is co-researcher and
contributes to creative thinking at all stages. It may be weak, in the
sense that the subject is thoroughly *informed* of the research
propositions at all stages and is invited to assent or dissent, and if

there is dissent the researcher and subject negotiate until agreement is reached. In the complete form of the approach, not only will the subject be a fully fledged co-researcher, but the researcher will also be co-subject, participating fully in the action and experience to be researched. (pp. 19 and 20)

These writers agree that the researcher can only do research on issues and with people with whom she shares certain defining characteristics. The researcher herself is the instrument rather than the questionnaires, interviews etc. which are more usually seen as such, and as the instrument she must be appropriate to the task. Appropriateness is defined through group membership or ideological commitment, rather than professional expertise. Reinharz (1979) argues that experiential analysis 'can be produced concerning any condition which would permit a researcher to be a temporarily affiliating insider' (p. 356)

It therefore follows that there will be issues and groups that it will be impossible for the researcher to do work on. In discussions about feminist research, male researchers frequently ask whether they could do such research. This is the wrong question. Anyone is free to adopt the model described as long as they accept the restrictions it imposes on the range of possible projects. Men, for example, would have to accept that it would be almost impossible for them to do work on mainly female situations. They could never fulfil the criteria to be a 'temporarily affiliating insider'. It also follows that you cannot do research on unwilling subjects. The researcher as a person is acknowledged to be crucial in interpreting the situation. Reinharz (1979) recommends that the researcher has some form of personal analysis.

If the researcher's self is the instrument by which the investigation proceeds, then that instrument must be well understood. For this reason I have urged the social researcher to undergo some form of systematic self-analysis as part of training. If the researcher's 'biographical presence' (. . . .) participates in a context to create perceptions or interpretations, then the biography of events, relationships and ideas that the researcher has experienced demands clarification. (p. 356)

The reports etc., produced by such a worker would be personal documents. Stanley and Wise (1983) compare such work to literature.

We see all research as 'fiction' in the sense that it views and so constructs 'reality' through the eyes of one person. We accept it because much literature is concerned with such an exploration of 'society' through the eyes of particular characters, but ultimately and frequently explicitly through the eyes of the writer. If this is the kind of literature that our kind of research is compared with then we accept the comparison and feel flattered . . . . If this kind of research can open people's eyes, can influence them and change them, to the extent that literature has done, then it will do better than any other social science research that has appeared to date. (p. 174)

However, this causes practical problems for an evaluator, who is often assigned a topic of investigation rather than being free to choose it. She also has clients whose needs, wishes and biases it is important to take into account. She is accountable to these clients for her final findings. Is it possible to resolve, honestly, the different needs and requirements of the client-sponsor and the client-subject?

I found an example of a different approach to research/evaluation in a Trades Union sponsored investigation into the stress involved in working on buses. The aim of the project was to locate the 'potential sources of stress in the working environment and in the work process' (TGWU, 1981, p. 6).

The investigation was initiated by union members and Worker's Educational Association[1] tutors involved in teaching Trades Union Congress[2] day-release courses. They felt that the common view of stress as a product of individual personality problems made it difficult for workers to argue for improvements to conditions in the workplace. There was also disagreement over what constituted evidence and who was expert about the problem. The workers felt, with some justification, that they were experts in knowing what caused stress in their workplace since they *experience* it. Therefore the form of investigation they wanted was a workers' investigation, that is 'not only one carried out by the workers themselves for themselves, but is also one that insists on the legitimacy of their "own way of experiencing and understanding the problem".' (TGWU, 1981, p. 7)

The rationale of such an enquiry was expounded further by two of the people involved in the investigation:

> Any workers' investigation must develop methods that can be understood by the workers and used by them on their own in other situations. The methods chosen must therefore involve learning transferable skills and not require expert control, for whatever reason, for example, accessibility, comprehensibility, cost, etc. (Forrester and Thome, 1981)

The areas of investigation were determined by the workers, and where they needed more information it was brought to them. For example, it was important to do an ergonomic survey of the cab of the bus so a seminar was held for the workers involved to explain the basic principles of ergonomics and to discuss how it might be used in the project. Another of the methods used was a questionnaire, designed by the workers and administered by certain trusted members. The questionnaire was also analyzed collectively. In this sort of approach the researched is also the researcher and the ordinary role of researcher is transformed into technician or resource. It is part of a process known as 'demystifying' expertise (as in Irvine *et al.*, 1979). 'Above all, a workers' investigation must attempt to challenge what is commonly accepted as science and to minimize/eliminate the mystique attached to the "expert".' (Forrester and Thome, 1981)

The researcher/evaluator becomes a resource and a facilitator whose job it is to develop the skills and confidence of all collective members of the project and to provide whatever support services are necessary to enable them to achieve what they want. This enabling role lends itself more obviously to evaluation situations where the declared purpose is to inform action and policy. It is a role that requires the researcher/evaluator to place the needs and experience of the researched first. It is least problematic when the researched and the client are both the same as in the busworkers enquiry.

There is no reason why the concerns and the methods of the feminist researchers quoted earlier could not be incorporated into such a workers' investigation. The remarkable and rare thing about this investigation is that the workers had the confidence to define the research problem and to control the research strategy. It could be seen as an example of strong cooperative enquiry.

With these models in mind I negotiated an evaluation of the first year of a women's studies course at the Open University, Course U221: *The Changing Experience of Women*. The circumstances, I felt, were ideal for me to explore the possibility of feminist evaluation since there was a convergence between the ideology contained in the course and held by the course writers, and that which I wanted to manifest in my role as evaluator. In negotiating a role for myself in evaluating the course I wanted to incorporate aspects of the models discussed above by developing a collaborative and reflexive way of working which was also flexible and responsive to the needs of the groups involved in the evaluation.

A Feminist Evaluation

Before I describe the evaluation I will briefly describe the course and its context. Women's studies is now an established academic area in Britain, with courses at all levels of education: school and post-school, formal and informal. It is still a developing area and there are debates over what constitutes women's studies and what its defining characteristics should be. (See Spender 1981; Bowles and Duelli Klein, 1980; and *Women's Studies International Forum*, Vol.6, No.3, 1983.)

Women's studies is a heterogeneous subject; courses which come under its protective umbrella can look very different from each other. What they all have in common is that they are part of the academic arm of the Women's Liberation Movement, to which they are accountable and whose aims they are intended to further. This is done through three activities and any women's studies course will be engaged in one, if not more, of these. One activity is that of presenting materials to compensate for bias and omission in courses as they presently exist. Another is to engage in consciousness raising activities which both validate the personal experience of the student as well as providing a base from which to develop theory in an experiential way. Finally, students on such courses are engaged in developing and extending feminist theory in all areas of knowledge.

Within the constraints of an academic institution and particularly one which teaches 'at a distance', *The Changing Experience of Women* contains some of the features of other women's studies courses. It is concerned with affective learning and developing non-hierarchical ways of teaching/learning as well as a commitment to personal and social change within the political context of feminism and the women's movement. I have been closely involved with the development of this particular course as an educational technologist and a feminist academic, and then as the evaluator of the course. I was concerned that strategies which I adopted for the evaluation take general criticisms of evaluation practice into account, as well as examine the special features of a women's studies course, and incorporate some of these features into the evaluation methodology. Indeed, an innovatory course which is involved with personal development and social change lends itself well to an evaluation where the role of the evaluator is to be closely involved with the experiences of the students.

I adopted a role that was experiential in a weaker sense than that used by Reinharz and Stanley and Wise, a sense closer to that of Heron, and which incorporated a commitment to cooperative working and to demystifying the evaluation process as in the workers' investigation. I would not claim that merging the different models produced a coherent final model but it provided me with a base from which I feel able to operate.

There were four major aims to the evaluation:

1 To provide insights into what students' expectations about this course are and how far the course fulfils them.
2 To identify particular aspects of course material which are not teaching effectively and to make recommendations for change and improvements.
3 To provide other people involved in women's studies courses with an evaluation of aspects of the course that are common to other women's studies courses.
4 To examine the special features of a distance teaching women's studies course to discover whether its distance teaching aspects detract from the success of the course.

One of the first problems was that of defining the clients of the evaluation. In an educational evaluation there are usually at least two groups of 'clients': one group is the sponsor and the people to whom the evaluator is accountable, the other group are the powerless, those whose interests the educational evaluator has at heart in being involved in the programme at all. I had three major clients: the central course team who wrote the course, the students and tutors who were using the materials, and the University. Although, in a loose sense the course team commissioned the evaluation, the greater body of the University was also a client because it *requires* that certain aspects of a new course must be evaluated and obliges the course team to use academic members of the Institute of Educational Technology as evaluators. This equalizes the power relationship between course team client and evaluator so that the evaluator has much more scope for negotiating the form of the evaluation and the strategies it incorporates. Therefore, in my first memo to the course team I outlined how I would like to operate and I also suggested that I saw my prime responsibility as being towards the other set of clients — the students on the course. I also briefly outlined the concerns that I felt would be central to the evaluation, the relationships involved, and the sort of qualitative methods I might use.

The memo was well received and negotiations with the course team were enthusiastic, although muted since the course was in the final throes of course production, struggling with tasks which were much more critical at that time than a projected evaluation study. Some members were enthusiastic *because* I was attempting a more unusual research strategy and because as feminists they were interested in being part of an evaluation which took account of a feminist critique of research.

There were 708 students from all over Britain on the course, of this 8 per cent (fifty-six) were men. Their ages ranged from the mid 20s to the mid 60s, the largest age range, 41 per cent, being between 30 and 40. The majority of students, 76 per cent (494), were studying the course as part of their undergraduate programme. The remainder were doing it simply out of interest. I chose to study in depth only two tutor groups, a total of forty students, one group in Kent, one in Oxford. They were not chosen as representative in any way, they were chosen so that they were within reasonable travelling distance and because the tutors were enthusiastic about an evaluation. Over the year my relationship with one tutor group was excellent and I developed a role that was completely integrated with the functioning of the group. With the other group my relationship was just satisfactory, but for much of the time I felt an outsider, and was not privileged to share the group's experiences. I believe that this was due to the different point at which I was able to first meet the groups, and the fact that I had already established a relationship with the tutor of group A.

My first meeting with group A students was at their first tutorial, we were all strangers together. I explained the aims of the evaluation and asked people to raise any doubts they had. There was overwhelming enthusiasm. In response to my request for people who wanted to talk or write to me to put their names and addresses on a piece of paper everyone did so. Many of the group wanted to talk to me during lunch in the nearest pub. From then on my position was fully accepted in tutorials and outside of them. I received letters from most of the group in which they wrote in great detail about their personal histories and their reasons for doing this particular course. I felt privileged to have had so much personal experience recounted to me. I believe no questionnaire could have elicited such a wealth of material, and I suspect that the form in which it was given — that of a letter — allowed the considered expression of personal details even better than an interview. I believe the use of unstructured personal letters as a form of data gathering and a way of explicating meaning has not been explored enough by social researchers. I also believe that my acceptance was helped by the fact of my membership of the course team and my identity as a woman (only five of the students in the sample are men and only one of these has ever written to me). This supports the arguments of Reinharz and Heron that it is only where the researcher is seen as a member of a group will she be allowed access to important information, and only as a group member will she be able to make sense of it. For various reasons, to do with the timing of my visits and my relationship with the tutor, I was unable to set up such good relationships with so many of the students in the second group.

My original intention had been to engage in as little written data collection: questionnaires, checklists etc, as possible. I had hoped that I would have enough personal contact or contact by phone to elicit as much data as I needed. However, this was not possible. Finding time to visit people in their homes in Kent was not feasible and women at home frequently have so many demands made of them that it is very difficult to choose a good time to phone them. I found that I wanted more detail about specific aspects of course material than I could get during and after tutorials and I resigned myself to writing letters. That in itself is also time consuming. Experiential research techniques, even with a sample as small as mine, demand a large amount of time from the researcher.

The original commitment to flexibility over data collection techniques proved very worthwhile. I tailored my needs for information to the students' need for privacy and for a technique which would not increase their workload. I have less sense of imposing on a student's good nature in this project compared to my previous experiences. I was also able to respond to the course team's changing needs for information and this increased their trust in the evaluation because of its responsiveness.

In order to involve people in evaluation they must feel that they are receiving some return to compensate for their time and energy. It is possible to get high levels of cooperation in situations where the researcher provides friendship, information, or support to the research subject. A powerful example of this is given by Ann Oakley (1981), in a discussion of interviewing women in a study of the transition to motherhood. She found that it was impossible to remain a detached interviewer and she resolved to be as involved with the women in her sample as they invited her to be. This engaged her in answering questions, being willing to talk about her own experiences, staying for dinner, and developing friendships. She considered that her behaviour was the major reason why she had such high levels of cooperation from her sample of women during the project.

I found I was able to involve those students who I could meet face to face at tutorials. And, although the response to my initial letter was very good (85 per cent), I was disappointed in the number of comments I received on draft reports that I circulated. Ultimately students were less involved in the final reports than I would have liked. It is important to realize when engaging in experiential research that, although the project is close to your heart and taking up the majority of your time, even if it interests the other people involved it is probably one of their least important activities. People must be free to have a limited involvement and therefore the researcher, since she has the prime responsibility for producing the goods, must be willing to exercise more control than she would ideally wish to do.

I was able to achieve the four aims I had set for the evaluation, although I cannot here go into any detail. The students' expectations of the course fell into three parts that can be loosely classified as academic, personal, and political. Academic expectations were referred to by expressions such as: 'getting a greater awareness and insight into women's position.' The personal expectations were to do with making sense of their own experiences as women. The political expectations where that the course would provide the student with language and the terms with which to argue the case for women with their friends or at work. This group saw themselves as already in agreement with feminist arguments, but needing to consolidate their understanding.

The evaluation suggested that the course was better at fulfilling the academic and personal expectations and less successful at fulfilling the political ones. One of the great successes of the course appeared to be that it introduced feminist ideas and arguments to women who very strongly did *not* identify themselves as feminists when they began, and to introduce these ideas in a way that the students felt was thought provoking and exciting without being threatening.

The evaluation, as well as raising some of these general issues, also identified weaknesses in parts of the course and contributed to suggestions for change. For instance, I was able to report strong feelings of annoyance from both tutors and students about the structure and wording of assignments. This was then backed up by personal conversations that members of the course team had with each other. The structure of assignments for the following year, as well as the examination, was redesigned in the light of this feedback I feel that the power of the material I was able to give the course team in terms of reports of anger, despair over completing assignments and extended verabatim comments from students about exactly what they thought was wrong, gave an urgency to the issue that would not have been felt in questionnaire responses alone. The flexible way of working with verbal reports to the course team also made evaluation data available quickly and the course team were able to respond soon after the details were known. There were other areas of the course, such as a particular audio-visual programme, which was not perceived as very relevant, and a textual component which was very difficult. Changes have been made to these for following years.

Teaching this type of course at a distance has proved difficult. The impact of the material is lessened somewhat when it is studied by the isolated individual. Those times when students were together, such as during the summer school, were experienced as the most powerful part of the course but were not always enjoyed. The course has retained its popularity in following years and has been studied by more people than any other women's studies courses in Britain.

Assessing the Potential of Feminist/Experiential Strategies for the Evaluation of Educational Programmes

It seems necessary, to me, that those of us who hold any ideological world view which is critical of the one commonly in operation in our own society, need to apply our criticism to our work. It has been argued that ideological commitment can change the choice of topic for evaluation and can influence the interpretation of evaluation results but not the methods by which data are collected; these will either be appropriate or inappropriate, well done or badly done. Feminists critics of research, as well as critical theorists, have argued that this is not the case and that particular methods of enquiry are inherently biased. For those of us who have political as well as methodological reasons to suspect that this is true, the time has come to stop throwing rocks at the 'patriarchal paradigm' and to begin building an alternative, feminist paradigm and see what the results look like.

However, attempting to do evaluation which is based on an ideal of cooperative non-hierarchical working in an educational situation that is both hierarchical and individualistic as is the Open University, resounds with contradictions. The ethos of the educational experience runs counter to the aims of the evaluation. The Open University has a model of the student as the isolated individual who has contact with a tutor and through the tutor with the university; a type of linear chain of command. It has been a problem to teach a women's studies course with this model since such courses have stressed the importance of the group learning environment and the educational value of students working cooperatively and sharing experiences, and the role of the tutor has been one of a resource rather than a pedagogue. The effect of the evaluation has been to open channels of communication which don't normally operate in the Open University. For example, I provided a channel between the central academic course team and the student groups so that some sort of dialogue could occur between them. My draft report which was sent to all the students and tutors involved in the evaluation allowed communication between students about themselves and their experience of the course. I therefore feel that those students involved in evaluation had an enriched experience which rubbed off in their enthusiasm for the course. However, the educational structure remains hierarchical and as the evaluator I have been placed in a position along that chain of command.

The attempt to re-negotiate accountability also contains contradictions. I tried to make myself and the evaluation accountable to the students much more than would be usual. But I had to recognize that in making myself more accountable to them I did little to change their power in the University structure. The freedom to renegotiate relationships at all is one, in a sense, only allowed by the central course team.

One of the main drawbacks of experiential research, as defined by Reinharz (1979) and Heron (1981) and feminist research as described by Stanley and Wise (1983), is that it is unrealistic in its expectations of the level of involvement of the co-researchers (the subjects). Even when problems are of major concern to people, they have work and private lives which usually take priority, whereas research *is* work for the researcher and evaluator. I suspect that frequently the evaluator will end up with more responsibility and power than she planned for. The TGWU model of a workers' investigation has great potential for involvement of the co-researchers in all aspects of the work, but it is unlikely that the majority of people have the confidence or the contacts to initiate such products, and it must be recognized that the Leeds busworkers' investigation was initiated by people made powerful by their membership of a union.

I also recognize that I am still undecided about the nature of generalizability of an evaluation. Stanley and Wise argue that generalization from research is impossible and an unrealistic aim. I do not feel as strongly as they do, but I recognize that all research design bargains validity against generalizability, and agree with Fife (1980) quoted earlier, that for evaluation validity is the more important measure. The assumption contained in the evaluation I have done, using indepth qualitative data from a small sample, is that if I am able to understand the experience of the sample and describe it in appropriate language it will resonate with the experience and understanding of others involved in women's studies. It will be 'meaningful' rather than 'true', and although perhaps not generalizable in the research sense it will allow others access to the experience of those in my sample in such a way that will contribute to such others gaining insight into their own situations. In phenomenological research the exploration of meaning to uncover truth is the primary aim of social research, although the methods I have used could be open to criticism for not probing meaning deeply enough. Despite these drawbacks, I believe that the models I have described, perhaps in a less pure form than presented by their original authors, offer ways of approaching both practical and ethical research problems.

I approached the task of evaluating course U221 *The Changing Experience of Women* from the position of identifying myself as a feminist and seeing the course as a feminist course. I am also a professional evaluator engaged in resolving problems inherent in the evaluation process. I have adopted strategies for this particular task that address both the problems of the evaluation process as well as the particular issues raised by the nature of the women's studies course. However, these experiential strategies can be used equally well in the evaluation of other educational programmes, as long as the necessity of the evaluator being a 'temporarily affiliating insider' is recognized, and in doing so the evaluator can honestly subscribe to the values of the programme.

The strategies have given me the opportunity to explore some of the contradictions I feel between my work and my ideological commitments. These contradictions have not been resolved and I doubt whether they can be as long as I accept work as an evaluator within the educational system. And, since I intend to carry on doing so, I put myself in the position of arguing that it is, in fact, the tension caused by these contradictions which provides the impetus for a more creative personal development of my role. I would also argue that there is some benefit to be gained by all groups involved in an evaluation in bringing these contradictions to the surface and examining them more closely.

Notes

1 WEA (Workers' Educational Association) *Aim*: 'to interest men and women in their own continued education and in the better education of their children' (*Directory of British Associations*, CBD Research, 1982). It does this by organizing and supporting a national system of adult evening classes.

2 TUC (Trades Union Congress) *Aims*: 'the promotion of interests of affiliated organizations; improvement of economic and social conditions of workers in all parts of the world; assistance in the complete organization of workers eligible for its affiliated membership and settlement of industrial disputes.' (*Directory of British Associations*, CBD Research, 1982).

References

ADELMAN, C. and ALEXANDER, R.J. (1983) *The Self-Evaluating Institution: Practice and Principles in the Management of Educational Change*, Methuen.

ARDITT, R. (1979) 'Feminism and science' in ARDITTI, R. BRENNAN, P. and CAVRAK, S. (Eds) *Science and Liberations,* South End Press.

BOWLES, G. and DUELLI-KLEIN, R. (1980) (Ed.) *Theories of Women's Studies,* Berkeley, University of California.

EVANS, M.(1982) 'In praise of theory: the case for women's studies', *Feminist Review,* 10, spring, pp. 61–75.

FIFE, J.D. (1980) in FEASLEY, C.E. *Programme Evaluation,* American Association for Higher Education.

FORRESTER, K. and THOME, C. (1981/82) 'Stress on the buses', *Science for the People,* 50, winter.

GAMARNIKOW, E. *et al.* (Eds) (1983) *Gender, Class and Work,* Heinemann.

GRAHAM, H. (1983) 'Do her answers fit his questions? Women and the survey method' in GAMARNIKOW, E *et al.* (Eds) *The Public and the Private,* Heinemann.

HABERMAS, J. (1972) *Knowledge and Human Interests,* Heinemann.

HERON, J. (1981) 'Philosophical basis for a new paradigm' in REASON, P. and ROWAN, J. (Eds) *Human Inquiry A Sourcebook of New Paradigm Research,* John Wiley and Sons.

HOUSE, E. (1977) *The Logic of Evaluative Argument,* CSE Monograph Series in Evaluation No 7, Centre for Study of Evaluation, UCCLA.

IRVINE, J. MILES, I. and EVANS, J. (Eds) (1979) *Demystifying Social Statistics,* Pluto Press.

KIRKUP, G. (1981) 'Evaluating and improving learning materials: a case study' in PERCIVAL, F. and ELLINGTON, H.I. (Eds) *Aspects of Educational Technology XV,* Kogan Page, pp. 171–6.

OAKLEY, A. (1981) 'Interviewing women: A contradiction in terms' in ROBERTS, H. (Ed.) *Doing Feminist Research,* Routledge and Kegan Paul.

PARLETT, M. (in press) 'Illuminative education', *International Encyclopaedia of Education: Research and Studies,* Pergamon Press.

PARLETT, M. and DEARDEN, G.J. (Eds) (1977) *Introduction to Illuminative Evaluation: Studies in Higher Education,* Washington DC, Council of Independent Colleges.

REINHARZ, S. (1979) *On Becoming a Social Scientist,* Jossey-Bass.

REINHARZ, S. (1981) 'Experiential analysis: A contribution to feminist research' in BOWLES, G. and DUELLI-KLEIN, R. (Eds) *Theories of Women's Studies II,* Berkeley, University of California.

SCHUTZ, A. (1972) *The Phenomenology of the Social World,* Heinemann. 'So far, so good — so what? Women's studies in the UK, (1983) *Women's Studies International Forum,* 6, 3.

SPENDER, D. (Ed.) (1981) *Men's Studies Modified: The Impact of Feminism on the Academic Disciplines,* Pergamon Press.

STANLEY, L. and WISE, S. (1981) 'Back into the personal or: Our attempt to construct feminist research' in BOWLES, G. and DUELLI-KLEIN, R. (Eds) *Theories of Women's Studies II,* Berkeley, University of California.

STANLEY, L. and WISE, S. (1983) *Breaking Out: Feminist Consciousness and Feminist Research,* Routledge and Kegan Paul.

Stress at Work (1981), an investigation carried out by shop stewards of the Transport and General Workers Union (TGWU) 9/12 Branch, final report, March.

SUCHMAN, E.W. (1967) *Evaluative Research,* Russell Sage Foundation.

4
Naturalistic Evaluation: Acting from Experience

Introduction

One of the significant events in the development of the evaluation field over the past twenty years has been the emergence of naturalistic evaluation. Led by such people as Barry MacDonald, Lawrence Stenhouse, David Hamilton and Malcolm Parlett in Britain, and Robert E. Stake, Louis Smith and Elliot Eisner in the United States, naturalistic evaluations have achieved some legitimacy. In Britain, in fact, this may be the dominant mode of evaluation. In the United States the overwhelming number of evaluations are still quantitative and formal, reflecting the strong positive science tradition of American social science. However, naturalistic evaluation has made inroads even in the United States.

Some of the differences between quantitative and naturalistic advocates arise over the different role that evaluation is expected to play in educational change. In the following chapter Stake presents the most comprehensive explication yet of his view of the role naturalistic evaluation is to serve. Stake sees educational change as fundamentally dependent upon the beliefs of educational practitioners. Unless they are persuaded to change, not much change will occur. Practitioner change will necessarily be gradual and evolutionary in developing, with practitioners modifying their practice over time based upon their own perceptions of what is the correct thing to do.

Traditional research which provides only general propositional knowledge statements has little relevance for practitioners. They are more interested in their own particular situation. What they will respond to, according to Stake, is vicarious experiences from which they can draw naturalistic generalizations about what to do. Hence, naturalistic evaluation should supply vicarious experiences that practitioners can understand and relate to. Through this new personal understanding, practitioners will be persuaded to act differently in their practice. Stake's view is quite different from that guiding most evaluation research, as for example that of Weiss in the next section of the book, who questions whether evaluation has anything to offer the practitioner. Stake would say that evaluation is useful only if it can relate to the practitioner's personal experience.

Rob Walker's chapter presents some of the difficulties he has encountered in conducting naturalistic studies. First, naturalistic case studies are highly interventionist in effect if not in intent. Interviewing and observing people greatly affect what people do. And sharing one's observations and conclusions with those people can cause intense reactions, as Walker illustrates. Second, naturalistic case studies often present distorted views of the world one is trying to portray. These distortions enter for a number of reasons and with sufficient power to transform the reality of the situation significantly. Finally, naturalistic studies are conservative in that they portray current practices and fix them in time although the reality of the actual situation changes even before the case study is written. Walker offers no panaceas for these problems of naturalistic research but suggests some ethical cautions the researcher/evaluator should attend to.

The last chapter in this section is by Stephen Kemmis. Kemmis was trained and apprenticed in the naturalistic tradition but the principles he explicates should apply to all evaluations in his view. He sees the role of evaluation as feeding information into a critical debate among program participants as to what that specific program should do. His account strongly emphasizes the rationality and autonomy of each participant, very much in the tradition of naturalistic evaluators. Kemmis also tries to go beyond individuals, however, and work towards the development of community. One of the difficulties of liberal theory has been that maximizing everyone's individual autonomy destroys the sense of community and the public interest. Kemmis tries to balance individualism by the development of community through self-critical debate. Thus action research by and for participants becomes a preferred method of investigation. In a sense with Kemmis's principles one begins to leave naturalistic evaluation and enter the realm of participatory evaluation, to move from an epistemological position to a political one.

An Evolutionary View of Educational Improvement[1]

Robert E. Stake
University of Illinois

As educational researchers and program evaluators, we are interested in improving instructional practice. In this chapter I will present an argument that naturalistic enquiry has been a *neglected element* in facilitating change and improvement in practice. In Brazil, as around the world, there is great desire to improve education, but also a reluctance to use our national treasuries for doing so. We need make the most of our research effort. And we need to realize the special need for an evolutionary style of correction, avoiding the implantation of devices and techniques into systems which cannot adapt to them.

Almost 200 years ago Immanuel Kant observed:

> . . . the whole mechanism of education has no coherence if it is not designed in agreement with a well-weighed plan, . . . it might behoove the state likewise to reform itself from time to time and, attempting evolution instead of revolution, progress perpetually toward the better.[2]

Evolutionary change is gradual, internally 'planned,' in harmony with the organic system, and adaptive to the habitat. I want to draw special attention to the choice between evolutionary change and 'creationist' change. The Moral Majority creationists sometimes call it 'cataclysmic' change. It is the kind of change exemplified by switching suddenly from traditional teaching to *Man: A Course of Study* or to 'competency based education.' Much of our course development work is based on a creationist notion of change. I prefer an evolutionary change, or at least, for any one organization, finding a better balance between evolutionary change and creationist change.

Later in the chapter I will present a schematic theory of action. I will connect naturalism and evolutionary change to teaching and administrative practice.

We researchers-evaluators-developers-consultants engage in serious business. We deal with people's lives — not only the lives of young people, but of teachers and other adults. We deliberately try to *change* them, and seldom exactly as they would change themselves. We interfere with their lives, convinced we are helping them toward something better. We are opposed to coercion, yet unattentive to the moral complexity of entice-ment. In the process of change how much should we give people opportunity to approve, to participate in controlling, the changes we would make in their lives? Contemplating, we will recognize that an evolutionary point of view (though of course not an assurance of it) can bolster self-determination.

In this chapter I will allude to a recurring science-education controversy in public schools in the United States involving the teaching of evolution of the species.

Anyone who examines the instructional technology literature and the operations research literature on 'planned change'[3] might come to the conclusion that there are only two ways to progress to the better: one way being to obtain *better information* and use it more rationally; the other way being to come to deeper *understanding of one's 'self'* and to find better ways of relating to and communicating with one's associates.

In the first way, the required better information is assumed to come from scientific studies which approximate — as nearly as conditions allow — the experiments of the natural sciences. A more rational use of this information requires carefully drawn plans with clearly stated goals and schedules. The second commonly recognized path to improvement involves self-analysis by individuals or groups, often guided by psycho-therapeutic expertise, and usually under conditions removing constraint on expression of personal feeling. There is merit to each of these remedies, and each can be carried to excess.

Almost absent from mention in the 'change literature' is the *common* way in which improvement *is* accomplished, a way followed intuitively by the greatest, and the least, of our thinkers. It is the experiential way, an evolutionary way, recognized particularly by John Dewey.[4] One may change practice when *new experience* causes re-examination of problems: Intuitively we start thinking of alternative solutions.

I observe that this third method of planned change regularly occurs, and that it is at least as important as the other two. I believe that program improvement efforts should more often rely upon the experiences and intuitions of the practitioners involved. I am *not*, on this occasion, advocating 'action research', which is research carried on by practit-ioners.[5] I *am* urging the design of studies to be carried out by trained researchers, carried out in such a way as to provide vicarious experience to the readers, done so that they easily combine new experience with old. One might say it is buying into the 'case method' of instruction. The role of the program evaluator or educational researcher on these occasions is to assist practitioners in reaching new experiential understandings, which in previous writing[6] I have called 'naturalistic generalization.'

One would expect this approach usually to lead to *evolutionary change* rather than to a replacement kind of change. In the literature on reform of social and educational practice it is regularly implied that problems are better dealt with by implanting new parts externally-created than by correcting practice. Here I call for aid to the *self*-correction of practice.

Before discussing evolutionary change and naturalistic generalization further, let me reflect on efforts to change educational practice in the United States. Most actual change continues to occur by the action of the individual instructor. But 'planned change' is usually thought of as an institutional or government responsibility. We have a thirty-year history of federal involvement in projects aimed at creating change in schools. These projects have ranged from the writing of new curricular materials, to creation of new programs for teacher education, to devizing new models for administering educational programs. Reviewing federal project rationales, Charles Lindblom and David Cohen[7] noted a heavy reliance on the aggregation of *new knowledge*. Researchers, developers, and evaluators were commissioned to produce new knowledge which was 'supposed to replace the ordinary and presumably deficient knowledge of local practitioners.'[8]

Concurrently with these federal projects, the schools and colleges felt pressures generated by a society facing serious dislocations. Professional people found their training insufficient, academics found old knowledge challenged. Even without external pressure almost all educational practitioners have felt needs for change. Many have wanted a greater opportunity to teach what they are good at teaching; many have wanted a greater security from overexpectation. Education is a presumptious profession. Often a practitioner never learns a task's ending. That needed feeling of accomplishment and completion is often lacking. A student's literacy is a life-long reaching. A faculty introduces a new curriculum but never finds out how far beyond nominal acceptance the teaching is changed. A teacher's time-tested exercises become of doubtful value, especially with changing ethnicities in the classroom.

Into uncertainty the educator plunges, clutching textbook or management plan, hoping to survive, hoping to help others survive. There is no way such a professional can be successful — however she defines success — with all problems, perhaps not even with the majority of them. Such a professional lives with the niggling sensation that she could do more, ought to do more. For most educational practitioners in my world, there exists an internal pressure to change, to improve, to do better next time.

During these thirty years we had across the country major federal projects and institutional pressures aimed at producing new knowledge to improve our universities and schools; *and* within their faculties a desire to change. One might expect this combination to assure a significant change. Lay observers and professionals alike, including Tom Hastings, David Cohen and John Goodlad, concluded, however, that it did not happen.

For one thing, within faculties there has not been a consensus as to needed direction and degree of change. The federal programs resulted in much less desired change than hoped for. I think the dominant research and development model was partly at fault.

Overemphasis on Knowledge-Based Change

It was curriculum specialist Madeleine Grumet[9] who said,

> What is most fundamental to our lives as men and women sharing
> a moment on this planet is the process of reproducing ourselves.

She was speaking of teachers and professors as well as parents. But she saw us parents and teachers as I do, more as builders of the nest, arrangers of cognitive furniture, actors in the same play — with a hand occasionally on the sculptor's chisel, but never as the *'creators'* of education. Enablers sometimes, but not creators. All important, yes, but not creators.

[Let me insert here that I think that it makes just as little sense to talk about *student learnings* as 'created' or 'produced'. Some of us in our technological roles get carried away by the notions of Genesis, expect-ations that we control what registers in a learner's mind. Learning is no more the creation of educationists than is the Atlantic Ocean the creation of the Amazon River.]

I am distressed by curriculum-builders who see curricula *created* by authors of guidebooks, textbooks, objectives lists, and by those who see the curriculum *created* by teachers. As is manifestly apparent in the extensive classroom studies of John Goodlad[10], the curriculum is not created — it exists.

It exists ever-changing, even in the most traditional schools, ever-changing — little because formal knowledges advance, changing more because learners create new images of themselves, with each group of youngsters forcefully different from last year's. The curriculum is ever-changing, more with the change in our social technology, changing only in some small degree by educators who strive to make it better.

It is true of course that:

Research can evoke Knowledge which leads to Improved Practice

But perhaps because education is so 'knowledge-oriented' many of us have a tenacious expectation that KNOWLEDGE can make sick educ-ation well, or primitive education modern. In a review of the impact of curriculum research a few years ago Edmund Short of Penn State said:

a number of researchers have redefined the scope of the phenomena and have conceived it, not as a problem of 'research into
practice,' but as one of 'knowledge production and utilization.[11]

In my mind appears the image of two towering enterprises,
KNOWLEDGE PRODUCTION and KNOWLEDGE UTILIZA-
TION, rising high, reaching out to one another, perhaps to form a golden
arch. It is an attractive image, particularly to someone justifying a research
budget or planning the implementation of a newly-written curriculum.
Certainly, this is sometimes the right model for managing research,
attempting to maximize the production of knowledge that would facilitate
a new consideration of practice. (And certainly, in retrospect, changes in
practice can almost always be described in terms of changes of
knowledge.)

But according to Short's findings, backed up more recently by
Lindblom and Cohen[12] and Carol Weiss[13], knowledge production and
knowledge utilization are seldom enjoined. Teachers and administrators
have little use for most research reports, and for the new knowledge
produced by large-scale change projects.

A frequent response to this situation is to assume people just do not
know how to understand research findings. Allen Schmieder, an official in
Washington, once commented:

> Very few people are professionally trained to build on research
> findings, or to market good educational ideas.[14]

What is needed — it seemed — was still another enterprise, *Knowledge
Dissemination*, to provide a scaffolding to connect our two towers.

It is a dream that distracts from the task at hand.

Directing attention to knowledge production and dissemination
diminishes attention to practice. Building the ERIC system and other
information services in the US appears to have increased the orientation to
researcher constructs and diminished emphasis on practice. Some policy
studies should continue to ask, 'Research into practice — how?'. But those
enquiries are unlikely to succeed in changing practice. The research
enterprise will be insufficiently useful as long as researchers have little
interest in studying the entwining, personalistic, and crisis-like problems
of daily practice. Unfortunately, researchers tend to conceptualize new
systems as ones that would operate in orderly circumstances and with
dispassionate practitioners. Planners have been fascinated with
schemata[15], with sophisticating technology. Unlike practitioners, and the
helpers of practitioners, the dissemination researcher's goal has not been
the well-being of daily practice.

Sometimes the well-being of daily practice requires changed practice,
sometimes preserved practice, but always an emphasis on practice. The
end-product desired is not knowledge-about-practice or any of the formal

generalizations most researchers strive for. Formal knowledge is *not* necessarily a stepping stone to improved practice. Such knowledge may be helpful in the long run, but for *each* educational situation the importance of formal knowledge about teaching or about administration remains to be demonstrated.[16]

According to Michael Polanyi[17] and Donald Schon[18] practice is guided largely by personal knowings, based on and gleaned from personal experience. And change in pedagogical or administrative practice, or resistence to change, is often rooted in a sense of personal protection, even survival. Because of this personal aspect it will sometimes be more useful for research itself to be designed so that:

Research can evoke Vicarious Experience which leads to Improved Practice.

You in my audience may prefer to define vicarious experience as just another form of knowledge, so that this latter statement does not conflict with the one before. But as spelled out by Polanyi the kind of knowings generated by experiencing, whether direct or vicarious, are different from the knowings which come from encounter with articulated statements of knowledge. The knowings which arise from experience are more tacit, contextual, personalistic. These are self-generated knowings, *naturalistic generalizations*, that come when, individually for each person, for each practitioner, new experience is added to old.

Formal research reports *may* contain the detailed description necessary to generate vicarious experience for readers, thereby modifying the reader's ever-developing naturalistic generalizations. But the author of the formal research report seldom assumes a commitment to facilitate this vicarious experience. Naturalistic case studies[19] *are* impelled by this commitment. The naturalistic researcher presents an exhibit of raw data — portrayals of actual teaching and learning problems, witnessing of observers who understand the reality of the classroom, words of the people involved. These raw data provide readers with vicarious experiences which interact with existing naturalistic generalizations formed from previous experience. Naturalistic research leads to vicarious experience.

Vicarious Experience

The vicar is a substitute, performing a service for those not well-placed to perform for themselves. The naturalistic researcher observes and records what readers are not placed to observe for themselves, but who, when reading the descriptive account, can experience vicariously the various perplexities and efforts to remedy. Mary Lee Smith, one of the 'vicars' of our *Case Studies in Science Education,* quoted a science teacher in Colorado:

> Teachers are extension of the parent and as such should teach the value system that is consistent with the community. The community has a vested interest in the schools, and has a right to demand that certain values be taught and certain others not to be taught.[20]

And a teacher in rural Illinois told field-researcher Alan Peshkin:

> I've been accused of being a Communist and an atheist. Once the science teacher and I brought two classes together to discuss Darwin. We were studying the twenties in history and talking about the Scopes trial. A few periods later a kid came by and asked if I was an atheist. These students are riled by a discussion of evolution.[21]

Situations such as these of high school science teaching can be studied by researchers either in knowledge-producing *or* experience-producing ways.[22] A researcher whose aim is to create formal generalizations, propositional generalizations, would probably do a content analysis of these quotations, attending to a few key variables such as 'curriculum authenticity' and 'teacher sensitivity.' Such a researcher seldom presents personal testimony as evidence. The data to be collected are more directly representative of the stated hypotheses, more in the form of pre-selected variables. Situational and contextual information often are considered irrelevant.

For the experience-evoking kind of research, for naturalistic-generalization-inviting research, a wider net is cast — gathering direct testimony, 'thick descriptions,'[23] time-bound, place-bound, personality-bound information, data of a phenomenological bent. The naturalistic researcher chooses the most coherent and immediately relevant information and puts it — in more-or-less natural state — into the resulting report.

Certainly, naturalistic researchers must focus and delimit their study, attending to one or a few major issues. But naturalistic researchers will present the data in more, rather than less, natural form, leaving in the richness and ambiguity and conflict which are part of ordinary experience. The readers then can weigh the given data against their own experience and perhaps confront previous interpretations and temper convictions formerly held. Changes affecting the naturalistic generalizations of each reader may relate to the interpretations of the researcher, but they may be in response to aspects of the data not considered by the researcher. Consider, for example, the nuances and suggestions which come to mind because of the quoted teacher's concern about being called an 'atheist.' An administrator's naturalistic generalization might be: 'I can't leave the

95

teachers alone to work out such sensitive issues with the public.' A teacher's might be: 'Most students are terribly dependent on a teacher to deal rationally with the science-religion controversy.' Such contextualized vignettes inform the practitioner much differently than do comparisons of groups on variables.

If the classroom practice of a teacher becomes something tomorrow it otherwise would not have been, convictions may have been altered by such vicarious experience as a naturalistic research report evokes. More of our research should be objective study serving the teacher's subjective experience. To quote Thomas Flanagan in *The Year of the French*:

> We possess ideas, but we are possessed by feelings. They lie too deep for understanding, astir with their own secret life, and carrying us with them.[24]

The Determinants of Action

Evoking vicarious experience may be useful — you might say — but is it really the place to make our investment? To consider the alternative investments of educational research let us survey the various ways a researcher might facilitate practice. Let us carefully analyze the determinants of action. Keep in mind the outcome is action — or more specifically, professional practice.

Action

The practitioner or actor, for example, a teacher or administrator, is someone responsible, in part, for an educational 'system,' for example, a classroom, a state department of education. This person is moved to act, to change an activity, to refrain from acting, or to resist acting, only when sufficient external demand or internal conviction arises. Otherwise inertia keeps her doing the same as before.

Most efforts to change educational action, certainly most of those supported by state and federal agencies in the USA, have been authoritarian in orientation. An 'order' to change is issued from higher administrative level, often as a condition for receiving certain funding. The literature on program innovation discusses the problems of such mandates. Some of these external demands come softened and sweetened with attractive workshops or fellowships for practitioners.

Figure 1.

But still, practitioners consistently reject (often by non-acknowledgement) new approaches, reorganizations, or curriculum reforms, even when use is mandated. For good or bad, the supervisory system is just too weak to guarantee compliance. External demand is weaker than most people think, and almost no demand can be impressed by the research community. If research is to influence, usually it will be via change in the practitioner's convictions.

In our *Case Studies in Science Education* we found that reforms were rejected in secondary school classrooms mostly because the new teaching styles did not leave teachers in command of responsibilities they considered critical, including those of fostering student obedience and seeing adolescence as a time of preparation.[25] These organized change-efforts fell short in part because personal experience and conviction were not accommodated. A practitioner's convictions are influenced by *understanding* and *voluntarism*. Voluntarism is a basis of action rooted in faith and personal feeling — conation ranging from momentary impulse to abiding devotion. The research community tries to influence practitioners' feelings, especially about rationality and technology, but its opportunities to influence understanding are much greater than its opportunities to influence feeling.

Figure 2.

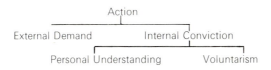

In his book *Explanation and Understanding*[26] Finnish philosopher George Henrik von Wright stressed that understanding is arrived at through dialogue and rumination, drawing from pools of knowledge both experiential and propositional. Or as I indicate in the schematic, personal understanding comes from both naturalistic and formalistic generalizations.

Figure 3.

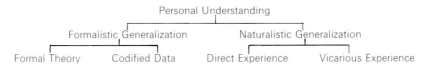

Continuing the analysis, we might say that theory and codified data are the main constituents of our formal, verbalized generalizations — whereas experience, real and vicarious, is the main constituent of the naturalistic generalizations. The interaction of determinants of action of course is

much more complex and turbulent than shown here; yet these representations should help us identify points at which there may be infusion from
research. In the first half of this chapter I argued that our efforts to
provide formalistic generalization through theory and empirical data have
had too little impact on practitioners. Little, on the other hand, has been
tried by researchers to influence practitioner *experience*.

Here now is my combined schematic diagram of the determinants of
action. If we consider every entry point, if we consider every major
leverage available to the researcher to influence practice, *one* stands out as
neglected, an undercultivated category of knowledge. It is the disciplined
collection of that experiential knowledge that might lead a reader
vicariously to naturalistic generalization.

Figure 4.

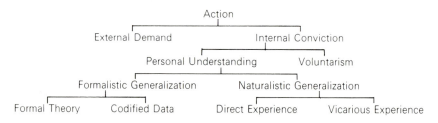

I note again that in their reports and research designs, educational
researchers emphasize formal generalizations, explanations. Those knowings are indeed essential to communication and in a complex world,
essential to practice, but they are too exclusively relied on by researchers
and educational authorities, too regularly presumed to be preferable
messages.

The intention of most educational research is to provide formalistic
generalization. A typical research report might highlight the correlation
between time spent on team projects *and* gain in scores on an achievement
test. The report might identify personality, affective and demographic
variables. Even with little emphasis on causation this report is part of the
grand explanation of student learning. It provides one way of knowing
about educational practice.

A more naturalistic research report might deal with the same topic,
perhaps with the same teachers and pupils, yet reflecting a different
epistemology. The naturalistic data would describe the actual interactions
within student teams. The report would probably portray project work —
conveying style, context, and evolution. A person would be described as
an individual, with uniqueness not just in deviant scores, but as a key to
understanding the interactions. A reader senses the experience of team-
work in this particular situation. It is a *unique* situation in some respects,
but ordinary in other respects. Readers recognize similarities with

situations of their own. Perhaps they are stimulated to think of old problems in a new way.

Curriculum evaluation and instructional research *can* be organized, by intent and with sophistication, to provide the raw data to furnish vicarious experience which should help the reader/practitioner develop new naturalistic generalizations to guide practice.

In this chapter I have *not* suggested that teachers and administrators are impervious to change suggested by formal knowledge. Some will respond, for example, to the essay of a curriculum specialist, others to an article documenting student attitude scores. Some instructors respond well to logic, codified data, and regulatory statement — but usually too few of them to satisfy campuswide and nationwide need for change.

Practitioners can be moved by what fellow practitioners elsewhere are experiencing, by what community residents expect, and by how their students respond. In one of our rural secondary schools the science teacher said:

> Evolution has never come up as an issue. I don't know. My personal view is probably 'safe.' I don't see any divergence between the theory of evolution and a religious viewpoint. I suppose I'm not really radical. Maybe that's the reason I haven't had any 'feedback.' If I were an atheist, I suppose *that* might present a problem. And the students don't make it a problematic discussion either. Never had any one do that. Here again, our students are pretty much of one mind. They're pretty 'closed' in the ideas they have. I've barely had any 'feedback' from the community.[27]

Now think again of the teacher quoted by Peshkin a few pages back. She too was moved-to-act by student response, but her reaction was quite different from that of this teacher. Each decision as to how to treat 'Evolution' in science class is influenced by particular experiences. Teachers will react, but not always of course in the way that specialists in 'planned-change' desire. Providing more opportunity for naturalistic generalization is not likely to increase the uniformity of practice. But improvement and standardization are separate and different goals, of course.

Research which attends to the complexity and contextuality of daily practice can reasonably aspire to provide the best possible knowledge for in-service education, i.e., for modifying practice. According to Lawrence Stenhouse, a British curriculum specialist:

> ... in-service development needs curriculum development and research in teaching. The error has been to see in-service education as the servant of curriculum reform rather than curriculum as a research field to serve in-service education.[28]

My argument that vicarious-experience data are neglected knowledge for the understanding and improvement of practice has a political side effect — which I should mention again. To emphasize the uniqueness of each classroom is to support autonomy for the classroom teacher.

But the argument for 'naturalistics' is not primarily political, nor humanistic. It is pragmatic. Even in situations where teachers are pleading, as were CSSE teachers, for someone else to specify their curricular responsibilities[29], it is likely that neither parent nor state will be served if external demands on the teacher are inconsistent with their convictions. We cannot expect a substantial change in practice if teachers and administrators lack understanding of new problems and new needs.

In the science classes of the United States and in the rural schools of Brazil we find few teachers expecting that researchers can provide either formal generalizations or vicarious experience capable of helping them solve their problems. Substantive change often will require arrangement of circumstances in which teachers engage in solitary and mutual self-study, i.e., action research. But action research needs more than first-hand knowledge and immediate experience. It needs problem representations and experiential descriptions that disciplinary-based researchers can provide[30]. To generate that back-up research is the plea of this article.

Our assistance of course needs to accommodate career-long investments-in-practice the teachers have already made. They cannot be expected to sacrifice much in the way of technical readiness or social standing in the adventitious hope that students would learn better. But vicarious experience, if relevant and interesting, is widely accepted by teachers and other practitioners. Thus this rationale that new vicarious experience might mix with old, and lead to evolutionary changes in conviction and practice.

To summarize then: we have seen that many efforts to produce change in the schools have failed to do so, frequently despite practitioner desire to change. It appears this is partly because the major ways of implementing planned change have been rejected by practitioners. Among researchers the dominant belief is that formal generalizations are the essential ingredient of improved practice. Too often they have designed new, perhaps theory-based, programs rather than modifying practice within its relatively fixed context. Researchers should have a stronger sense of both the appetite for change *and* the survival instincts of our teachers and administrators.

My argument has been that practice is largely guided by tacit knowing, by naturalistic generalization, formed from experiencing, often implicit. Formative evaluation and other change-effort research has often failed to honor naturalistic generalization. Too seldom has it presented practitioners with the vicarious experience which helps alter conviction and practice. Evolutionary change is slow, but it can capitalize on a still remaining abundance of fitness, uniqueness, personal understanding and a universal desire to survive.

Notes

1 This chapter was the keynote presentation at the National Symposium on Evaluation, Federal University of Espirito Santo, Vitoria, Brazil, August 1984. Earlier versions had appeared as 'Naturalistic generalizations' by myself and Deborah Trumbell in the *Review Journal of Philosophy and Social Science*, VII, 1982 and as 'Generalizations', a paper presented at the Annual Meeting of the American Educational Research Association, April 1980. My interest in an evolutionary approach was first awakened by Tom Hastings' ideas of the role of program evaluation in instructional research and nursed along by Stephen Kemmis' 1976 University of Illinois dissertation, 'Evaluation and the evolution of knowledge about educational programs'.

2 From a 1798 essay entitled 'An old question raised again: Is the human race constantly progressing?' and quoted here from translations edited by BECK, L.W. (1963) *On History*, Indianapolis, Bobbs-Merrill, p. 152.

3 See for example the summative review by FULLAN, M. (1982) *The Meaning of Educational Change*, NYC, Teachers College Press; and management science literature emphasizing group dynamics since Kurt Lewin.

4 DEWEY, J. (1916) *Democracy and Education*, NYC, Macmillan.

5 As usually defined, action research has *practitioners* planning, changing practice, observing and reflecting. See for example, 'Action research: notes on the national seminar' by BROWN, L., HENRY, C., HENRY, J.A. and McTAGGART, R. (1982) in *Classroom Action Research Network Bulletin*, 5, Cambridge Institute of Education.

6 STAKE, R.E. (1978) 'The case study method in social inquiry', *Educational Researcher*, 7, 2, February, pp. 5–8.

7 LINDBLOM, C.E. and COHEN, D.K. (1979) *Usable Knowledge: Social Science and Social Problem Solving*, New Haven, Yale University Press.

8 Quoted in COWDEN, P. and COHEN, D.K. (1979) *Divergent Words of Practice: The Federal Reform of Local School in the Experimental Schools Program*, Cambridge, Mass, Center for the Study of Public Policy, summer.

9 GRUMET, M. (1980) 'Conception, contradiction and curriculum', paper presented at the Annual Meeting of the American Educational Research Association, Boston, April.

10 See GOODLAD, J. (1984) *A Place Called School*, NYC, McGraw Hill.

11 SHORT, E.C. (1973) 'Status of knowledge production and utilization in curriculum', paper presented at the Annual Meeting of the American Educational Research Association, New Orleans, February.

12 *Ibid.*

13 WEISS, C. (Ed.) (1977) *Using Social Research in Public Policy Making*, Lexington, Mass, Lexington Heath.

14 SCHMIEDER, A.A. (1975) *Journal of Teacher Education*, spring, pp. 18–23.

15 THORNDYKE, P.W. (1981) *Schema Theory as a Guide for Educational Research: White Knight or White Elephant?*, Rand Paper Series, March 1981. Invited address presented at the Annual Meeting of the American Educational Research Association, Los Angeles, April.

16 See ATKIN, J.M. (1973) 'Practice-oriented inquiry: A third approach to research in education, *Educational Researcher*, 2, pp. 3–4.

17 POLANYI, M. (1958) *Personal Knowledge*, Chicago, University of Chicago Press.
18 SCHON, D. (1982) *The Reflective Practitioner: How Professionals Think in Action*, NYC, Basic Books.
19 See my entry 'Case study' in NISBET, J. (Ed.) (1985) *World Yearbook of Education*.
20 In STAKE, R. and EASLEY, J (Eds) (1978) *Case Studies in Science Education*, Urbana, Ill, CIRCE, University of Illinois, Booklet II, Volume I, pp. 2–13.
21 *Ibid*, STAKE, R.E. and EASLEY, J., Booklet IV, Volume I, pp. 4–51.
22 This is not quite the distinction made by Cronbach and Suppes between conclusion-based and decision-based research. Both they and I have been attentive to: whose thinking is climatic, researchers or practitioners? But they accentuated differences in 'problems' pursued in research and practice, whereas I am accentuating differences in epistemological structure between formalized abstraction and informal experience. See their (1969) *Research for Tomorrow's Schools: Disciplined Inquiry for Education*, New York, Macmillan.
23 See GEERTZ, G. (1973) *The Interpretation of Culture*, NYC, Basic Books.
24 FLANAGAN, T. (1979) *The Year of the French*, New York, Holt, Rinehart and Winston.
25 STAKE, R.E. and EASLEY, J. (Eds) XIII, 16–3.
26 Von WRIGHT, G.H. (1971) *Explanation and Understanding*, London, Routledge and Kegan Paul.
27 STAKE, R.E. and EASLEY, J., *op cit.*, Booklet IV, Volume I, pp. 4–11.
28 STENHOUSE, L. 'Review of the status of precollege science, mathematics, and social studies educational practice in US schools', Norwich, England, Centre for Applied Research in Education, University of East Anglia, unpublished manuscript.
29 STAKE, R.E. and EASLEY, J. *op cit.*, XII, pp. 14–22.
30 In his theory of action Jurgen Habermas presupposed a 'real relationship of communicating (and cooperating) investigators, where each of the sub-systems is part of the surrounding social systems, which in turn are the result of the sociocultural evolution of the human race', (1974) *Theory and Practice*, (translated by John Viertel), London, Heinemann, p. 14.

Three Good Reasons for Not Doing Case Studies in Curriculum Research

Rob Walker
Deakin University, Australia

While case-study methods of research have a long history of use in educational enquiry, they have a particular attraction for those with an interest in curriculum for, in curriculum research, case studies offer a means of integration across the disciplines of the social sciences. They also offer an emphasis on synthesis rather than on analysis and a means of approaching hidden curriculum, informal social structures and unintended consequences of action on the same terms as formal curriculum, social, and management structures. In other words, those who share a view of the curriculum field as organized around issues rather than around theories, find in case study an empirical genre appropriately flexible, eclectic and capable of creating surprises.

The view of curriculum studies as organized around analysis of issues has undoubtedly been stimulated by the experience of the curriculum development movement and, perhaps curiously, in no way diminished by its demise. The past ten years has, therefore, seen the development of increased interest in case-study research,[1,2] an interest often associated with a particular view of curriculum research as 'process',[3] for this view lends itself least easily to conventional research approaches.

The attraction of case-study research also derives from a central dilemma in the curriculum field, for in recent years (in Britain, Australasia and the USA at least) we have seen a number of attempts to centralize and to standardize what is taught in schools at specified age and grade levels. Paradoxically, this growing tendency toward centralization has been accomplished by an apparent growth of diversity in the curriculum practice of individual schools and individual classrooms. In this context, case studies offer both some measure of diversity, and of the processes which give rise to it (and so to the administrator and the politician they may appear to promise some measure of control). To those at the periphery, case studies seem to celebrate diversity and so to endorse it, often when other avenues to legitimacy offer less promise of progress.

It will be clear from what I have written that I have a view of case-study research in curriculum as marked by the attempt to get beyond illustrative examples of more general phenomena to the particularities and idiosyncracies of the instance, though not necessarily to turn to social science theory in the process. Case studies are, to me, primarily documentary and descriptive in character, but are marked by the attempt to reach across from the experience of those who are the subjects of study to those who are the audience. As so conceived, case studies are not limited to an illustrative role in relation to current theorizing, but may be one step ahead of it.

One of the incidental qualities of case studies is that they usually reveal that the person writing them is, to an extent, changed by doing the research and this is reflected in the present chapter, which draws on my own attempts to try and do case-study research. It is written less for those who are looking for a justification for case-study research, than it is for those who, like me, feel the end is justifiable but who have difficulties with the means. Its focus is on what some might call methodology; it is about the practical, and it is written in the hope that it might help others be successful where I have failed.

A Common Problem

Given the aspirations of the kind of case-study research I have outlined, a common problem is how to get beyond routine data to the stories that make the case come to life. This is an especially common problem in interviewing, where people often find it hard to break out of the constraint of telling you what they think you want (or ought) to know in order to tell you what you want to hear. Most of us more or less consciously adopt tactics for trying to close down one line of discussion in order to open up other, quite different lines. Barry MacDonald, for example, has a favourite question. When the interviewee is in full flight in what to the interviewer is a wrong direction, Barry will pause, look hard at the interviewee, and ask; 'But what keeps you *awake* at night?' This sharp break in formal discourse allows people to recollect their thoughts and to set out in the direction of a more personal and intimate discussion. It is an effective question. So effective I find myself asking the same question in relation to research. Like many of those who write in what loosely is called the 'naturalistic tradition' I tend to talk and write a lot about methods of research; but what keeps me awake at night? The truth is, very little, but over the years there have been a number of occasions when things have gone wrong in the course of carrying out case studies and this paper started out simply as a list of the events that have troubled me to the point where I lay awake worrying about them. As I thought about them and talked about them the list narrowed to three headings: three good reasons for not doing case-study research. They are that:

(a) Case-study research is an intervention, and often an uncontrolled intervention, in the lives of others.
(b) Case-study research provides a biased view, a distorted picture of the way things are.
(c) Case-study research is essentially conservative.

In the rest of the chapter I shall fill out each of these headings with examples before asking myself if three good reasons for not doing case-study research are in fact enough to stop me doing it.

An Uncontrolled Intervention in the Lives of Others

It is something of a paradox that, while we tend to fret at our failure as researchers/evaluators to get the messages through to those in policy-forming positions (see, for instance, Jenkins *et al.*[4]), we simultaneously face the problem that research/evaluation is highly intrusive in the lives of those who are its subjects. Indeed one of the main reasons why so much of the literature is taken up with pursuing questions of a methodological kind is in order to find ways of reducing the threat of intervention.

To take the simplest examples, to interview someone, to observe someone teaching, to talk with teachers about the head, or with pupils about teaching, are each potentially undermining of the façades which individuals and institutions construct in order to make the management of schooling possible. Those who have done research in schools will know and recognize the power of the interview as a means of intervention in the lives of others; an intervention often denied but no less real for that. And it is important to stress that intervention does not need to be an aspiration on the part of the interviewer in order for its effect to be felt. It is in the nature of the situation that power is vested in the questioner. The *kinds* of questions that are asked are usually enough to set trains of thought going in the interviewee's head that do not stop when the interview ends. Those who have been interviewed will know that it is quite common, for some hours, or even days after the interview has ended to keep rethinking lines of thought that first came to light in the interview itself. The question is a powerful tool for change, sometimes more powerful than the recommendation or the conclusion.

The same is true of being observed. The fact of being observed alone is enough to heighten some self-perceptions and sensitivities at the cost of others, even when the observer gives little clue as to what is being looked for. And while the literature often reports the problem of access and acclimatization (which are essentially researchers' problems), other problems are associated with the processes of exit and withdrawal, especially when the observation takes place over long periods of time.

This much is perhaps common knowledge, but when I think about the things that have gone wrong in research studies I have done, a number of them fall into the category of uncontrolled intervention. An example might help.

Some time ago I did a school case-study in order to try out the notion of 'condensed fieldwork' which Barry MacDonald and I devized as a key method for use in applying naturalistic approaches within evaluation studies (see MacDonald and Walker[5]). The plan was that I should make a one-day visit to the school in order to explain the study and return sometime later to make a three-day data-collection field visit; then I would write up the first draft of the 'case study', take it back to the school for comment and spend a further three days collecting responses and further data as directed by the school. The final case study would be a rewrite of the first draft taking into account all that this account stimulated by way of a response.

Compared to conventional 'ethnographic' field studies, the model here was intentionally interventive in character, but the intention of the design was to control the intervention by use of an extensive set of procedures for the uses made of information. Each of the subjects was promised total confidentiality during the initial fieldwork phase, in the sense that any information that was to go into the first draft of the case study would be sent to them so that they could examine it for relevance, fairness and accuracy, and so that they had an opportunity to edit and to censor any parts they did not want to be seen by their colleagues. At the second stage, the school as a whole was offered the opportunity to make similar changes to the draft before it was seen by anyone outside.

The first phase went reasonably well. I spent three days in the school, mainly tape-recording interviews with teachers. I returned to the University and spent three weeks writing up the first draft of the study from the transcripts, organizing the report in such a way that I could take the sections back to the individuals concerned before collating a version for the school to see. Past experience had though led me to some worries about this kind of design. As David Jenkins has pointed out, although the design makes it sound as though a lot of power is being handed to the subjects of the study, in practice, because the researcher/evaluator actually holds the information, all kinds of ploys and suspicions can come into play.[6] The effect can be to feed the power of the researcher, perhaps to an even greater extent than in a conventional participant-observation study, where the subjects have greater freedom to withhold commitment to the research enterprise.

In the early phase of the study one problem that worried me particularly was that, in condensing the interview material into a case-study format, I was free to commit all kinds of methodological violence on the data which was difficult for the subjects to control. Simply in translating from the spoken to the written word, in editing out sections and in rearranging the text, it is possible to arrive at meanings that go beyond what the speaker intended. Aware of this problem (and of my penchant for dramatic reconstruction), I duplicated all the tapes and left copies with each of the subjects. As I left the school at the end of day three of the field-work period, I said 'I am going away to write the first draft of the study, but I am taking away with me no more than I have left you. We have equal access to the data. If you are unhappy with what I write for whatever reason, if you think I have misquoted you, misunderstood or misrepresented you, you and I can both return to the tapes to check what has happened and to correct it'.

I admit I felt rather pleased with myself. Because I was aspiring to make the relationship between researchers and their subjects more 'democratic' (see MacDonald and Walker[7]), I felt this device of sharing access to the data was rather a neat one, especially as some of David Jenkins's criticism was still rattling around between my ears. I was also pleased with the idea because it put pressure on me to push past the data into interpretation. The way I saw it, as each teacher already had the data, I had to do more than regurgitate it if I was to retain their interest in the study. I wanted them to read the study and to be surprised by it, and as they already had the data I felt I would have to really work on it to produce accounts they found insightful and interesting. As someone who needs a sense of competition in order to generate motivation, I found this a good device for stimulating my own enthusiasm. I should add that I went to great lengths to stress to each of the teachers that it was important that they keep their tapes to themselves. I said that even if they felt quite happy to share their tapes with their colleagues, I would not want a situation to arise where someone who wanted to suppress what they had said found it difficult to resist staff-room social pressure to pre-release the data. Everybody accepted this as reasonable and agreed to wait until the written reports were available.

When I returned to the school some four weeks later I knew something was wrong. People who had been friendly during the earlier visit ignored me or paid me the minimum of attention. When I started to show people the written reports they were off-hand and dismissive. They did not seem to want to know anything about them. I was puzzled, but by mid-morning the story broke. One of the teachers took me on one side and told me that immediately after my previous visit the head had asked each of them to hand over their tapes. Some refused but eventually gave in. Within a few days the head had all the tapes but one, and locked them in his office.

My response was one of disbelief, followed quickly by confusion. What should I do? Should I confront the head and demand an explanation? Should I wait and see what happened, pretending I didn't know? How could I best rescue the study? Later that day I managed to talk to the head, and to let him know that I knew what had happened without actually confronting him with a sense of anger or disappointment. His explanation was a good one. He had been the last person I had interviewed during the previous visit. He claimed it was only when I talked to him that he realized some of the implications of the questions I had asked other teachers. While he did not object to being asked such things he realized that the total set of the data was potentially explosive. 'But I had promised you I would not show it to anyone until you had a chance to see it, as individuals and as a school', I protested. 'I think I trust you', he said, 'but I am not sure I trust everyone else involved'. The way he saw it there were teachers who might get together and share their tapes and find ways of using them that were not in what he saw as the interest of the school. As head, he did not feel he could take the risk of having such information loose in the school while I was 'away in the university'. If something went wrong, he argued, he had to be in control of the situation. If information leaked to the local press or to the office, he had to know what was happening. He realized he had broken the procedures of the research, but claimed that he had a greater responsibility for the running of the school, which overrode any agreements he might have with me.

It was a direct collision between the 'democratic' model built-in to the design of the research, and a bureaucratic model built-in to the organization of the school. It caused me some anguish and loss of sleep. I recovered the situation enough to be able to complete the study. I don't think that any of the teachers suffered as a result of what happened or the school was in any way changed by the events I had precipitated, though whether the school let any later researchers through the door I don't know. I certainly haven't left any tapes behind anywhere since.

There is another kind of intervention that case-study research can make into people's lives, and that is intervention that cuts the other way, across the researcher's side of the counter. I have recently completed a case study of the work of a local authority advisory team. My interest is in the observational work of advisers and inspectors. What kind of opportunities do they get to observe schools and classes? What do they look for? What kinds of infomation do they collect? What do they do with the information when they have got it? For two years I followed one team of advisers around schools, into meetings and into the office in order to understand better how those in a field role in a large social service organization function as the 'eyes and ears' of the Authority.[8]

Before I began, people warned me I would have a lot of problems with access and with the release of data, partly because the area is a sensitive one and partly because advisers constitute a relatively high-status occupational group. With this in mind I again designed the research to maximize the control that the subjects had over the use of the data. Part way through the study I became worried about the situation I was in, and in an annual progress report I wrote to the sponsors that, while I was collecting a lot of interesting material, I could not promise to make it available either in the period of the grant or in the final report, because, given its sensitivity, the advisers were unlikely to give me permission to use it. No researcher likes to hide good data, any more than journalists like to sit on a good story. But I was going further still. I was telling a funding agency whose good (tax-payers') money I had spent, that I was unlikely to deliver the goods I promised in the proposal. No-one likes offending funding agencies, especially at the present time, though perhaps tenured members of university faculty should feel free to take such risks. What is more worrying is the consequence of my loss of credibility in the research community among those of my colleagues who may be looking to me for their next contract. Among researchers I am in a privileged position, but I feel a keen sense of responsibility to those who do not share it. Case-study research carries some high risks, one of which is apparently just this kind of intervention in the life of researchers, especially those unprotected by regular jobs.

Case Studies Give a Distorted View of the World

Most case studies in education rely heavily on interview material and concentrate their focus on the immediate workings of organizations, particularly schools. As I have already indicated, the interview is a powerful and interventive research tool but it is also highly productive in that it allows you to cover a lot of ground at speed and, given modern recording technology, to emerge with a lot of data from a short field visit. The dangers of relying too heavily on interview data, from the problem of who you select to interview, to what they select to tell you, to how you select what to write, are well rehearsed in the social-science fieldwork literature. They are no less real or important for that, but they are problems well documented elsewhere.

Whatever the recommendations to be found in the standard textbooks in case-study research it is not always as easy to balance interview data against observations as it might seem, especially when the subjects of the study have some control over the process of assembling the study. I recently ran into a classic case of this problem in a case study I worked on with Saville Kushner and Clem Adelman. Part of this study involved a 'portrayal' of a school which served the Spanish-speaking community in an American city: the portrayal being assembled from interviews with the teachers, observations of teaching, and 'field-time' spent in the school. We chose to write up the study using, at one point, a series of transcripts from lessons taught to different classes in order to give some sense of variation within the school; variation in teaching approach, in age/grade/level of the children, in subject area and in bilingual competence.[9]

One of the teachers who taught younger children let us record her lessons and we emerged with a set of transcripts which revealed a competent teacher who strongly emphasized a didactic, instructional approach. Our reading of the transcript was that she did not come over from the transcript alone as very warm or sympathetic, as compared with some of the other teachers. But set against this observational data we had some interview data which showed her in a very different light. She was a nun who had devoted her life to the immigrant community, not just as a teacher, but as a social worker, friend and advocate. She was acutely aware of the problems faced by the children in her class and their families, and highly respected in the community and in the school system. We tried to write around the transcript some of the biographical material we collected in order to give the reader a means of seeing beyond the limited image presented in the transcript. The teacher was distressed by what we did, mainly on a question of principle. As a Catholic she resented any implication that she had worked for any self-serving purpose. At one point in the account we wrote I quoted one of her one-time colleagues describing her as the 'Mother Theresa of the school system'. She wanted this comment removed from the study, in fact she wanted everything removed except the transcript. We tried to persuade her that, to an outsider, the transcript showed her in an unsympathetic light; she was well aware of this, but wanted it that way. 'That is the way I am', she said, 'I can't deny that'. If people misrepresented her because they lacked access to the information that the pupils, parents and other teachers had, which meant they saw her in a different light, she said she felt that was their problem and she had limited sympathy for them.

It was a difficult situation to find a way through. I got locked into it without an escape route, and it was left to Clem and Saville to negotiate some kind of compromise, but it caused me to worry about the consequences of selection. It caused me to worry too about research as an intervention in the lives of others. It was one of those research relationships I mishandled, and it was fortunate that others were involved to resolve it. Usually we work on our own and that route is not available.

When I have told this story as a moral tale it has disturbed those who take a strong view of the sense of responsibility that the researcher owes to the research enterprise. A good deal of the freedom we have, they argue, is contingent on our ability to find the truth and to tell it without fear. In arguing for the need to compromise 'the truth' with the need to protect the subject they say I am not making a methodological point, but one which cuts through to an assumption that is fundamental to the whole enterprise.

As often happens with arguments of this kind I find myself persuaded by the rhetoric, but find the working of its practice less clear-cut than might appear. In the case of the story I have just told it would seem that the end result was a compromise of 'the truth' in order to soften the intervention of the research in the lives of the subjects. But this in itself is only part of the story, for when I look at the final report I have to admit that it is a much better depiction of reality than the overdrawn stereotype I first had in my head of an apparent paradox between the person the teacher is and the way in which she teaches. That paradox was primarily a feature of *my* perception of the reality, and not a good account of the reality itself. As I got to know it better, to think about what I saw, and to talk to others about it, I realized that it was inadequate. So, in the end, it was not just a question of being talked out of a strongly held belief about what was 'true', but of coming to realize that my interpretation was partial and limited and that it did not serve the case study well to make too much of it.

There is a problem of distortion at another level that stems from the heavy emphasis case studies tend to place on what teachers say. As such studies accumulate the interview responses of teachers come to loom large in the image that builds up of the way the system operates. It can be argued that this is no bad thing, and that such a perspective is long overdue, but the problem of balance remains. How much emphasis should be placed on the reports given by teachers as opposed to those given by pupils, by parents, by chief education officers, by civil servants . . .? What often happens, I think, is that those who figure most fully in case studies are those who have, or who are given, most power in the negotiation process that lies behind the writing and release of the study. Those who have little power (for example the pupils) tend not to figure centre stage. Those who have a lot (teachers and head teachers) tend to occupy a lot of space and often to use their position to influence the way they are presented.

In evaluation this is often not a problem, for the evaluation may see itself as providing opportunities for those in schools to make just that kind of use of the studies. Distortion is significant and balance important, but there is little sense of responsibility for any conception of a level of truth that lies behind it. In practice the process of negotiating the account often *is* the process of evaluation.

The distortion problem is more worrying for the case-study worker writing to a research audience, especially when a situation arises where there are two accounts; a public account the school agrees to release, and a private account that it requires the researcher to keep private. Evaluators may be prepared to sign away their right to contribute their own viewpoint within the study so long as they can maintain a position of independence in relation to some overall conception of balance. Researchers, however, usually feel the need, not just to maintain an independent stance, but also for an opportunity to promote what they see as independent view.

If evaluation case studies tend to rely too heavily on interview data, observational research studies often underestimate the significance of what people say, and make too much of what the researcher claims to observe. Either way we end up with very distorted pictures of the way the system works. In the first case we make too much of the perspective of those who are located within the system at certain selected points. In the second we get a view of the way schools and classrooms work which minimizes the significance of the human actors in the situation.

It is difficult to make this criticism as specific as I would like to, because what I am talking about is an image built up from the accumulation of studies and experiences rather than the characteristics of particular studies. But if I can fall back on personal experience again, I worked for several years in what has become known as 'classroom research'. I spent a lot of time closely observing what I had selected as being classrooms with distinctive pupil-teacher relationships, a particular approach to the use of resources, and a learning philosophy that might be typified as 'exploratory' or 'discovery', or 'creative'. I certainly do not regret the time I gave to that research. I learnt an enormous amount and I think it was important research to do. After some time, though, I did begin to get a feeling of unease about the effects of what I was doing. When I asked myself what the purpose of the research was, the answer I gave myself was that it was to understand better what was happening in those classrooms. Here, I told myself, were teachers devizing ways of teaching that marked a break with the way they had been taught, and a break very often with what else was going on in their schools. Set alongside the writings of radical innovators, what was happening in these classrooms had a complexity that made the writings look inadequate. Rather than write polemic that might influence teachers I thought that a strong justification for the research I was doing was that it would both help the teachers I was studying push further along the lines of their own development, and provide others with more valuable 'case studies' than I could find elsewhere in the literature.

That argument sustained my enthusiasm for several years, but there came a time when it looked inadequate. As I began to piece the case studies together I realized that, while it was true they depicted rather well what was happening in the classrooms I had observed and filmed, they also made them extremely vulnerable. I found it harder and harder to write about them because I began to realize that you don't need to assume a conspiracy against innovation in order to locate its enemies: providing an adequate description is enough. I had committed the classic error of what Gouldner rather brutally calls, 'underdog sociology'.

The only way I could 'balance' the account I gave was to pursue the process of documentation throughout the system. The classes I had studied needed to be balanced by equally penetrating studies of locations I hadn't studied. It is not enough to reveal what happens in classrooms if you do not at the same time reveal what is happening in staff meetings, in the head's office, in the local education authority and perhaps in the Department of Education and Science (DES). To be fair you almost need a requirement specifying what would count as 'equal exposure'. This is in part what I mean when I say that case studies give a distorted view of the world. The view they give *always* emphasizes one set of views rather than another; in fact the very power of the case study comes from just that selective bias, especially when the view taken is not one shared by the reader. But when we look at what we have case studied, it seems to me it has nearly always been vulnerable areas of the system: innovations, teachers, classrooms, and schools. Where are the really penetrating case-studies of the DES, of the National Union of Teachers, of local authorities, of examination boards, or of influential academics? The only ones I can find have been suppressed, remain unpublished or are awaiting transformation into history. Most of those academics who have an interest in these areas are too concerned with acting on the stage to risk observing what is happening, and the rest of us tend to leave that responsibility to journalists, who are inevitably limited by time, space and the editor's scissors.

Case Studies are Conservative

I have reached a point where my categories are beginning to merge, as part of what I have said already points to a conservatism built-in to the notion of case-study research. Certainly, in the recent literature what has been case studied has been the margins of the system, and that is particularly true of educational innovations. Not, I hasten to add, that those who have done the studies have wished particularly to increase the vulnerability of innovations to the political process, in fact the contrary is almost certainly true. But that has often been their effect: the unintended consequence of their publication.

Case studies are, though, conservative in a deeper sense than this. It is not simply that case studies of innovations have been used to bring them under control, but that it is in the nature of the case study to embalm what is established practice simply by describing it. The very process of conceiving, writing and publishing a case study solidifies and crystallizes a reality in the minds of readers and writer which is, initially tenuous, fluid and dissolved in another medium. The act of case study (and perhaps of any research) is to describe reality in order to create it. The implicit is made explicit, the intuitive is made self evident and the abstract is made concrete. Once fixed, the case study changes little, but the situations and the people caught in it have moved even before the image is available. The case study is therefore 'conservative' in much the same way that a photograph is conservative. It captures an instant in time and space which can then be held against a moving changing reality. As readers we can turn to Louis Smith's account of Kensington School,[10] Hargreaves' case study,[11] Shipman's account of the Keele Project[12] or MacDonald's studies of Rosehill or of Canon Roberts Schools[13] and read them as though those schools and projects exist now as they did then. The case study freezes something of their vitality for later readers. Yet none of these studies reveal the situations they describe as they are now, they live only in the literature and the minds of their readers.[14]

I have written of this 'conservatism' as though it was a limitation in case-study research. That is because my theme has been to link up aspects of the research that have caused me concern, and one of the aspects of case study that has worried me on several occasions in the past has been a feeling of being overtaken by events. For example, having worked hard to portray the state of a number of curriculum issues in a school, to be told by the school at the fifth draft of the report, 'You've got it. That is right. That is an accurate account of the way things were a year ago. But since then everything has changed'. And while I know it cannot have changed that much, I know in many respects the school is right, and even that the process of writing the case study has contributed to its own redundancy. Even in evaluation, with a strong emphasis placed on fast reporting, we deal in models and images, and even in history, more often than we allow.

Looked at another way this 'conservatism' has more positive aspects, though it involves rethinking the purposes and the possibilities of the enterprise. Just as the still photograph has value as a record, as a point of identification, and as an image in its own right; so the case study has more uses than I think we often allow. The mistake is to assume that the case study is a mirror, rather than to acknowledge that it is analogous to a cumbersome and primitive plate camera that we have scarcely learnt to handle. To continue exploring the potential of case-study method requires enthusiasm and a degree of trust. We are experimenting with a method we do not fully understand (and it is a method related to, but very different from the field methods developed in the social sciences).

It is that sense of potential that provides my main excuse for continuing to work in the area of case-study research, despite awareness of mistakes I have made in the past, and certain knowledge that I will make others in the future. It is not easy to make yourself relive those things that have gone wrong, especially where they involve relationships with others, but when opportunities occur for doing further studies my enthusiasm always gets the better of my sense of caution. The important lesson to be learned is, I think, to make every effort to learn from our mistakes.

What resolutions should be carried through from the mistakes I have recounted here?

(a) First, not to underestimate the interventive power of the case study and its methods. Where possible to make use of multiple observers, to act to protect the lives of participants, and to hold to procedures which build in countervailing forces in order to strengthen the position of those who are subjects of, and to, such research.

(b) Second, to take care not to neglect the fact that the conduct of research is a social process, a temporary system, which has to find space for itself and so to be accommodated by other interests. Case-study research is not simply interventive as a process, but as the presence of people and relationships impinging on existing patterns of authority and of social relations. In the academic world we tend to lay great stress on the value of information for understanding, and to stress democratic rights of free access to information. In the worlds we study, research information is often conceived as the currency of power, and right of access to it controlled by bureaucratic boundaries. The interaction of these two sets of conflicting assumptions is frequently a more significant part of the research process than we admit or allow. It is not simply noise in the system, or the consequence of poor designs, but marks a fundamental discontinuity between the worlds of the researcher and of the subject.

(c) Third, where possible to design studies such that those with power over the lives of others included in the scope of the study are required by the design to see the nature of their responsibilities. In particular, to design studies that give those at different levels of the system equal access to, and control over, the resources that the research provides.

(d) Fourth, we should constantly look for ways of underlining the fact that case studies tell *a* truth but not *the* truth. They may offer certain claims to truth, depending on the nature of the evidence they provide, but they are always partial accounts; constructions of reality; representations. Though, as I have argued here, they may well become part of the culture they describe, in that they provide shared memories and perceptions for their subjects, and so are likely to become a part of institutional mythology.

Acknowledgement

This paper was written during a period as visiting lecturer at Monash University. I am grateful to Lawrence Ingvarson, Stephen Kemmis, Colin Power, Don Hogben and their students for discussions on its themes.

Notes

1 WALKER, R. (1982) 'The use of case studies in applied research and evaluation', in HARTNETT, A. (Ed.) *The Social Sciences in Educational Studies*, London, Heinemann.

2 SHAW, K.E. (1978) 'Understanding the curriculum: the approach through case studies', *Journal of Curriculum Studies*, 10, 1, January–March.

3 STENHOUSE, L. (1975) *An Introduction to Curriculum Research*, London, Heinemann.

4 JENKINS, D. *et al.* (1981) 'Thou nature art my goddess', *Cambridge Journal of Education*, 11, 3.
5 MACDONALD, B. and WALKER, R. (Eds) (1974) *Innovation, Evaluation, Research and the Problem of Control*, SAFARI Interim papers, Norwich, Centre for Applied Research in Education, University of East Anglia.
6 JENKINS, D. (1980) 'An adversary's account of SAFARI's ethics of case study' in SIMONS, H. (Ed.) *Towards a Science of the Singular*, occasional publication 10, Norwich, Centre for Applied Research in Education, University of East Anglia.
7 MACDONALD, B. and WALKER, R. (Eds) (1974) *op cit.*
8 WALKER, R. (1981) *The Observational Work of LEA Inspectors and Advisors*, final report to the SSRC, copies available from the Centre for Applied Research in Education, University of East Anglia.
9 MACDONALD, B. *et al.* (1982) *A Study of Bilingual Education in the USA*, Norwich, Centre for Applied Research in Education, University of East Anglia.
10 SMITH, L. and KEITH, P. (1971) *Anatomy of Educational Innovation*, New York, Wiley.
11 HARGREAVES, D. (1967) *Social Relations in a Secondary School*, London, Routledge and Kegan Paul.
12 SHIPMAN, M. (1974) *Inside a Curriculum Project*, London, Methuen.
13 MACDONALD, B. (1978) *The Experience of Innovation*, occasional publication 6, Norwich, Centre for Applied Research in Education, University of East Anglia.
14 SMITH is, however, currently writing *Kensington Revisited* (to be published by the Falmer Press), a revised view of the school and of those who taught there at the time of the first study.

Seven Principles for Programme Evaluation in Curriculum Development and Innovation

Stephen Kemmis
Deakin University

Different definitions of evaluation abound. The Australian Curriculum Development Centre (CDC) Study Group on curriculum evaluation reviewed a variety of definitions with currency in the evaluation literature and adopted the following one as the most useful guide for the evaluation of CDC's own projects and programmes and for curriculum evaluation more generally: 'Evaluation is the process of delineating, obtaining and providing information useful for making decisions and judgments about educational programs and curricula'.[1]

This definition highlights the function of evaluative information in assisting decision-making. It reflects a fairly widespread agreement among evaluation theorists[2] about the role of evaluation in informing action at discrete decision-points. But it is important to recognize that a curriculum programme and its evaluation are highly interactive, not only in 'summative' decisions, but throughout the process of curriculum development. In short, the discrete decision points are few and far between and evaluation permeates development: the two processes are not discontinuous. Accordingly, a desirable definition of evaluation will acknowledge the mutuality of the relationship between evaluation and curriculum development and its continuous, organic and reflexive contribution to thought and action about a curriculum. Other definitions of evaluation, while more general than the one adopted by the CDC Study Group seem more likely to recognize the pervasiveness of the evaluation function, and less likely to treat it as discontinuous and separate from development. Stake and Denny (1969), for example, have this to say:

> Considered broadly, evaluation is the discovery of the nature and worth of something. In relation to education, we may evaluate students, teachers, curriculums, administrators, systems, programs and nations. The purposes for evaluation may be many, but always evaluation attempts to describe something and to indicate its perceived merits and shortcomings ... Evaluation is not a

search for cause and effect, an inventory of present status, or a
prediction of future success. It is something of all of these but only
as they contribute to understanding substance, function and
worth.[3]

This definition, emphasizing 'nature and worth', 'perceived merits and
shortcomings' and 'understanding', goes further towards acknowledging
evaluation as an ever-present aspect of considered action. One might
quibble over the use of the word 'discovery', suggesting as it does that the
nature and worth of the thing evaluated antedate the evaluative search for
them, but the force of the term is mitigated by the notion that merit and
shortcomings are 'perceived' rather than intrinsic or imminent.

It is critical in deciding upon a definition to guide evaluation efforts to
give due importance to the pervasiveness of the evaluative dimension of all
human activity, and to the fact that it is present in a range of individual
and public judgment processes which exist whether or not an evaluation is
formally commissioned or expected of project and programme participants. Indeed, when evaluations of particular programmes *are* commissioned, they should approximate (and focus and sharpen) these informal
critical processes, not ignore or supplant them. Though the formality of
commissioning or requiring an evaluation imposes certain obligations to
formalize and discipline the individual and public judgment processes
which occur naturally in considered activity, formal evaluations should
attempt deliberately to preserve something of the conviviality of the
informal processes.

Preserving conviviality is no easy task. These principles attempt to
provide a framework within which conviviality can be preserved by
emphasizing the continuity and mutuality of concern between programme
participants, a programme sponsor, an evaluation sponsor and an
evaluator. They also attempt to emphasize that evaluation forms a natural
part of the critical thinking that guides the development process. This is
not to say that formal evaluations can lack rigour, discipline or honesty;
rather, it is to assert that their critical edge should be tempered with
humane values rather than narrowly technocratic or bureaucratic
concerns.

Accordingly, the definition of evaluation which has informed and
guided the development of these principles is this: *Evaluation is the process
of marshalling information and arguments which enable interested individuals
and groups to participate in the critical debate about a specific programme.* So
construed, evaluation consists in harnessing and refining the ubiquitous
processes of individual and public judgment, not in resolving or replacing
them with a technology of judgment.

There is a certain kind of seduction in discussing principles: one is
often inclined to share the aspirations they embody simply because they
seem worthy ones or because the rhetoric of principles is lofty and stirring.

For this reason, the discussion of each principle includes a reference to two alternative principles. Each of the three resulting sets of principles (the set advocated here and the two alternative sets) are more or less self-consistent.[4]

The reader is invited to choose between the three sets and to consider in choosing that the choice may be a revealing one: it will indicate a preference for the interests and concerns of one group over another when evaluator, sponsor and programme participants interact in the evaluation process.

1   The Principle of Rationality as Reasonableness

Programme participants act reasonably in the light of their circumstances and opportunities. It is the task of an evaluation to illuminate the reasoning which guides programme development and evolution, to identify the contextual and historical factors which influence it and to facilitate critical examination of these matters in and around the programme community.

Evaluation is always guided by the impulse to understand and to act on the basis of understanding. It thus has a major role to play in articulating justifications of action. Properly speaking, the justification of action is not merely a backward-looking enterprise, to be equated with post-rationalization. On the contrary, it is concerned with demonstrating both *how* things have come to be as they are (that is, with illuminating the reasoning which has guided the activities of those associated with a programme and identifying the circumstances which shaped and constrained them) and with providing information and arguments which can justify contemplated action.

In evaluating an educational programme it is critical to explicate the reasoning which has guided the activities of those associated with it. Unless there are very good reasons for assuming otherwise, the evaluator and the evaluation sponsor should assume that persons will act reasonably in the light of their current circumstances and the available opportunities. That is to say, it should be assumed that those associated with a programme are committed to acting with understanding; in ways informed by their values and beliefs; wisely and prudently. By explicating the reasoning of those in and around a programme, an evaluation may therefore share the understandings of those who are deeply concerned with it. It may help to disclose the nature of the programme and the values it embraces and give those associated with it an opportunity to have their perspectives on it represented.

The truths to be told about educational programmes are social truths. They are negotiated among those who claim to know it and those who want to know better. The principle of 'rationality as reasonableness'[5] draws attention to this negotiation process. Claims about the programme are defended and challenged in a process of critical debate or conversation. What will count as the truths to be told about the programme will depend upon the quality of the debate. Rational debate consists in giving reasons and defending reasoning with information and arguments.

An evaluation may make a substantial contribution to this critical process. It can gather evidence relevant to programme aims and claims, and subject it to critical cross-examination. It can elicit, articulate and share understandings about why the course of development, implementation and dissemination is as it is by reference to the purposes of participants, the constraints of circumstance and the available opportunities, and reflect on these understandings in the light of the wider context and experience of the programme as a whole. Likewise, it can subject the views of programme audiences — supporters, detractors and those who have not yet a basis for making judgments about it — to critical scrutiny so a 'conversation' between the perspectives of those associated with it can be created and maintained.

The implication of the principle of rationality as reasonableness is that evaluators will attend to a wide variety of perspectives on a programme, to the diverse claims made about it, to its context and to its history. They will thus be in a position to harness and refine the individual and public judgment processes by which the programme comes to be understood and by which its value is determined. The quality of the evaluation may be judged by the quality of its contribution to informing and improving the critical debate about the programme.

Evaluation should thus aim to contribute to programme improvement both directly and indirectly: by its direct interaction with programme participants and by feeding and refining the interaction between programme praticipants and their audiences.

An alternative principle to the principle of rationality as reasonableness, and one which is not advocated here, is that of 'rationality as rule-following', Stake's (1975) label of 'preordinate'[6] fits evaluation approaches which have prior rules for judging a programme and which do not respond to immediate value-perspectives, information-needs and circumstances. For example, some evaluation approaches are based on the notion of rational consumption and set out criteria and standards which must be met before a programme can be considered a 'good buy'. Scriven's 'product evaluation checklist'[7] is perhaps the best example of this. It lists thirteen considerations in the evaluation of products, producers and proposals, and sets standards of adequacy for each. They are: (1) need; (2) market; (3) performance: true field trials; (4) performance: true consumer; (5) performance: critical comparisons; (6) performance: long term; (7) performance: side-effects; (8) performance: process; (9) performance: causation; (10) performance: statistical significance; (11) performance: educational significance; (12) cost-effectiveness; and (13) extended support.

These are powerful considerations and the model provides a useful set of questions to be asked of a programme or product. But the criteria are subject to interpretation in application and they do not respond sufficiently to the nature of the critical debate which actually attends a programme. How would such an evaluation model account for the controversy over SEMP (the Curriculum Development Centre's Social Education Materials Project), for example, where different value premises underlie the opposing positions which cannot be resolved on the basis of a common criterion test? Furthermore, the criteria are extremely stringent in practice and few curriculum developments are able to justify themselves in terms of the standards Scriven sets. Rhetorically, one might claim that these standards should always be met, but since they cannot be met in real curriculum development how can what actually happens be justified? It must be by appeal to something else, that is, by something other than the criteria the checklist proposes.

There are other forms of rationality as rule-following. Evaluations guided only by considerations of testing and measurement are rule-following, drawing their rules from psychometrics. Cronbach[8] has pointed out their limitations for real curriculum evaluation which depends on more information than simply data about student performance on carefully-designed tests. More generally, Hastings[9] has drawn attention to the fact that research methods, inspired by their own rational models (for their own purposes) often distort evaluation problems by twisting them to fit the methods they employ. Clearly, methods which are designed to handle closely-defined, special problems are of limited help in handling poorly-defined, multiform programme realities. The problem about specifying the rules for rational justification in curriculum is that the rules are likely to be limited; rationality as reasonableness makes no such prescription about what particular rules must be applied, though it recognizes the usefulness of such rules as far as they seem relevant.

A second alternative principle, also not advocated here, is the view of rationality implied in 'rational planning'. This view sees justification as based on the notion of satisfaction of needs. If a need can be identified and regarded as an urgent one, then programmes can be designed to satisfy it. Relatively few educational programmes can be said to satisfy urgent needs, though education as a whole responds to a general social need. But the rational planning approach tends also to take a contractual view of programmes: to see them in terms of the obligations imposed on those brave or foolish enough to accept grants to develop programmes. Within such a view, measurements of need-reduction or aims-achievement, coupled with fulfilment of contractual obligations, are sufficient to demonstrate that a programme is successful.

Potential grantees exploit the invitation this approach suggests, 'manufacturing' needs, over-promising, and using limited or biased measures. The exploitations are not always deliberate; rather, they are inspired by a cultural tendency towards legalism and concepts of exchange rooted in economics. Such values have their place, of course, and programme evaluations which do not attend to the contractual obligations of grantees may fail to take account of important aspects of the programmes.

But the 'rational planning' approach to evaluation may treat educational programmes in a bureaucratized way which does not do justice to the organic and reflective character of social and educational life. Programme objectives change, as they should, in response to changing circumstances and opportunities; educational programmes rarely specify the sole means by which goals can be achieved; 'needs' are usually relative in education, not absolute. The 'rationality as reasonableness' approach is likely to take a more open-minded view of programme justification which is sensitive to the relativity of educational values and their adaptation to social contexts.

To adopt the principle of rationality as reasonableness is thus to take the view that social truths are socially-negotiated and historically- and culturally-relative. It is to reject the notion that any discrete set of rules can be formulated which will provide universal criteria of programme adequacy. Similarly, it is to reject the notion that programmes can be justified solely by reference to their own goals, objectives and obligations or by reference solely to needs-reduction. Evaluations based on either of these alternative perspectives are likely to be limited and partial, providing an inadequate basis of information and argument for those who want to enter the critical debate about a programme.

2   The Principle of Autonomy and Responsibility

Moral responsibility for an outcome can only be ascribed to a person to the degree that his or her free choice of action as an autonomous moral agent was a cause of that outcome. Curriculum development projects and programmes are co-operative enterprises. Evaluators must illuminate the interactive character of accountability for a programme.

Just as the evaluator may assume that those involved with a programme act rationally in the sense that they are open to arguments based on reason, so it may be assumed that those involved with the programme are autonomous and responsible moral agents. This has implications for the way programme participants, evaluators, evaluation sponsors and programme sponsors view accountability issues in evaluation.

Most programme sponsors use or distribute public funds for programme development and implementation. They are publicly accountable for their use of these funds; programme participants must also account for their use of the resources allocated to them. Financial and management procedures usually accompany development project fundings to ensure that accountability demands are met. A 'maximalist' view of accountability requires programme participants to justify every decision about the use of resources by reference to programme goals, social needs and the consequences of each decision (especially in terms of programme outcomes for students and teachers). But it is sufficient to adopt a 'minimalist' view of accountability as keeping financial and other records which show that programmes have operated within their budgets and according to their terms of reference, and to make these records open to view.[10]

More generally, the minimalist view of accountability is based on the principle of autonomy and responsibility. According to this principle, moral responsibility for an outcome can only be ascribed to a person to the degree that his or her free choice of action as an autonomous moral agent was a cause of that outcome. To the degree that the person's choices were constrained by others, or by circumstances outside his control, then to that degree the person cannot be held responsible (or at least not solely responsible) for the outcomes.

In a climate where the accountability dragon has reared its head and begun to roar in education, it is as well to be clear about these issues. Any programme sponsor is always implicated in the accountability issue. By constraining the choices open to those who carry out its work, it reduces their autonomy as agents. It must therefore accept a part of the responsibility for the outcomes. Accountability is always bilateral: it concerns provision as well as performance.

Accountability is not a matter of the distribution of praise and blame. Curriculum development is a co-operative enterprise between programme sponsors and participants; the co-actors share responsibility just as they jointly constrain one another's opportunities. Nor will it do to take an overly-personalized view of responsibility. Structural constraints of programme design and organization impose constraints on free action whose effects are sometimes difficult to predict; circumstances which surround development are often beyond the control of participants and may restrict free action in unanticipated ways. One task of programme evaluation is to identify such structural constraints and to determine their effects. A programme evaluation should therefore be highly sensitive to historical and contextual issues so that the work of the programme can be seen against its background of constraints and opportunities.

One alternative principle concerning accountability not advocated here would be one based on ideals of truth and justice. According to such a principle, an evaluator or programme sponsor might adopt some view of what constituted true and just work, perhaps spelling out criteria for truth and justice. These would then constitute a view of what 'the good' (or best) in curriculum development might be. Programme participants could be held accountable for deviations from this ideal.

This sort of principle is clearly unsuitable given the commitment already declared to the notion that social truths are socially-negotiated. And it is unsuitable in a pluralist society where different value-perspectives, with different patterns of coherence and legitimacy, coexist. Curriculum development always expresses social and educational values and it is proper that they be critically analyzed and examined in each case. Far from asserting what values are proper for a programme and then judging it according to those values alone, evaluations should attempt to explore the diverse values and value-perspectives expressed in a programme and the work of those involved in developing it, setting these in a context of the diverse values of the wider society beyond the development group.

A principle concerning accountability based on ideals of truth and justice and concerned with attributing blame for deviations from these ideals thus seems both inappropriate and unworkable. The principle of autonomy and responsibility allows for interaction among value-perspectives; it does not close off critical debate by imposing an ideal because this happens to be the ideal of the evaluator or the programme sponsor. Programme sponsors will no doubt have their own curriculum values and hope to express them through their work, but they should not assume that these values can be imposed unilaterally — they must stand up to the test of critical debate among a plurality of value-perspectives.

A second alternative view of accountability, likewise not advocated here, might be one based on the notion of contractual obligation. Such a view would seem to be based more on notions of prudence and expedience than on principle. Nevertheless, it is worth exploring briefly. The accountability issue as it has been aired in education has frequently been discussed in these terms. According to this view, there is a chain of obligations from the classroom teacher through education systems to ministers of education and ultimately through parliaments to the people. Each superordinate agency is seen as totally responsible for the actions of all subordinates. This view is based on a notion of management which might be described as highly positivistic, that is, the notion that management causes events to occur. This managerialism is contrary to the facts of development, of course: subordinates are not mere operators whose every action is determined by job specification. It is also contrary to the values of professionalism in education: teachers are not operatives but relatively autonomous professionals. (This value reaches its peak in the notion of academic freedom; it is moderated by notions of social responsibility.)

If a programme sponsor were to adopt this contractual and manager-ialistic view of accountability it might present itself as a 'responsible' authority yet preserve the capacity to disavow responsibility when things go wrong, claiming that operatives in its projects and programmes stepped outside their specified tasks and responsibilities. Naturally, it cannot do so: the principle of autonomy and responsibility embodies an acknowledgement of the interactive character of accountability, and the fact that it is bilateral or multilateral, not unilateral.

Ideals for action as a basis for accountability are thus inadequate as are purely contractual views. There is merit in both alternatives: the one puts a premium on the value-commitments of programme sponsors, the other puts a premium on the responsibility of programme staff to meet their contractual obligations. But each is insufficient, failing to recognize value-plurality and the co-operative character of development work (a programme sponsor is not simply an initiator of development activity; it negotiates the character and amount of development activity in planning and executing its programmes).

3   The Principle of Community Self-interest

When a curriculum development project is formed, it is a community of self-interests — it represents the self-interests of all participants within its terms of reference. The evaluator has a responsibility to illuminate the extent of commonality and conflict among the values and interests of participants in this community.

When a programme sponsor enters relations with other agencies (education systems or individual officers who work on its projects, for example) and negotiates the terms of reference which set up a project or programme, it forms a community of self-interests with them. Within the terms of reference of the programme, the (self-) interests of the sponsor and these other individuals or groups coincide. Programme organization always has this cooperative character. A programme sponsor is thus always only one among a number of participants in the communities of self-interests formed by its projects and programmes.

Individual self-interests, which exist outside the terms of reference of the cooperative, are irrelevant to it unless conflicts of interest prejudice the interests of the cooperative itself.

When a programme sponsor commissions a project or sets up a programme, it establishes a community of self-interests. Similarly, when a programme sponsor commissions an evaluation study, it should recognize that the role of the sponsor is a critical aspect of the programme to be evaluated. Sponsorship of development and evaluation confers no exclusive right to have the interests of the sponsor served at the expense of other participants in the community of self-interests. Both with respect to programmes and their evaluations, the actions of programme sponsors may be examined in terms of their fairness in agreeing terms of reference and negotiating contracts. House and Care[11] set out conditions indicative of fair agreement, one of which is community self-interestedness. The conditions are: non-coercion; rationality; acceptance of terms; joint agreement; disinterestedness; universality; community self-interestedness; equal and full information; non-riskiness; possibility; 'counting all votes'; participation.

If these conditions attend the process of reaching the agreement, then it is a fair one, House and Care argue. Agreements so reached are binding on all parties and can only be overridden by appealing to some higher moral principle. The conditions for fair agreement represent an aspiration, of course: sometimes for 'technical' reasons (for example, in relation to questions about who was able to attend a meeting where the organization of a project was discussed, how negotiations proceeded over time, and who was involved at what stages) and sometimes for prudential reasons (for example, the need to unilaterally define the terms of reference for some activity in order to let contracts), these conditions will not be met.

These conditions apply as much to programme evaluation as to programme development. In general, and in accordance with the principle of community self-interests, the evaluation of a project or programme should be regarded as a cooperative venture, not as an information service for a sponsor's own exclusive use. Sponsors should recognize that they will 'co-own' the information generated by an evaluation study with other participants; and that their own role in shaping a programme is relevant in evaluating it.

There are respects in which programme sponsors' evaluative efforts will not be entirely governed by this principle, however. Firstly, sponsoring agencies generally have obligations to collect financial and other information which allows them to discharge their statutory obligations; sponsors do this (one might say) in their own self-interest. This will not generally conflict with the interests of other participants and it is simply a condition of sponsorship of developments. Secondly, sponsors initiate some forms of evaluative activity before a community of self-interests is formed. They do this as a necessary and private matter when they evaluate proposals for projects and programmes in the light of their own interests.

Once a community of self-interests has been formed, however, a programme sponsor's particular interests must be considered in an evaluation study alongside the interests of other participants. A sponsoring agency cannot expect to withdraw from the cooperative enterprise at the point of judgment in the guise of 'disinterested observer' (disavowing involvement). It is relevant to note that the concept of the interests of a sponsoring agency is a slippery one, at least in the case of government agencies, charitable foundations and the like. As institutions, these agencies are themselves communities of interests bound together by the common goals of their enterprise and the organization of their common work. They may be defined by an *Act*, charter or constitution, governed by a council, responsible to a minister, and express a variety of interests in their staff. Within them, a variety of individuals bring their interests to bear in shaping the overall common interest. At the same time, these diverse individuals are capable of disinterest, suspending their own values and interests as they try to understand and develop the common work. The notion of a community of self-interests is an important one simply because it emphasizes these 'internal' and 'external' negotiations. Programmes are cooperative efforts among participants and thus sponsors cannot disavow their involvement when commissioning evaluation studies.

The foregoing paragraphs have emphasized the sponsor's involvement in the cooperatives formed in project and programme work, primarily because it should be clear both to project workers and to evaluators that the work *is* cooperative. Naturally, the same might be said of all other participants in the cooperative: all are bound by it unless they withdraw for some other overriding reason.

Two alternative principles to the principle of community self-interest could be proposed, based on the one hand on the notion of 'the public interest' (defined outside the interests of participating individuals and agencies), or, on the other, on the notion of the sponsor's self-interest. The first might depend on some definition of what is supposed to be in the public good and specify criteria by which programmes might be judged; the second might assert a narrow definition of value according to the sponsor's own perspective. For reasons already outlined in the discussion of earlier principles (social negotiation of social truths, pluralism, the importance of contributing to the critical debate about a programme), neither of these approaches is a reasonable option. Since the sponsoring agency is a participant in the development process along with other groups and agencies, it is interested in improving the quality of critical debate about curriculum. To do so, it requires evaluations which share information among those involved in the process (with due regard for the protection of the rights of individuals) rather than evaluations which serve only its own purposes or only those of other particular groups within the cooperative. (Equally, it is not interested in evaluations which serve only the purposes of those outside the communities of self-interests it forms.)

4 The Principle of Plurality of Value-perspectives

A range of different value-perspectives becomes relevant in judging a programme. An evaluation should identify these different perspectives and be responsive to the different concerns they imply.

Programme participants' values and interests are served by their participation in curriculum development. The particular individuals and agencies cooperating in a project or programme have their own values and interests which may be independently justified. Other audiences for the work of a project or programme will likewise judge it by reference to their own values and interests. A programme sponsor can claim no monopoly on the values or criteria by which a programme is to be evaluated.

According to the principle of plurality of value perspectives, programme evaluators should recognize that a range of perspectives may be relevant in making a judgment of it. Any judgment of the value of a project or programme will be made in the light of the value commitments of the judge; programme evaluators should therefore inform themselves and their audiences about the value perspectives of relevant judges, be responsive to their concerns, and provide information which is appropriate (and valued most highly) as evidence according to their criteria of judgment. If the information and arguments collected in the course of the evaluative study are relevant and significant to the audiences of the evaluation, there is a greater likelihood that they will be used in the critical debate about the programme.

As an alternative to this principle, the view could be taken that judgments of a programme should be the prerogative of those best-equipped to judge: for example, competent authorities in curriculum as a field, curriculum development processes, the subject-matter of the programme, or teaching and learning processes. While these specialists may well be able to provide valuable information and insights into the programme, they are not the only ones entitled to judge it. An evaluation should embrace such perspectives but should go beyond them to take into account the perspectives of other interested parties (for example, students, parents, community groups or employers). The mature judgment of specialists may be of great value to audiences less familiar with specialist debates about the nature and worth of a programme, but lay concerns demand attention too: as clients or observers of the programme, laymen must have their questions treated seriously in an evaluation study, have specialist issues made accessible to them, and see how these specialist issues fit into the broader context of the issues concerning the programme as a whole.

Still another principle which could be adopted would concern a sponsor's own right to judge, and the primacy of its right as a sponsor of development to have its own questions answered. To be sure, a programme evaluation should address questions which the sponsor regards as important. But such a principle, pursued single-mindedly, would have a conservative and defensive effect. It would make the evaluation a service for the sponsor at the expense of other audiences with legitimate rights to be heard. In order to feed the critical debate about the programme and to refine it, an evaluation must engage the perspectives of a variety of audiences.

5 The Principle of the Self-critical Community: Internal Evaluation, Evaluation Consultancy, Meta-evaluation, External and Independent Evaluation

> Critical debate about the nature and worth of a programme already exists within and around its programme community. It is the task of programme evaluation to refine this debate and improve its bearing on programme action. Evaluation consultancy may provide additional tools for this purpose. Meta-evaluation efforts may help to improve the quality of the contribution of programme evaluation. An external evaluation may contribute to the critical debate by increasing awareness of a particular set of values and interests relevant to a programme; it should not be thought of as an alternative to the self-critical process. An independent evaluation may help to harness programme self-criticism where the programme community is diffuse or divided by controversy. Self-criticism by the programme community is the primary basis for programme evaluation; other evaluation efforts extend it in different ways but do not supplant it.

The community of self-interests formed by a curriculum project or programme is likely to embrace a variety of value-perspectives which, through their interaction in its life and work, create a continuing conversation about its nature and worth. This conversation provides a basis for systematic self-criticism within the community; it is nourished by contact with perspectives from the wider social and educational communities outside.

A major task for programme evaluation is to harness this self-critical conversation: to collect the perspectives and judgments of those associated with a programme, to reclaim meanings and concerns from the flux of programme experience, and to make this store of understandings available to participants and other audiences. Describing the programme, formulating issues regarded as significant by those associated with it, collecting judgments and portraying these in ways which are accessible to evaluation audiences — these are activities through which the evaluator can contribute to the critical debate about a programme and improve the quality of the critique.

Such activities acknowledge that critical debate already exists independently of the evaluation of a programme, within and between programme staff and interested observers. Far from attempting to supersede 'natural' critical debate, an evaluation should attempt to capitalize on it, harness it and refine it. In doing so, it can engage the perspectives and concerns of those within and outside the programme (without imposing perspectives which are regarded as 'foreign' by those within). By bringing these perspectives in contact with one another and opening up interaction across the borders of the programme, the evaluation may generate authentic knowledge about the programme — that is, knowledge grounded in the life-circumstances of participants and understood as experience. Authentic knowledge is the only sure basis for programme improvement and for improvement of critical debate because it reflects personal understandings which will express themselves as free commitments in the actions of participants.

The implication for evaluators is that evaluations should be responsive to audience concerns and the real, experienced issues which surround a programme. The evaluation task is thus an educative one, informing and developing the understandings of those associated with the programme. The evaluation may accept as its primary task the formulation of programme issues in ways which clarify them for programme participants and audiences. It may report frequently rather than just towards the end of the evaluation, so that the perspectives of participants and audiences can be engaged more or less continually rather than in a single confrontation of perspectives. The recurring 'reports' of the evaluator can be regarded as a conversation which develops the points of view of those it engages. In this conversational process, interim reports should be less formal and regarded as ephemeral (rather than highly authoritative) by participants and audiences. A final report should reflect the evolution or history of the critical debate in and around the programme. Evaluation reporting should be regarded as a dynamic process rather than static or discontinuous; the evaluation findings as contributory and reflexive rather than confrontational or inert; the evaluator as a facilitator of debate rather than as an 'objective' outsider who represents truth against one-sidedness or complete understanding against the partial understandings of participants.

Regarding the programme as a self-critical community does not mean that it is an insular group feeding only on its own perspectives; using the self-critical debate within the programme as a basis for the evaluation does not mean that the evaluation becomes simply a kind of self-report. Through the evaluation (as well as through programme initiatives), participants should be brought into contact with the perspectives of other relevant judges and audiences, some of whom may be quite distant from the programme. The self-critical community of the programme can incorporate the perspectives of 'outsiders' by creating a conversation with them through which both sides can learn each other's perspectives. This can occur if the programme and the evaluation create opportunities for outsiders to see the work (or portrayals of the work), to consider it, to judge it, and to explain their judgments.

The principle of the self-critical community establishes self-criticism as the cornerstone of programme evaluation. All participants in the community of self interests formed by the programme have a right to be heard in the critical process. As already indicated, the value of self-criticism does not preclude external judgment, rather, it attempts to create mechanisms whereby external judgments can be incorporated into project or programme thinking. To emphasize the value of self-criticism is not to advocate programme insularity; on the contrary, it is to emphasize the value of authentic knowledge as a basis for development and debate and to encourage participants to take a broad, critical view of the programme in its wider historical context. But it is also to stress that once a programme surrenders self-knowledge to external authority as a basis for development, it loses its autonomy as an intellectual community.

As a corollary to this principle it follows that each participant agency in the cooperative enterprise of a programme regards itself as a self-critical community, and evaluates its own activities in a spirit of self-criticism.

The primary implication of the principle of the self-critical community is that curriculum projects and programmes should establish 'internal' evaluation mechanisms which can systematically record and develop the critical debate about their work. These 'internal' evaluations may be augmented in four ways: by evaluation consultancy; by meta-evaluation; by external evaluation; and by independent evaluation.

(a) Evaluation consultancy

Where specialist evaluation expertise is available, programme participants and evaluation sponsors may want to take advantage of it. Using such advice is by no means precluded under the principle of the self-critical community. For many evaluation tasks (like interview techniques, questionnaire design, planning and sampling), technical assistance is highly desirable. But this advice should not be thought of as definitive, finally authoritative or legitimating. As Hastings pointed out[12] the nature and scope of an evaluation can all too easily be limited to the capacity of the particular evaluation methods, techniques or instruments with which an evaluation specialist is familiar. Programme participants should consider the extent to which the advice of specialists and the evaluation processes and findings they propose will contribute to the critical debate about the programme and 'programme decision-making' (that is, whether the information and arguments collected will help in guiding and refining action in the programme.)

In short, evaluation consultancy can help considerably in the planning and execution of a self-critical evaluation. But programme participants should consider who is helped and how and when they will be helped by particular evaluation methods and techniques. In the end, the community of participants bears responsibility for the programme, so evaluation plans must be judged by reference to their impact in the community of participants and on those who interact with it.

(b) Meta-evaluation

A programme sponsor is a co-participant in the community of self-interests formed by a programme. But as an agency authority accountable for the expenditure of its resources, it will generally need to be satisfied that the evaluation arrangements proposed for a project or programme are adequate and appropriate. Programme sponsors therefore have an interest in meta-evaluation (the evaluation of evaluation), to determine whether a programme evaluation can meet the demands of the critical debate to which the programme is subject. This is in part an internal management question, but it will naturally include an interactive element through which project or programme evaluators confer with programme sponsors (who are often also sponsors of programme evaluations). In exceptional cases, programme evaluations may be formally evaluated by evaluation sponsors, but most often the meta-evaluation process will be in the nature of informal monitoring and interaction.

According to the principle of the self-critical community, the primary responsibility for programme evaluation is 'internal' to the programme. Programme or programme evaluation sponsors may want to ensure, however, that adequate evaluation consultancy is available to the programme community, and they may want to encourage some form of meta-evaluation which can monitor the responsiveness of evaluation efforts to the concerns of the programme community and interested observers. Like the programme evaluation function, the meta-evaluation function can be 'devolved' from the sponsor to the programme community in order to ensure that the range of concerns, perspectives and interests present in the programme community is being considered in the critical debate about the programme. It is possible that a meta-evaluation will guarantee that sponsors' interests in the evaluation are met at the expense of other interests in the same way that evaluation consultancy can serve some interests at the expense of others; thus, a meta-evaluation must be judged by reference to the same criterion as the primary programme evaluation: How does it contribute to the improvement of the critical debate about the programme as a whole, for the whole community of programme participants and interested observers?

(c) External evaluation

Following negotiation with other participants in the community of self-interests of a project or programme, a programme sponsor may sponsor distinct evaluation studies which are outside (or in addition to) the self-critical evaluation of the programme. These evaluations will take two forms: external evaluation and independent evaluation.

External evaluation studies may be commissioned when the community of self-interest of a programme wants advice, critical review or validation from substantive specialists, or when the judgment of recognized authorities in a field is necessary for a project, programme or evaluation to be regarded as credible. In such cases, care should be taken in negotiating an evaluation contract with potential external evaluators to see that the evaluation study respects the interests of the programme community as a whole (as expressed in these principles). Most programme evaluations undertaken today are of this form. Regrettably, they tend not to take account of the values embodied in these principles (for example, rationality as reasonableness, autonomy and responsibility, community of self-interest, etc.). In consequence, they may further some interests in a programme at the expense of others, impose a 'foreign' perspective on its work, or deny the authentic knowledge of participants. We should not be too xenophobic about this state of affairs, though: often such perspectives prefigure the views of the wider community outside the programme (indeed, they often shape outside views). A healthy self-critical community should incorporate these external perspectives and, where necessary, correct them by reference to the concerns and circumstances of the programme as a community with particular goals, terms of reference and contexts.

Just as it is a mistake to assume that an external evaluation represents the 'true' perspective on a programme (though it may aspire to objectivity, its very purpose will align it with particular interests in or around the programme at the expense of other interests), it is a mistake to think of a self-critical evaluation as a complete amalgam or synthesis of relevant perspectives. Both kinds of evaluation are fluid and interactive, not susceptible of completeness or ruling definitively on the worth of a programme. A self-critical evaluation aspires to awareness of the diversity of values and interests in and around a programme and more conscious negotiated control of programme development and evolution; an external evaluation aspires to awareness of particular values and interests, and to influencing programme development or evolution in the light of these particular values and interests. The mistake is to think that either represents a unified or complete perspective on the programme which can form the basis of an unequivocal plan for action.

(d) Independent evaluation

Sometimes a project or programme will be so large or diffuse that its sense of being a community of self-interests or a self-critical community is sharply attenuated. It may be able to develop only a very poor sense of itself as a whole. In other cases, programme participants may prefer a 'specialization of function' in evaluation, so that one person or a small group take responsibility for the conduct of the evaluation (though programme participants will naturallly continue to participate in the critical debate). In such cases, an independent evaluator may be appointed or commissioned in order to harness and refine the critical process on behalf of the programme. Such an evaluator may prefer to be regarded as an evaluation 'facilitator'.

Moreover, when the community of a programme embraces a wide variety of viewpoints which must be articulated and explored before a joint perspective can be reached about the value and meaning of the work, an independent evaluation will be appropriate. Similarly, an independent evaluation will be appropriate when the work of a programme is particularly controversial and a variety of value perspectives within or outside a programme must be considered before an evaluation can be regarded as relevant and credible by audiences with differing value commitments.

Independent evaluations will often require the services of evaluation specialists capable of dealing with conflicting value perspectives, political pressure, complex theoretical conceptualizations, and the real and difficult issues of curriculum associated with a particular programme. They may need to adopt refined evaluation procedures capable of generating and maintaining negotiation among the conflicting theoretical, practical, and organizational interests of those in and around the programme. It is necessary to take great care in negotiating evaluation contracts with potential independent evaluators in order to ensure that the contract (as much as the evaluation) respects the values and interests of the range of participants in the community of the programme.

The principle of the self-critical community is a recognition of the natural existence of self-reflection within a programme, on the one hand, and the natural critical debate around it, on the other. Such a principle may encourage those involved in project and programme evaluation to be 'responsive' in the sense that Stake (1975)[13] uses the term. He says:

> An educational evaluation is *responsive evaluation* if it orients more directly to program activities than to program intents; responds to audience requirements of information; and if the different value-perspectives present are referred to in reporting the success and failure of the program (p. 14).

But in addition to this, such a principle may encourage evaluators to see their work as part of a naturally-occurring process of evaluative activity in a programme, not distinct from it.

It would be possible to adopt alternative principles to this one. On the one hand, curriculum programmes could be evaluated solely by teams of expert external evaluators, thus putting the validation function of evaluation before all others. Or programme sponsors could adopt a form of evaluative activity based on their own perspectives of what projects and programmes should be, thus establishing the primacy of their own value-frameworks (as seals of approval) in every programme evaluation. But neither of these principles will suffice. The cooperative nature of curriculum development and the diffuse control of educational organizations (with different participants having different sources of legitimacy — teachers' professionalism, schools' autonomy, ministerial responsibility for state systems, parents' and community roles in school councils, students' rights etc.) mean that curriculum evaluations must encompass wider views than those of substantive experts or programme sponsors' particular predilections. Programme evaluators simply cannot afford to ignore the wider debate about a programme in its social and educational context.

Current trends in the history of evaluation have been significantly influenced by the demands of project evaluation, where outside groups of evaluators have been called in to observe and evaluate curriculum development work in order to provide external validation of the quality of development. As a consequence, much recent evaluation literature reflects an expectation that evaluations will be 'objective', disinterested, expert and validatory. But external evaluation cannot provide unilateral validation. There is an older trend in evaluation based on school accreditation, inspection and appraisal which is more organically related to school curriculum work. But the techniques these purposes generated are not well suited to the evaluation of innovative curriculum projects or programmes. The older tradition stabilized itself around the organization of a school rather than around the organization of a new curricular activity or product.

Project or programme evaluation must be able to negotiate between the demands for curriculum validation and the conditions of schooling in different systems. Programme evaluation cannot treat curricula as discrete products, to be considered as if they existed independently of their contexts of application, nor can it focus all its attention on the conditions in schools adopting particular innovations. The principle of the self-critical community recognizes that innovations enter adopting systems by a process of negotiation; evaluation should facilitate negotiation by refining the critical debate.

The people who work on, use and sponsor a particular programme form a natural focus for its evaluation activities; their work provides a natural forum for critical thinking about it. The principle of the self-critical community may encourage those associated with innovative programmes to regard their natural evaluative work as a primary, not a secondary, evaluation function; accordingly, it is proper to expect that 'internal', self-critical evaluations will provide the primary basis for judgments about the nature and worth of programmes. Evaluation should not be regarded as a specialist activity tagged on to development to monitor and observe from a position of privilege (the outside observer) as if the interests which guided evaluation work were unrelated to the interests of those which guide the developers (that is, that there are no confluences or conflicts among their values and interests). Evaluation is interactive and reactive; it should not be construed as 'objective' and outside the whole system of social relationships which constitute curriculum development programmes in practice.

6 The Principle of Propriety in the Production and Distribution of Information

Evaluation processes inevitably affect the political economy of information in a programme (the production and distribution of information about it). Because information and arguments justify or legitimize decisions, evaluation affects the distribution of power and resources in programme situations. Programme participants and interested observers live with the consequences of the use and abuse of evaluation information. An evaluation should have explicit principles of procedure which govern its conduct and its processes of information production and distribution.

As suggested in the introduction to these principles, evaluation is often defined as 'delineating, obtaining and providing information for making decisions and judgments about educational programs'. Indeed, formal evaluation efforts may well be included among the management and decision-making processes of a project or programme. Though it has been an explicit purpose of these principles to widen that definition, it would be naïve to assert that evaluation was not normally regarded as an important management and decision-making tool. Evaluation processes thus link the generation of information and arguments about a programme with the power to decide: those responsible for deciding the shape and conduct of a programme, whether it should be implemented, or even whether it should be continued or discontinued will look to evaluation studies as sources of information and arguments when they make their decisions. Evaluation is thus inevitably a political process, affecting the flows of information in a situation and having life-consequences for those who inhabit it.

The point was made dramatically by ethnographer Harry Wolcott in a throwaway line at the Annual Meeting of the American Educational Research Association in 1976. Discussing several papers on ethics and methodology in fieldwork, he remarked: 'Some people define evaluation as the collection of data to guide decisions to continue, revise or terminate programmes. If you were an ethnographer, how would you like your material to be used to continue, revise or terminate another culture?'

The production and distribution of information about people, projects and programmes through evaluation must be regulated according to a principle of propriety capable of taking into account the moral, social and political consequences of information use and abuse. The evaluator must find procedures appropriate to each context by which he or she can negotiate the disputed territory between the public's 'right to know', management's 'right to relevant information', and the individual's 'right to discretion'. Even in cases where innovators are anxious to have their work more widely known, or where teachers regard their work as exemplary, there may be consequences of the release of information which may jeopardize their future opportunities. Evaluators must treat seriously the problems raised by the political economy of information production and distribution — the role of evaluation in the distribution of power in particular settings and in the support or denial of already-existing power-structures. It is not sufficient to take a moralistic stance on open information, on privacy or on the rights of sponsors: the production and distribution of information inevitably affects the politics of the programme situation and it is up to the evaluator to find procedures which are defensible within the particular context and technically feasible given the constraints of time and resources.

The principle of propriety in the production and distribution of information implies that evaluators must set out their intended procedures for information control in the form of an evaluation contract or a statement of procedural aspirations so that everyone who becomes involved in the evaluation process knows how the information is to be produced and distributed, what risks are involved in cooperating with the evaluator, and what safeguards exist against the misuse of evaluative information. Such procedures should specify how information is to be collected, analyzed, interpreted and reported. It should indicate the status of the evaluator's interpretations *vis-à-vis* the interpretations of programme participants (including programme sponsors). The contract should make clear who will come to know what about whom as a result of the evaluative process and its products. (The process is just as important as the product in shaping the views of participants in the evaluation.) It should make it clear what procedures will govern access to 'data-sources' (people, records, events), the conduct of the evaluation and the determination of its boundaries, the ownership of the evaluation data and findings, the release of information, rights to publication, confidentiality rules and mechanisms for accountability of the evaluation. It may also be possible to specify safeguards against abuse of the intended procedures (like rights of appeal or the sanction of denying the evaluator further access to the situation).

Alternative principles can hardly be framed in terms of 'impropriety': no-one could accept the notion that an evaluation should use information improperly. The principle of propriety presented here does specify the rights of participants in a programme to know how the information is to be used and controlled. It attempts to set up a model of equitable distribution of information based on the rights and obligations of all those involved in an evaluation study. Evaluations would operate in a spirit contrary to the present principle if they were an exclusive information service for evaluation sponsors rather than a service to a range of audiences associated with the programme, if they used secret reporting, if they failed to take into account the diverse perspectives and interpretations of participants and evaluation audiences, or if they published reports in forms suitable only for research audiences. The principle thus establishes a view of evaluation opposed both to the view that evaluation is an arm of the educational research industry serving some general ideal of truth or 'the public interest', and to the view that it is a tool to be used in the service of bureaucratic responsibility.[14]

Furthermore, the principle of propriety in the production and distribution of information establishes the view that evaluators have the responsibility to be aware of the consequences of information production and distribution and to respond in defensible ways by developing appropriate procedures for information control.

7   The Principle of Appropriateness

> Evaluation design is a practical matter. An evaluation must be appropriate to the programme setting, responsive to programme issues, and relevant to the programme community and interested observers. An evaluation design must be renegotiated as the study progresses in the light of changing circumstances, issues and interests, and in the light of its own consequences (as they become apparent).

The contemporary scene in evaluation theory and research abounds with evaluation models and approaches with a bewildering variety of foci and employing a diversity of specific techniques. While this variety and diversity must be acknowledged, evaluators and evaluation sponsors should not adopt an unconstrained eclecticism with respect to evaluation just because no dominant orthodoxy has emerged in the field. These principles, and the value commitments they embody, identify some forms of evaluation as unacceptable. To be acceptable, particular evaluations should embody the six principles previously presented, but they must also be appropriate to their objects. That is to say, evaluation studies must suit the curriculum projects, programmes, processes or products to be evaluated and the contexts in which they appear. The design of an evaluation is a practical matter, depending on considerations of purposes; audiences; substantive issues raised by programme theory, aspirations, organization and practice; resources; issues of information control in the particular political economy of the programme and its evaluation; relevant evidence; methods for data-collection; issues and approaches to analysis and interpretation; and modes of reporting.

Evaluators and participants in curriculum projects and programmes must take all of these topics into account in designing or commissioning evaluation studies. The appropriateness of evaluation designs is a practical matter, not a technical or theoretical one. Decisions about the form an evaluation should take cannot be made by reference to the 'internal logics' of evaluation models and approaches alone; such decisions must take into account the needs, preferences, obligations, circumstances and opportunities of those who will be most closely involved in the evaluation process (as evaluators, programme participants, sponsors, evaluation audiences).

As in the case of the sixth principle, it is hardly possible to propose an alternative principle of 'inappropriateness'. But inappropriate evaluation designs are often proposed for the evaluation of curriculum projects and programmes. Such designs are ones which suffer from 'methodological tunnel vision', employing evaluation models dogmatically or inflexibly when more sensitive attention to the critical debate about a programme or the circumstances of its operation would suggest a different approach. Evaluation designs are also inappropriate when they fail to serve those most closely involved in the work of a programme, reporting instead only to sponsors or research audiences. These audiences have a legitimate claim for evaluative information, to be sure, but evaluations frequently fail to serve the needs and interests of those most directly affected by the work.

If the evaluators of curriculum projects and programmes take seriously the thrust of the definition of evaluation proposed at the beginning of this chapter — that it is the process of marshalling information and arguments which enable interested individuals and groups to participate in the critical debate about a specific programme — then it is less likely that they will err on the side of inappropriateness. Appropriate evaluations will take into account the social and contextual conditions under which educational programmes operate and include a meta-evaluation component: the evaluation will thus include an element of self-reflection which allows those involved with the evaluation and the programme to monitor its effects on programme development and evolution and on the social life of the programme as a community. The aim of this self-reflection is to treat the appropriateness of the evaluation as problematic and dynamic, not as something which can be decided once and for all at the design stage. It is to recognize that evaluation programmes, like curriculum programmes, are negotiated between interested individuals in the light of their consequences.

Acknowledgements

The author wishes to acknowledge the contribution of those people who offered criticism and commentary on earlier drafts of these principles; Max Angus, Ed Davis, Ernest R. House, Caroline Hueneke, Clare Hughes, Neil Russell, Malcolm Skilbeck and Ralph Straton. In particular he wishes to thank Barry MacDonald for many valuable discussions about principles of procedure in evaluation.

He is also grateful for the support of the Australian Curriculum Development Centre to which he was evaluation consultant at the time when the first draft of the principles was prepared.

Notes

1 *Curriculum Evaluation: A CDC Study Group Report* (1977) CDC professional series, Curriculum Development Centre, Canberra, p. 24.
2 See for example CRONBACH, L.J. (1963) 'Course improvement through evaluation', *Teachers College Record*, 64, pp. 672–93; MACDONALD, B. (1973) 'Briefing decision-makers' in HOUSE, E.R. (Ed.) *School Evaluation: The Politics and Process*, Berkeley, Calif, McCutchan; STUFFLEBEAM, D.L. *et al.* (1971) *Educational Evaluation and Decision Making in Education*, Itasca, Ill., Peacock.
3 STAKE, R.E. and DENNY, T. (1969) 'Needed concepts and techniques for utilizing more fully the potential of evaluation', *National Society for the Study of Education Yearbook*, LXVIII, Pt II, Chicago, University of Chicago Press, p. 370.
4 The two 'alternative' sets may be somewhat less internally-consistent since they parallel the first set.
5 See WEIR, E. (1976) *Rationality as Reasonableness*, University of Illinois at Urbana-Champaign, Office for Instructional Research.
6 STAKE, R.E. (1975) 'To evaluate an arts program' in STAKE, R.E. (Ed.) *Evaluating the Arts in Education: A Responsive Approach*, Columbus, Ohio, Charles E. Merrill.
7 SCRIVEN, M. (1974) 'Evaluation perspectives and procedures' in POPHAM, W.J. (Ed.) *Evaluation in Education: Current Applications*, Berkeley, Calif., McCutchan.
8 CRONBACH, L.J. (1963) *op. cit.*
9 HASTINGS, J.T. (1969) 'The kith and kin of educational measures', *Journal of Educational Measurement*, 6, pp. 127–30.
10 See STAKE, R.E. (1973) 'School accountability laws', *Evaluation Comment*, 4, pp. 1–3. The present definition is based upon Stake's.
11 HOUSE, E.R. and CARE, N.S. (1977) *Fair Evaluation Agreement*, University of Illinois at Urbana-Champaign, Center for Instructional Research and Curriculum Evaluation, mimeo.
12 HASTINGS, J.T. (1969) *op. cit.*
13 STAKE, R.E. (1975) 'To evaluate an arts program' in STAKE, R.E. (Ed.) *Evaluating the Arts in Education: A Responsive Approach*, Columbus, Ohio, Charles E. Merrill.
14 See MACDONALD, B. (1976) 'Evaluation and the control of education' in TAWNEY, D.A. (Ed.) *Curriculum Evaluation Today: Trends and Implications*, Schools Council Research Studies, London, Macmillan; MacDonald distinguishes 'autocratic', 'bureaucratic' and 'democratic' forms of evaluation in his political classification.

5

Participatory Evaluation:
The Stakeholder Approach

Introduction

By the late seventies the extensive evaluation activities of the federal government in the United States had been roundly criticized by a large number of people. The National Institute of Education decided to try a significantly different approach to evaluation that might address some of the strongest criticisms. The fundamental idea was to have others participate in the evaluation itself, and this participatory attempt was called the stakeholder approach because these who were to participate were those who had a stake in the program. The story of this particular attempt to democratize evaluation is encapsulated in this section of the book. It is not an entirely happy story.

In her first chapter in this section, Carol Weiss traces the criticisms and government action that led to the development of the stakeholder approach. Critics had contended that program evaluation was unrealistic, in that it held programs to standards of success impossible to attain; irrelevant, in that much evaluation information had no connection to the people involved; unfair, in that the powerless were held accountable by the powerful; and unused, in that the evaluation results seldom influenced decisions about the programs.

Responding to these criticisms federal officials within the National Institute of Education thought that involving stakeholders in the evaluation would sensitize evaluators to local needs, give the information requests of the local stakeholders high priority, and provide some local control over the evaluation itself. Hence, the local stakeholders would be empowered by the evaluation, thus improving the evaluation's realism, relevance, fairness, and utility. Evaluation was recognized as partly a political process, and the stakeholder approach was a political solution to evaluation problems.

As Weiss notes, there was perhaps another motivation working as well. Some evaluations had been hotly contested politically. By sharing control of the evaluation with local stakeholders, the federal bureaucrats could partially defuse the political fall-out and criticisms directed at them by critics of past evaluations.

The first two programs chosen to employ the stakeholder approach were intensely political. One was the Cities-in-Schools program, a favorite of Rosalyn Carter and strongly supported by the Carter White House. The other was PUSH/Excel, the educational program of the Reverend Jesse Jackson, the highly charismatic leader of the black minority in America and possibly the most controversial person in the United States. Both programs were clearly politically loaded. The stakeholder approach was tried with these two.

The chapter by Farrar and House relates what happened when the stakeholder notion was applied to PUSH/Excel. Essentially, the contractors who won the bid to do the evaluation did not engage the stakeholders in any meaningful way. Although calling the study a stakeholder evaluation, the evaluators actually employed a more traditional, technocratic approach to the evaluation. The evaluators claimed that they tried but could achieve no meaningful participation from the stakeholder groups. Farrar and House claim the evaluators' efforts to involve the stakeholders were minimal and inept. In any case, the PUSH/Excel program could not meet the standards imposed by the evaluators and was called a failure. The evaluation results were widely reported in the mass media and eventually had an effect upon Jesse Jackson's campaign for the presidency. The high promise of the stakeholder approach was converted into something quite different in the course of events.

In reassessing the stakeholder approach to evaluation in the light of the experiences of the Cities-in-Schools and PUSH/Excel evaluations, Weiss concludes that the stakeholder approach holds modest promise. It can improve the fairness of the evaluation, democratize access to data, and equalize whatever power knowledge provides. However, it will not ensure that appropriate, relevant information is collected nor increase the use of the evaluation results, she concludes. Weiss wonders whether the planning of evaluations is the proper place to redress the inequitable distribution of influence and authority.

Weiss also contends that several smaller studies by different groups would have been preferable to one 'blockbuster' study. The single blockbuster study places too much weight upon one group of evaluators. A group of studies, perhaps each examining the program from the perspective of one stakeholder group, might have several advantages. Finally, Weiss speculates that qualitative designs would be better for involving stakeholders than the quantitative design employed in these evaluations.

Overall, the stakeholder evaluations of Cities-in-Schools and PUSH/Excel were not satisfying experiences for anyone involved. They remain controversial and hotly contested. In my opinion these two evaluations were badly done, and the stakeholder notion never truly employed. In general, evaluators have a very difficult time including broad public participation in what they conceive as a technical act.

The Stakeholder Approach to Evaluation: Origins and Promise

Carol H. Weiss
Harvard Graduate School of Education

The National Institute of Education's advocacy of the stakeholder approach resulted from decades of criticism of evaluation practice. For more than twenty years, observers have noted serious shortcomings in the manner in which evaluations were conducted. Almost everyone associated with the evaluation of social programs seems to have written a critique of some aspect of the enterprise. Indeed, it sometimes seems that more papers have been published criticizing evaluation practices and procedures than reporting the results of studies conducted. Educational evaluators have been in the forefront of the criticism industry. For example, with dramatic sweep, Guba (1969) titled one early paper 'The Failure of Educational Evaluation.'

Many critiques have centered on methodological inadequacies. In addition, there have been complaints about the lack of fit between evaluation and the sociopolitical context of the program world. Critics charge that evaluation is narrow because it focuses on only a small subset of questions of importance to program people; unrealistic because it measures the success of programs against unreasonably high standards; irrelevant because it provides answers to questions that no one really cares about; unfair because it is responsive to the concerns of influential people, such as bureaucratic sponsors, but blind to the wants of others lower in the hierarchy, such as front-line staff and clients; and unused in councils of action where decision are made. These concerns motivated NIE to develop the stakeholder approach. Because they provide the intellectual underpinning for the stakeholder notion, we will examine them briefly to try to discern where critics lay the blame for shortcomings.

Narrow

Of necessity, evaluations select a limited number of issues for examination. No study can encompass all the issues that come up in the hurly-burly world in which programs function. Inevitably, arbitrary limits are set, and some of the things that turn out to be crucial to program people are not addressed by evaluators.

Critics claim that evaluators too often select for attention the issues that are easy to study with available social-scientific tools, not the issues that are important. Evaluators, they contend, choose their issues and variables for reasons that have little to do with the needs of people who make decisions about the program (Berk and Rossi, 1976; Patton, 1978).

One of the ways in which evaluators narrow their focus is by concern. trating on measurement of program outcomes. In doing so, critics claim, evaluators give insufficient attention to what goes on inside the program. Thus, they ignore issues of operation that program people can do something about (Williams, 1971). Further, even when it is appropriate to limit attention to outcome indicators, evaluators tend to select a narrow set of indicators (Stake, 1978). In education, for example, the standard measures are student scores on standardized tests. Yet, many programs have much broader goals than improved test scores, and these other goals (improvements in social competence, health, persistence in school, and so on) are often disregarded. Some programs that aim only peripherally at educational improvement, such as changes in school governance, still find themselves evaluated by the available standby-tests.

Unrealistic

Evaluators, it is claimed, often choose outcome measures that are difficult to budge. As a result, if the program is a relatively modest effort, it is unlikely that changes will be of sufficient size to move the indicators into the zone of statistical significance (Caro, 1971; Schwarz, 1980). To expect a reading program that meets two hours a week to affect reading scores significantly or to expect a counselling program for delinquents to prevent all further delinquent behavior is to impose standards of success that are unreasonable. By the choice of such measures, the evaluator almost dooms the program to a judgment of failure.

Irrelevant

Critics contend that much of the data that evaluators collect and analyze is unresponsive to the real needs of people involved in the program (Cochran, 1980; Datta, 1981; Parlett and Hamilton, 1976). For example, data on program outcomes do not give program staff much information about what they can do to improve the program. Program staff may want to know why they are not attracting more people, which strategies of programming are more helpful, why people drop out, what kinds of staff are more successful, and how long the program should run. An evaluation that relies on test scores provides data that can be useful for summative decisions, but these data give program people little insight into the operational issues with which they must deal every day.

Unfair

Evaluations, critics allege, usually address questions that concern federal staff or program managers. They rarely consider the needs and wants of less powerful groups such as program recipients (Coleman, 1980; House, 1980). It is possible for clients to enter a program with expectations that differ in important ways from the official goals of the program. Yet, the evaluator rarely takes such expectations into account or judges the program from the clients' perspective.

Similarly, evaluators usually report study results to superordinate groups — the Congress, the sponsoring federal agency, managers of the local agency. They seldom report findings to line staff members who actually give services and even less often to clients whose lives are affected by what the program does and does not accomplish. Evaluation addresses the concerns at the top levels of the hierarchy, while the people whose lives are affected most deeply by the program's success or failure are bypassed.

Even when federal staff do not try to dictate the scope and dimensions of the evaluation, evaluators tend to be responsive to what they perceive as federal priorities. They have a vested interest in satisfying the office that funds evaluations. If they are to receive further evaluation contracts, they see their role as one of responding to the concerns of the sponsoring body. Thus, even when the federal presence is not active, evaluators tend to ignore issues of moment to other actors in the program context.

Unused

Critics allege that evaluation results seldom influence decisions about the course of the program (Rutman, 1980; Scott and Shore, 1979; Weiss, 1972). The evaluator conducts the study, completes the report, and leaves. Program managers take comfort from the findings that are positive and bury or forget the findings that suggest a need for major reform. At policy levels, there are few examples of evaluations that lead decision makers to expand a successful program or to terminate a program that shows few beneficial effects. Despite all the rhetoric about the utility of evaluative evidence for improving the rationality of decision making, evaluation often seems to leave the situation unchanged.

Carol H. Weiss

Early Reform Attempts

NIE was not the first federal agency to become exercised about the shortcomings of evaluation practice. Other federal agencies have made efforts to improve the craft. The President's Committee on Juvenile Delinquency, the Office of Economic Opportunity, the Model Cities Administration, the Office of Education, and the National Institute of Mental Health, among others, have all attempted to respond to the criticisms. Over the years, they have tried to institute three types of reforms.

Sensitizing Evaluators to Local Needs

Repeatedly, evaluators have been advised to involve user groups in the development and conduct of evaluation studies (Glaser and Backer, 1972; Windle and Ochberg, 1975). Drawing on the array of traditions that advocate user involvement as a means of increasing commitment to study results, staff in several agencies promoted active participation by program people in the design of studies. They urged evaluators to provide periodic feedback on study results to participant groups and to devote a major effort to the dissemination of results (Davis and Salasin, 1975; Zweig and Marvin, 1981).

Such advice was frequently heeded. Sensitive evaluators immersed themselves in the local situation and came to understand the concerns of various parties. They shaped their studies to respond to local needs and to represent the diversity of local issues. When they had information to report, they made strenuous efforts to bring it to the attention of the people involved and to interpret it in ways that were meaningful. Many other evaluators paid no attention. Their primary commitment was to the canons of social science. Whether they satisfied program people was of secondary concern. They had been trained in proper methodology, and they were not willing to sacrifice their standards in order to satisfy the whims of people who knew little about validity and causality and who cared even less.

Evaluators who worked for local agencies were more likely to attend to local issues, although not necessarily to the concerns of people far down in the hierarchy such as teachers, students, and parents. Evaluators who conducted nationwide studies rarely had the motivation to involve themselves in concerns below the federal level.

Funding Separate Evaluations for Different User Groups

A number of agencies officially recognized the divergent information needs of federal policy makers and local program managers. In evaluations

148

of ESEA Title I, school districts were expected to do their own evaluations for their own purposes, while federal staff sponsored nationwide studies. The Office of Economic Opportunity recognized and funded three different types of evaluation. Type I evaluations were designed to assess the overall effectiveness of a national program. Type II evaluations inquired into the relative effectiveness of different strategies of programming. Type III evaluations, which monitored the performance of individual projects, placed the emphasis on assessment of operational efficiency (Wholey and others, 1970; Williams, 1971).

A few adventurous agencies provided funding to client groups to do their own evaluations of the programs in which they participated. The Model Cities Administration, for example, funded neighborhood participant groups in a few cities to evaluate the programs in their neighborhoods. The funds were meant to enable these groups to study the program from their own perspective and thereby satisfy their own interests, information needs, and criteria of success.

Separate evaluations for purposes of federal policy making and local program management tended to have reasonable success, although the quality of local evaluations was erratic. Experience with the funding of client groups to conduct evaluations was less satisfactory. Most client groups were not convinced that evaluation was useful. They tended to be more interested in changing conditions than in studying them. Even when money was available for study, these groups rarely followed through on the laborious and time-consuming process of evaluation. Information was not their priority. They wanted action. They believed that they understood the problems and the types of interventions that would make headway against them, without all the rigmarole that evaluation seemed to entail.

Systematic Canvass of User Group Values and Information Priorities

Another way to see that evaluation addresses the full range of issues that matter to participants is to undertake a systematic canvass of each group's concerns and criteria for success. Such procedures as multiattribute utility scaling were developed to collect data about the program features that each group valued and the relative weight that they assigned to these features. Once evaluators knew which goals were important and how important they were, they could collect information on matters of concern to each group of actors, and they could use the utility weights assigned by the different groups to assess the program's success (Edwards, 1971; Guttentag, 1973).

Evaluators who use this procedure have generally used it to learn about each group's goals for the program, rather than any broader set of concerns. They report that systematic weighting of participants' definitions of goals provides a useful basis for evaluation (Edwards, Guttentag, and Snapper, 1975; Snapper and Seaver, 1978). However, the process demands large amounts of time and considerable input from participants, and the final results do not always satisfy participants. When they see the numbers attached to their preferences by the process of assemblage, iteration, and calculation, they frequently find that the aggregate does not represent what they meant to convey (Guttentag and Snapper, 1974). And when the evaluator recommends the alternative that scores highest on their utility weightings, participants sometimes reject it in favor of an alternative that is intuitively more acceptable (Lock, 1982).

The stakeholder approach to evaluation attempted to build on much of this experience. It took the several pieces — involvement of people holding different positions in the social structure of programs, attention to their interests and utilities, representation of their priorities, emphasis on feedback and dissemination — and tried to shape them into a coherent package. Stakeholder-oriented evaluation was to remedy the assorted ills of old-style evaluation without running afoul of the pitfalls of some of the newer ventures.

Development of the Stakeholder Model

As it matured through staff discussions within NIE in the mid 1970s, the stakeholder approach to evaluation was designed explicitly both to increase the use of evaluation results for decision making and to bring a wider variety of people into active participation in the evaluation process. The former aim, increased use, was to be accomplished in large part by achievement of the latter aim, involvement of a diversity of prospective users in the design and conduct of the study.

How well does the stakeholder approach deal with the complaints leveled at evaluation practice? First, it addresses the issue of fairness directly. By empowering an array of concerned groups to play an active part in the evaluation, the stakeholder approach makes fairness a central tenet. Since it gives high priority to their definitions of information requirements and to timely feedback of the information that they want, it democratizes the evaluation process.

The stakeholder approach should also improve the relevance of information, because it gives stakeholders a strong voice in deciding what information shall be collected. In the process, and by their very diversity, stakeholders will help to avoid the narrowness of measurement that occasioned many complaints.

The unrealistic character of evaluation measures is not quite so easily disposed of. Gold (1981) notes that newly enfranchised groups can have their own unrealistic expectations about the size and scope of program effects. He devotes considerable attention to procedures for continual 'reality testing.' The evaluator is charged with responsibility for reviewing the developmental history of the program and other programs of similar type and for helping stakeholders to understand from the outset which expectations are reasonable. At a number of points during the evaluation, the evaluator is to provide information on the progress of program implementation. All parties to the evaluation are expected to become more realistic as the evaluation provides successive readings on indicators of program success and as stakeholders and evaluators learn to regard program development as an evolving process.

Wider and more immediate use of evaluation results is the driving force behind the stakeholder model. It assumes that giving people the information that they want when they want it and in a form that makes sense to them will increase their commitment to its use. When people have decisions to make, they will have relevant information that they had a say in developing and that responds to their interests.

There is a delicious flavor to the concept. It tackles some of the pervasive problems that have plagued evaluation, and it addresses them with high-minded intent and plausible strategies of action. However, many of its operating features are not well specified. There is ambiguity about a number of central concepts, and evaluators who are expected to implement the stakeholder approach confront a series of unresolved issues. This was true in 1977, when the first attempt to implement stakeholder-oriented evaluation began, and it still seems true today.

Some Unresolved Issues

Definition of Stakeholders

Who exactly are stakeholders? NIE documents sometimes describe them as people who make decisions about the program. However, the same documents also describe them as all the people whose lives are affected by the program and its evaluation. Thus, groups identified as stakeholders in these documents include teachers, school administrators, students, parents, school board members, the mayor's office, the Congress, the research community, the Department of Education, state officials, national program managers, and community organizations. Wide latitude for interpretation remains.

The research community is included in NIE's list of stakeholders because one of NIE's abiding aims is to use evaluations to build a body of generalized knowledge about what does and does not work in education. Are the interests of this community — primarily in valid, generalizable knowledge — compatible with the concerns of people engaged with the program? Can a single evaluation study satisfy such disparate needs? Can any team of evaluators, however skilful, provide information of immediate utility for various sets of program participants and at the same time conduct an adequate test of a replicable program model?

The justification for stakeholder involvement relies heavily on the idea that it can increase the use of evaluation results in decision making. But not all the groups associated with or affected by a program have program decisions to make. Students, parents, and community groups all have little say in the future of the program. Teachers, principals, youth workers, counselors, and other direct service staff do make decisions, but their decisions are generally about issues for which evaluations give little guidance.

Having a stake in a program is not the same thing as having a stake in an evaluation of the program. The kind of information that many people who have a stake in the program want is data that prove their worth. They want program vindicators, not program indicators. Even clients, who probably should want to know whether the program is likely to do them any good and whether they should participate, usually make up their mind on the basis of firsthand experience, not evaluative data. If they enjoy the program and the special attention it gives them, they, too, are likely to want data that justify its continuation.

Another question that arises is: Who defines which groups are stakeholders and which groups are not? Does NIE make the determination, or do evaluators? And does the right to decide who is in and who is out reduce the efficacy of stakeholder evaluation as an instrument of democratization? Since the concept arose from above, in the rarified halls of NIE — not from demands for inclusion from below, can a truly representative orientation be sustained?

Compatibility with Traditional Evaluation Procedures

Another unresolved issue is the extent to which the stakeholder approach is compatible with conventional evaluation practice, particularly with goal-oriented summative evaluation. The stakeholder approach puts a premium on flexibility and on the ability to respond to emergent information needs. Traditional evaluations develop indicators of program effectiveness in advance, so that they can take before and after measures on the same variable. Does the stakeholder approach make demands that conventionally trained evaluators cannot fulfill? Can evaluators integrate formative and summative concerns within a single study, at a level of competence and with a degree of richness that satisfy their varied audiences?

The stakeholder approach requires time for negotiation. NIE foresaw the additional demands and tried to accommodate them in the schedule.

Did they make ample allowance? Or did they underestimate the time and resources necessary to keep the elaborate process moving along?

The stakeholder approach changes the role of evaluators. They are asked not only to be technical experts who do competent research. They are required to become political managers who orchestrate the involvement of diverse interest groups. They must be negotiators, weighing one set of information requests against others and coming to amicable agreements about priorities. They must be skilful educators, sharing their knowledge about appropriate expectations for program development and program success while giving participants a sense of ownership of the study. Are the expectations for evaluators unreasonably high?

Finally, the stakeholder approach marks a change in evaluation priorities. The salience of quantitative, summative assessment of the value of the program concept is reduced. People still care about outcomes. NIE continues to care, as do stakeholders who have to make decisions about whether to support the program in their school district and with their funds. They retain — or they should retain — a concern for the technical quality of the research and for the validity of its results. But such interests are jostled for dominance by demands from other stakeholders for current information on a barrage of practical questions. Can evaluators juggle the competing demands?

These were some of the issues left unresolved when the stakeholder concept was launched. Still, all things considered, the concept was worth a trial. Important evaluations were coming up, and NIE decided to put the idea into practice. Experience would help to flesh out the concept. The potential benefits seemed promising enough to warrant taking the stakeholder approach into the field.

Promise of the Stakeholder Approach

In many ways, the idea marks a decided advance in awareness of the purposes and potential of program evaluation. Above all, it represents a recognition of the political nature of the evaluation process. Unlike early formulations of the mission of evaluation, it does not cast evaluation as the impartial, objective judge of a program's worth. It does not claim that scientific research methods can reveal a single unvarnished truth that, by the sheer force of its verity, can lead decision makers to the right course of action.

The stakeholder concept represents an appreciation that each program affects many groups, which have divergent and even incompatible concerns. It realizes — and legitimizes — the diversity of interests at play in the program world. It recognizes the multiple perspectives that these interests bring to judgment and understanding. It takes evaluation down from the pedestal and places it in the midst of the fray. It aims to make evaluation a conveyor of information, not a deliverer of truth; an aid, not a judge. Realization of the legitimacy of competing interests and the multiplicity of perspectives and willingness to place evaluation at the service of diverse groups are important intellectual advances.

Furthermore, the stakeholder approach represents an awareness of the developmental nature of large-scale social programming. It does not assume that programs are laboratory-like interventions — clearly formulated and replicable entities whose effects can be judged once and for all. Embedded in the concept is a realistic sense of the growing, changing, shifting course that programs follow and of the variety of information needed in the development process. The concept emphasizes quick response to emerging questions and quick feedback to aid in program design and redesign.

One of its most engaging characteristics is the shift in power that it signals. No longer is the federal agency to have a monopoly on control. The concept enfranchises a diverse array of groups, each of which is to have a voice in the planning and conduct of studies. Local as well as national concerns are to be addressed. Issues specific to individual sites and generic issues common across sites receive attention.

The reasons for NIE's willingness to cede authority were not all altruistic. As it had learned through sorry experience, full responsibility for the evaluation of programs could put the agency on the hot seat, particularly when the program being studied was a pet project of an influential political figure and evaluation found it wanting. The stakeholder approach could spread the responsibility. Several observers have suggested that a reduction in NIE's political vulnerability was a significant if unstated goal of the stakeholder approach. By sharing control over the direction of evaluations and therefore over the findings that emerged, NIE was trying to defuse political pressures on itself, on the evaluators, and on the program agencies.

However, the means with which NIE chose to share its responsibility was slightly incongruous. The stakeholder approach imposed a bureaucratic procedure on participation. Stakeholders were to be identified, convened, given set tasks, and required to participate in scheduled and routinized activities. The procedure was a far cry from the disorderly contest of ordinary interest group politics. The potential for conflict among groups was recognized, but it was to be constrained by orderly proceduralism. NIE appears to have assumed that harmony could be achieved by focusing on the definition of the information needs of different groups and by restricting attention to the issue of who needed to know what and when.

Implicitly, NIE seems also to have expected the stakeholder approach to reduce the level of conflict in decision making about the program. Multi-lateral participation in the evaluation process would help the several groups involved in the program to develop mutual understanding and to appreciate one another's viewpoints. Even more important, since they had to agree on the design of the evaluation they would all have to accept its results. The facts would be settled. In later discussions, they could discuss divergence in the values that they attached to the facts, but they could not argue about what the facts were. The area of contentiousness would be bounded.

Furthermore, the federal program office would be removed from the conflict. NIE was no longer judging local performance through evaluation, not weighing or criticizing. Local people were shaping the evaluation themselves. Thus, relations between local and federal authorities should be more relaxed and collegial.

The stakeholder approach was expected to build support for and commitment to the findings that evaluations produced. People who had helped to plan and design an evaluation would have bought in. They would take the results seriously. If and when they took part in subsequent decision making, they were expected to use the data that evaluation provided. At the very least, they could hardly say that the evaluators had studied the wrong things or that they had ignored the effects that mattered. Thus, the stakeholder approach was expected to increase the use of evaluation results in decision making. This had been the stimulus for reform in the first place, and its attainment would represent the real test of the efficacy of the concept.

The Stakeholder Approach in Action

The stakeholder approach received its first trials in evaluations of the Cities-in-Schools and Push/Excel programs. Both programs were highly complex, and both had politically sensitive connections with important people. That the stakeholder approach should be tested in connection with these two programs was partly due to chance; they were the evaluations that happened to come along as the stakeholder approach reached maturity. In another way, however, the concatenation was not at all accidental. NIE had developed the stakeholder approach in part to deal with just such contingencies — politicized program, diverse constituencies, the incipient risk to NIE of an evaluation that might antagonize powerful people. The stakeholder approach would yield an evaluation that was responsive to multiple concerns, and it would protect NIE's bureaucratic interests.

It is relevant, however, that both programs were very difficult to evaluate. They tended to be inchoate, emergent, characterized by high levels of ambiguity. Their activities differed from day to day and from site to site. The programs were administered not by orderly school bureaucracies according to predictable sets of rules but by outside, movement-like groups. They depended in considerable part on the dedication of committed workers and the charisma of leaders. To evaluate such programs as these with conventional evaluation techniques appeared to be courting trouble. Yet, if the programs were to receive federal money, the rules said that they had to be evaluated. Thus, they became the first tests of the stakeholder approach.

References

BERK, R.A. and ROSSI, P.H. (1976) 'Doing good or worse: evaluation research politically re-examined', *Social Problems*, 3, pp. 337–49.

CARO, F.G. (Ed.) (1971) *Readings in Evaluation Research*, New York, Russell Sage Foundation.

COCHRAN, N. (1980) 'Society as emergent and more than rational: An essay on the inappropriateness of program evalution', *Policy Sciences*, 12, 2, pp. 113–29.

COLEMAN, J.S. (1980) 'Policy research and political theory', *University of Chicago Record*, 14, 2.

DATTA, L.E. (Ed.) (1981) *Evaluation in Change*, Beverly Hills, Calif., Sage.

DAVIS, H.R. and SALASIN, S. (1975) 'The utilization of evaluation' in STRUENING, E. and GUTTENTAG, M. (Eds) *Handbook of Evaluation Research*, Beverly Hills, Calif., Sage.

EDWARDS, W. (1971) 'Social utilities', *The Engineering Economist*, summer, symposium series.

EDWARDS, W., GUTTENTAG, M. and SNAPPER, K.J. (1975) 'Effective evaluation: A decision-theoretic approach' in STRUENING, E.L. and GUTTENTAG, M. (Eds) *Handbook of Evaluation Research*, Beverly Hills, Calif., Sage.

GLASER, E.M. and BACKER, T.E. (1972) 'A clinical approach to program evaluation', *Evaluation*, 1, pp. 54–9.

GOLD, N. (1981) *The Stakeholder Process in Educational Program Evaluation*, Washington DC, National Institute of Education.

GUBA, E.G. (1969) 'The failure of educational evaluation', *Educational Technology*, 9, 5, pp. 29–38.

GUTTENTAG, M. (1973) 'Subjectivity and its use in evaluation research', *Evaluation*, 1, 2, pp. 60–5.

GUTTENTAG, M. and SNAPPER, K. (1974) 'Plans, evaluations, and decisions', *Evaluation*, 2, 1, pp. 58–64 and 73–4.

HOUSE, E.R. (1980) *Evaluating with Validity*, Beverly Hills, Calif., Sage.

LOCK, A.R. (1982) 'A strategic business decision with multiple criteria: the Bally men's shoe problem', *Journal of Operational Research Society*, 33, pp. 327–32.

PARLETT, M. and HAMILTON, D. (1976) 'Evaluation as illumination: a new approach to the study of innovatory programs' in GLASS, G.V. (Ed.) *Evaluation Studies Review Annual 1979*, Beverly Hills, Calif., Sage.

PATTON, M.Q. (1978) *Utilization-Focused Evaluation*, Beverly Hills, Calif., Sage.

RUTMAN, L. (1980) *Planning Useful Evaluations*, Beverly Hills, Calif., Sage.

SCHWARZ, P.A. (1980) 'Program devaluation: Can the experiment reform?' in LOVELAND, E. (Ed.) *Measuring the Hard-to-Measure*, New Directions for Program Evaluation, no 6, San Francisco, Jossey-Bass.

SCOTT, R.A. and SHORE, A.R. (1979) *Why Sociology Does Not Apply: A Study of the Use of Sociology in Public Policy*, New York, Elsevier.

SNAPPER, K.J. and SEAVER, D.A. (1978) *Application of Decision Analysis to Program Planning and Evaluation: Technical Report*, Falls Church, Va, Decision Science Consortium.

STAKE, R.E. (1978) 'Responsive education' in HAMILTON, D. and others (Eds) *Beyond the Numbers Game*, Berkeley, Calif., McCutchan.

WEISS, C.H. (1972) 'Utilization of evaluation: Toward comparative study' in WEISS, C.H. (Ed.) *Evaluating Action Programs: Readings in Social Action and Evaluation*, Boston, Allyn and Bacon.

WHOLEY, J.S. and others (1970) *Federal Evaluation Policy*, Washington, DC Urban Institute.

WILLIAMS, W. (1971) *Social Policy Research and Analysis*, New York, Elsevier.

WINDLE, C. and OCHBERG, F.M. (1975) 'Enhancing program evaluation in the community mental health centers program', *Evaluation*, 2, 2, pp. 30–6.

ZWEIG, F.M. and MARVIN, K.E. (Eds) (1981) *Educating Policy Makers for Evaluation*, Beverly Hills, Calif., Sage.

The Evaluation of Push/Excel: A Case Study

Eleanor Farrar and Ernest House
Huron Research Institute and University of Illinois

Jesse Jackson, interviewed on the CBS television program *Sixty Minutes* on 4 December 1977, said: 'Now, the challenge is upward mobility, and that is why the focus on not only getting in school but producing in school becomes a new kind of challenge ... We must struggle to excel because competition is keener, because doors that once opened are now closing in our faces. It's my judgment we need a massive revolution in our attitude.

'But we cannot do it alone ... Many other people must get involved ... We pulled together a group of ministers [and] massive parent involvement. We've begun to mobilize disc jockeys and key athletes and artists and entertainers ... So, in a real sense, what we're doing is not operating alone; we're simply using our talent and energy to mobilize involvement to take on a massive problem.'

Hubert Humphrey was watching *Sixty Minutes* from his hospital bed in Minneapolis on that night, and he heard Jesse Jackson speak of the need for a movement to convince black youth to excel in school. He watched Jackson's impassioned appeal to a stadium full of wildly applauding teenagers in Los Angeles; he heard Jackson's call to the black community to join in the endeavor. The next day, Humphrey called his old friend Joseph Califano, Secretary of Health, Education, and Welfare. Califano (1981) reports: 'In a weak voice, his strength consumed by his battle with cancer, [Humphrey] asked me if I had seen the *Sixty Minutes* program. When I responded, he said, "Well, then, you saw what I saw. I want you to talk to Jesse Jackson and help him. He's doing something for those kids. I've talked to him this morning and told him I'll talk to you. Now, you get him down to your office and help him. Will you do that for me?" I told him I would.' (p. 294)

This case study was supported in part by the National Institute of Education (NIE), but the study presents the views of the authors, for which the NIE is not responsible. This case reflects AIR's account of Push/Excel's early history. The authors are indebted to Maria Sachs and Stephen Raudenbush for proof that the story can be told at a fraction of its original length.

Thus began the federal government's involvement in Push/Excel, a motivational program for black youth started by Jackson two years earlier and supported by individual, corporate, and foundation contributions. One month later, the National Institute of Education awarded two grants to the Push Foundation: a $25,000 grant to plan a Push/Excel conference and a $20,000 grant for preliminary program evaluation and project design. Five months later, NIE awarded another $400,000 for the design of projects in Chicago, Kansas City, and Los Angeles and for expansion to additional sites. Next, the US Office of Education began planning for a $3 million demonstration project to begin in January 1979. By early May 1978, more than twenty local education agencies had expressed interest in taking part in the demonstration.

Not long after, at Califano's request, NIE began to plan a national evaluation of Push/Excel. For some observers, the government's involvement, although uninvited, seemed to be a big boost for Push/Excel. But was it? An editorial in the *Washington Star* ('A Shove Comes to Push, 1978) expressed reservations: 'We must admit that HEW Secretary Joe Califano's announcement that his department is giving two modest grants to the Reverend Jesse Jackson's Push program strikes us as a good news/bad news event. Our delight, accordingly, is not unmixed with worry. With even modest federal grants, especially from HEW, come bureaucratic intruders; and with bureaucratic intruders come "guidelines"; and with guidelines come stale, meddlesome orthodoxies and ideologies that are quite capable of rubbing the sharp edge off the best ideas. Jesse Jackson's movement is, we think, one of the most hopeful things that has happened to this country in years and has been so because he marches to his own drummer. The last thing we need is the federalization of Jesse Jackson.'

The editorialist's worry was prophetic: Less than five years later, Push/Excel was struggling to survive. Budgets and staff had been reduced, and federal and philanthropic support had shifted to other interests. The few remaining local programs had severed connections with the national office, abandoned the Push/Excel name, and reduced Jackson's crusade for total community involvement to familiar school programs for under-achieving black youth.

The story of Push/Excel's demise is complex. It involves shifting political winds and straitened school finances, Jackson's unpredictability and insensitivity to school politics, and struggles between various groups of program participants. The national Push/Excel staff sought to persuade local districts and schools to share program control and decision making. It was a reasonable goal, but it failed to allow for school politics and the need of local Excel staffs for central direction. The federally sponsored evaluation of Push/Excel and its press coverage are also part of the story. Government support required Excel to undergo an evaluation, and despite all evidence that it was a movement, it was evaluated as a program. The evaluators tried to help it to become one, but for three years, as they guided and advised Excel staff, their reports documented Excel's inability to produce the desired effect on students and the community. These findings were widely reported in the national and local press, and in less than three years, before the final report appeared, the verdict was in: Jesse Jackson's inspirational movement had failed.

This is a case study of the federally sponsored evaluation of Push/Excel. The authors of this chapter had no involvement with Push/Excel prior to this case study. In the course of our work, we interviewed staff and participants in two local Excel programs and made several trips to NIE, the Department of Education, and the evaluators' offices. We reviewed documents, press articles, and program files, and we were generously granted hours of interviews by NIE and AIR. Their views of Push/Excel and its evaluation are, we hope, fairly represented, but those of the national program office are not: Our requests to meet with Push/Excel national staff and with Jesse Jackson remained unanswered.

The story begins with the federal government's involvement in Push/Excel two years after Jackson began the movement, and it concludes with publication of the final evaluation report some fifty-two months later. The study was commissioned by the National Institute of Education as part of an examination of the utility and productivity of urban secondary school program evaluation. To ensure that the evaluation would be useful to Push/Excel stakeholders, NIE sought to involve them in the evaluation process. Stakeholders included federal officials and national Push/Excel staff and sponsors as well as local participants — students, parents, school people, churches, funding sources, and other community segments. The evaluation was to show not only how Push/Excel affected students, schools, and communities but also how these groups influenced the evaluation.

The Federal Involvement

Not everyone shared Humphrey's enthusiasm for a federal role in Push/Excel. A few days after Humphrey's conversation with Califano, Califano called Patricia Albjerg Graham, director of NIE, to ask about funding for Excel. According to Graham (personal interview, June 1981), 'I called [various] people and said, ... "Should we put money into [Jackson's] operation? It seems to me that the basic question is 'Can you bottle charisma and organize it?'" And people said, "Well, yes." And they said he'd also had trouble keeping his books straight. [Subsequently, I told Jackson], "There's money for you to plan a program ... which we will evaluate ... If you take federal cash, then you have to ... account for how [it] is spent and specify what it is you're going to do with [it]. And the

gist of the evaluation is whether or not you did [that]" ... This is
shortened, of course. It was about an eight-month discussion.'

Mary Berry, Assistant Secretary of HEW, recalled (personal interview, July 1982) that, after speaking with Humphrey, Califano offered to
fund Push/Excel. However, Jackson refused the money, saying, 'No, I
have no program.' Califano told Jackson that was not important; he could
hire a writer to prepare a proposal to HEW, and the government would
provide technical help to develop a program. Jackson accepted.

Several weeks later, Jackson met with a group that included Mary
Berry, Ernest Boyer, US Commissioner of Education; Jeff Schiller and
Patricia Graham from NIE; and James Comer of Yale, who was completing an evaluation of Excel funded by the Ford Foundation. They
discussed the evaluation, including the possibility that it would attempt
'to show that Jesse was no good and that Push/Excel was no good'
(Graham, personal interview, June 1981). Some of those present argued
that there should be no evaluation. As Graham recalls this meeting, 'I said
[that] the gist of evaluation is not to figure out whether the program meets
the evaluator's goals, but for the evaluator to figure out what your goals
are, which means that you've got to figure out what your goals are.'
According to Graham, an evaluation had to be done. How extensive it
should be and what form it should take were arguable, but some form of
accounting, both substantial and financial, was required.

NIE decided to use the stakeholder approach in the evaluation of
Push/Excel. There was little discussion of other possibilities. According to
Jeff Schiller, assistant director of NIE's Teaching and Learning Program,
this was due to a concern for evaluation utility. Conflict between
evaluators and program staff had frequently undermined the credibility
and usefulness of evaluation for decision makers. The NIE group, and
particularly Norman Gold, believed that stakeholder involvement could
prevent such problems. NIE had contracted with the American Institutes
for Research (AIR) to use the stakeholder approach in evaluating the
Cities-in-Schools Program under Gold's direction, and NIE wished to
explore it further. Push/Excel was selected for the same treatment —
chiefly, as Schiller remembers it (personal interview, July 1982), 'because
it was there.' According to Schiller, 'The stakeholder notion was a good
one to try with Cities-in-Schools and Push/Excel anyway. We knew
there'd never be any federal policy in this area. [Excel] would always be
locally modified, implemented, and supported, and it had to be evaluated
against their goals. Also, it was very developmental. The stakeholder
approach would improve the implementation process and [evaluation]
utility.'

Norman Gold was responsible for drafting the request for proposals
for evaluation of Push/Excel (National Institute of Education, 1978).
Gold, who has been described as 'handling all the politically sensitive
evaluations at NIE,' gave potential bidders considerable latitude. Since

the evaluation would have several audiences — parents, teachers, community members, policy makers, and evaluators — the contractor was to consult with panels representing these groups during the design and implementation of the evaluation. Noting that this approach implied no 'technical compromises which will satisfy consumers but [lack] methodological rigor and clarity,' the request for proposals outlined seven questions that the contractor was to address (National Institute of Education, 1978):

1   To what extent have the programs been implemented; what implementation problems were there, and how were they addressed; and how does the implementation vary within and between cities?

2   How have students benefited from the program both in and out of school in terms of long- and short-term gains?

3   How have participating schools been affected by the Excel program and support? What were the effects on the delivery of educational services, staff morale, and the general climate of the schools?

4   Excel stresses close involvement of parents, families, and the community in schools. What has been the impact of the program upon these groups?

5   What has been the impact of Reverend Jackson, Push, and other unique aspects of Excel upon programmatic outcomes?

6   What are the marginal extra costs of schooling attributable to Excel? How much of these are start-up costs and how much ongoing costs?

7   To what extent can the processes, structures, and costs of Excel be accommodated within normal school administrative procedures and budgets? (pp. 8–9)

The intention was that other stakeholders would add to this list. According to Norman Gold (personal interview, January 1982), '[I was attempting to] set up a process by which the evaluators would not dominate the evaluation as much as they had in the past, [nor would] the federal government; . . . [one in which] we would empower others to have more say.'

The work was to proceed in two phases: four months to design the evaluation and thirty-two months to carry it out. The total level of effort was 12.5 FTE/person-years. The first phase would familiarize the contractor with the programs, the expectations of stakeholders, and the basis for decisions about continuing support. This phase had the explicit aim of increasing the evaluation's usefulness by enabling stakeholders' information needs to be incorporated into the final design.

Award of the contract was swift. The request for proposals was issued in September 1978, proposals were due in October, and the contract was signed in January 1979. The budget was $750,000. NIE received seven proposals. According to Gold (personal interviews, October 1980 and July 1982), it was 'not a hot competition. The proposals weren't great.' AIR was chosen because 'they understood what the stakeholder concept was all about,' although NIE was uneasy about relying on the same principal investigator for two similar evaluations, and although the stakeholder approach was not prominent in AIR's proposal.

The wisdom and the appropriateness of formal evaluation of Jesse Jackson's movement had been questioned, but evaluation had to accompany the serendipitous federal involvement in Push/Excel. The stakeholder approach was selected because NIE was exploring it as a way of reducing conflicts and of increasing the utility of evaluations. NIE's information about the program was sketchy: Since most Excel documents were designed for promotion, the request for proposals relied heavily on Jackson's proposal to the Department of Health, Education, and Welfare, which had been developed at Califano's urging with HEW help and funding (National Institute of Education, 1978, p. 3). NIE staff had visited the Los Angeles site, where they had been impressed by reports of improved attendance and by the student activities that they found (personal interview with Jeff Schiller, July 1982). NIE concluded that, while the program was still loose and unstructured, it made sense to begin collecting 'a data base around some [useful] conceptual structure for evaluation' (personal interview with Norman Gold, July 1982). The evaluators were to develop the structure after investigation of program activities and objectives at five sites. Armed with NIE's impressions of Excel and its possibilities, AIR began its three-year study.

Push/Excel: A Movement and a Program

The evaluation of Push/Excel was not destined to be straightforward. Excel had been launched as a movement — a grass-roots, self-help effort to achieve a broad set of goals through personal and community commitment. It was not a structured education reform with an implementation blueprint, and Excel's national staff were not educators or program developers. Their experience lay in the civil rights movement and its strategy and tactics. They lacked the skills and the perspective needed to develop a school program. The fact that program objectives and activities differed across schools was a further complication, which ruled out the usual methods of multisite evaluation. When the evaluation contract was awarded, what existed was an eloquent, charismatic leader of national reputation who had attracted a staff of committed followers, considerable public and private funding, and several school districts willing to make an attempt to translate a self-help ideology into a school program that could regenerate black youth — an unlikely subject for scrutiny by social science.

The Origins of Excel

Push/Excel was the offspring of Operation Push, a social action organization founded by Jesse Jackson in 1971 after his break with the Southern Christian Leadership Conference. It grew out of a demonstration staged at the White House on 15 January 1975, for full-time employment and jobs for blacks. The demonstration ended abruptly when Reverend Jackson told the marchers to go home. Subsequently, a letter from the Push/Excel board of directors to potential donors explained Jackson's decision: 'Walking through file after file of protesters, a tall, athletic young black minister — a man who had been in the vanguard of the civil rights movement for years — was shocked to see that a great many of the youths were drunk or on drugs, visibly out of control. That man, the Reverend Jesse Jackson, realized then that the time had come for him to change his target for reform. As he painfully said: "The door of opportunity is open for our people, but they are too drunk, too unconscious to walk through the door"' (Reverend O. Moss, Jr., letter, n.d., cited in Murray and others, 1982, p. 12).

Ten months later, Jackson appeared before a student assembly in Chicago's predominantly black Martin Luther King High School. His message was blunt: It was up to blacks to ensure that they did not waste the opportunities that they had. Or, as Jackson put it, 'No one will save us for us but us.' It was the first stop on a cross-country tour that the *Washington Post* later described as Jesse Jackson's 'crusade' (Murray and others, 1982, p. 12).

The Movement

Jackson's crusade carried a timeless message: that hard work, self-discipline, delayed gratification, and persistence were qualities that youth needed in order to succeed. Jackson believed that black youths in particular blamed society for their failures and that they expected society to provide redress. He hoped to replace this futile aspiration with one based on sacrifice and commitment to a larger personal goal.

Jackson believed that the resources of the entire community had to be mobilized. He urged parents to take an interest in their children's schooling, to establish regular study hours at home, and to pick up report cards at school. Schools were admonished to raise their standards for behavior and academic performance. The community was urged to participate in program events, to contribute time and money, and to offer rewards and opportunities. In brief, Jackson celebrated a striving toward solid middle-class virtues through total involvement by students and communities, especially the church. The prominence that Jackson assigned to the church reflected his Southern background and the origins of his movement. He elaborated his beliefs in ten 'commandments,' later renamed *the ten principles* (Push for Excellence, Inc., n.d.):

1 It is essential that a public institution clearly define itself, to say unequivocally what it believes in and stands for.
2 The development of responsible adults is a task requiring community commitment. It cannot be left solely to the public schools.
3 The principal tasks of the public schools cannot be achieved if a disproportionate amount of time and resources must be given to maintaining order. Public schools are not obligated to serve students who persistently disrupt schools and violate the rights of others.
4 The full responsibility for learning cannot be transferred from the student to the teacher.
5 Parents must consistently support the proposition that students have responsibilities as well as rights and that the schools have an obligation to insist upon both.
6 High performance takes place in a framework of expectation.
7 There is nothing inherently undemocratic in requiring students to do things that are demonstrably beneficial to them.
8 Involvement in and commitment to meaningful activities which give one a sense of identity and worth are essential to all human beings and are especially critical to adolescents.
9 The practice of convenience leads to collapse, but the laws of sacrifice lead to greatness. This applies to students, teachers, parents, administrators, and community leaders.
10 A sound *ethical* climate must be established for a school system as a whole and for each individual school, because the death of ethics is the sabotage of excellence. Politicians, school board members, superintendents, central office staff, principals, teachers, parents, and ministers have the obligation to take an aggressive lead in setting such ethical standards. (pp. 4–5)

Jackson's message of self-help and high standards of achievement struck responsive chords wherever he went. Stadiums were filled. Television and newspapers recorded his successes. Editorials praised the wisdom of his pronouncements, and appearances on nationally televised talk shows followed. A rally in the New Orleans Superdome drew more than 65,000 people; 20,000 watched Jackson, joined by entertainers Marlon Brando and Aretha Franklin, in Los Angeles. Education editor Art Bronscombe (1979) described the Denver rally in the 12 September 1979, issue of the *Denver Post*: 'Leading about 4,000 students in chants of "I am somebody ... Down with dope, up with hope," the Reverend Jesse Jackson opened his Push for Excellence program in the Denver public schools Tuesday.

The slim, dynamic Chicago Baptist minister ... told the multiracial throng that his generation has largely conquered the mountain of equal opportunity ... "The mountain you must conquer is ... the mountain of effort." "The Lord makes oranges grow on trees," he shouted, "but you've got to squeeze the juice yourselves." He paused frequently to demand that the students join him in such chants as "Nobody can save us from us, for us, but us." And he told them, "There is nothing more powerful in the world than development of the mind and a strong character."'

In spring 1976, the Chicago Board of Education agreed to initiate Excel activities in ten schools, and a year later preliminary Excel activities began in Kansas City, Los Angeles, Washington, DC, and Chattanooga, Tennessee. Other cities made inquiries and began planning. In 1977 alone, Jackson made more than forty personal appearances at colleges, high schools, and educational conferences. These activities were supported largely by corporate and philanthropic contributions: Illinois Bell, the Joe Drown and Piton Foundations, the Ford Foundation, Lilly Foundation, Rockefeller Brothers Fund, and Chicago Community Trust. In record time, Jesse Jackson's crusade had become an educational movement of national proportions.

Jackson's base was Operation Push, of which he had been President since 1971. Push considered itself a 'civil economics' organization, aimed at achieving economic parity for blacks by using strategies that had proved so effective in the civil rights movement: selective patronage, boycotts of specific businesses, and the mass rally. The structure and modus operandi of Operation Push were reflected in the practices of the fledgling movement. As AIR later described it (Murray and others, 1982) '[The] Push organizational structure ... adapted continually to accommodate the issues and funds at hand. Programs and departments came and went, along with the ... staff that conducted them. Through it all, Jackson took the lead ... When he decided to seek reform among youth, the organization accommodated once more and added a new box to its organization chart — this time labeled *Push for Excellence.*' (p. 14) Push/Excel was a modest part of the Operation Push enterprise, which was a strong pressure in the black and third-world political scene, but for a time, Push/Excel was a source of national visibility for both the organization and its peripatetic leader.

The Program

If Jackson's movement caught on overnight, efforts to translate it into an organization that could implement his message proceeded slowly. Originally, Operation Push was to take care of fund raising and promotion, while local staff were to develop and manage local operations. But, it quickly became apparent that most local staff were inexperienced in community organization and unable to deal effectively with top-level school bureaucrats. They needed and expected help from a national office, which Operation Push finally established in spring 1977. A Push/Excel national director and administrative aide were hired to design program components, coordinate activities, develop a structured approach to Excel, and expand its resource base. But, almost from the start, they spent more time helping Jackson to spread his message than they did developing implementation tools for local staff.

Gradually, program descriptions became available. One of the first, an illustrated booklet providing 'just a few starter ideas,' suggested activities to involve community members and sustain student commitment: reward and incentive programs, career day forums, 'witness for excellence' meetings. It also recommended media campaigns, school plays emphasizing excellence, and field trips. A second publication (Push for Excellence, Inc., n.d.) was more specific. It discussed Excel's objectives, described activities to make the program work (teachers must 'expect quality work,' while churches must 'begin tutoring programs,' 'adopt schools,' and so on), and provided tips on how to begin local Excel programs.

Jackson placed six activities at the core of an Excel program (Push for Excellence, Inc., n.d.)

1   *State of the School Address.* At the start of each school year, the principal should give a state of the school address, setting the climate and the goals for the year. The principal must be the moral authority, teach discipline and academic achievement; and development will be the by-product.

2   *Student Pledges.* Students must pledge to commit themselves to study every school-day night a minimum of two hours from 7 to 9 P.M., with the television, radio, and record player off and no telephone interruptions. If we match our effort and discipline in athletics in the academic arena, we will achieve the same results.

3   *Parent Pledges.* Parents must pledge to accept the responsibility to monitor their child's study hours and agree to go to school to pick up their child's report card each grading period.

4   *Teacher Pledges.* Teachers must pledge to make meaningful homework assignments; to collect, grade, and return homework to students; and call the parent if a student is absent two days in a row or is doing poorly in school — all of which reflects increased expectations of students on the part of teachers.

5   *Written Ethical Code of Conduct.* A written ethical code of

conduct, which presents alternative life-styles to drugs, al-
cohol, violence, teenage pregnancy, and other forms of de-
cadence that detract from an educational atmosphere, must be
implemented.

6 *Voter Registration.* On graduation day, all eligible seniors
would receive a diploma in one hand (symbolizing knowledge
and wisdom) and a voter registration card in the other
(symbolizing power and responsibility), as well as ... nonpart-
isan information on how to vote and operate a voting machine.
(p. 2)

But, the methods that schools used to get the activities under way and to
increase participation were left to local invention.

The early Push/Excel material portrays signing the pledge as the
main event and the suggested activities as ancillary ways of keeping people
involved, of expressing the pledged commitments. The pledge appeared to
be critical to Excel — perhaps because it was viewed almost as a religious
experience, a commitment analogous to coming forward in the church and
pledging one's life to Christ. Underlying this commitment was the notion
of change as a conversion process. One converts and thereby changes one's
life forever in one swift action; subsequent activities are devices to
reinforce commitment. In its early efforts, Push/Excel seemed driven by
the belief that demonstrable change would naturally follow the pledge.

The AIR evaluators did not believe that change must follow conversion or that Excel activities were sufficient for demonstrated change to
occur. In commenting on program development at that time, AIR noted
(Murray and others, 1982): 'These [activities] were more in the nature of a
good place to start than a prescription for how to apply the Push/Excel
message concretely. The fledgling programs ... had been struggling with
the next steps ... Now, with the availability of federal money [and] the
flood of new requests for help, the need for a concrete, describable
program of activities became urgent. But, who was to produce it? Not
Jackson, who explicitly saw his role as catalyst, not program designer or
implementor. Not the existing Push/Excel staff, who at this point
consisted of a national director and a secretary. Program development was
a major job, calling ... for expertise in a variety of skills, a sizable staff,
and time.' (p. 25)

The development of an organizational model for local Excel programs
was the next step. (The national Push/Excel office takes credit for the
model, but the Chattanooga program director said that it originated in Los
Angeles and that it was refined in Chattanooga.) The model called for
close collaboration between school districts and local Push/Excel staff. A
Push/Excel site director hired by the national office was responsible for
local fund raising, liaison with the national office, coordinating activities,

and assisting program staff. Community liaison persons, employed by the national staff but based in schools, worked to involve the community. Each school had a teacher-adviser for recruiting and counseling, who, jointly with the community liaison, selected the advisory council, comprised of students, teachers, parents, and community members. A district administrator was named Push/Excel program director. Working with his Excel counterpart, he was to coordinate decision making and share responsibility for program operations. This organization presumed that school districts would be willing to give nondistrict personnel a major voice in school affairs and to commit resources to implementation of the concept of total community involvement.

The national office expected local staff to use this structure in devising a program and activities suited to the local context. Jackson's ten principles and six core activities gave them a place to start, and the mass rally provided an audience. It was then up to them to develop a Push/Excel program that would build and sustain commitment to the broad movement objectives.

Excel's Early Implementation

In practice, early implementation of the Push/Excel program model and activities varied from site to site. Frequently, it was problematic. When the NIE evaluation contract was awarded in 1979, six programs were affiliated with Push/Excel: the original pilot program sites in Chicago, Los Angeles, and Kansas City and sites in Memphis, Denver, and Chattanooga where programs were about to begin. Financial woes and political turmoil in other districts that adopted Push/Excel left few still operating after the first two years.

The Chicago program was initiated in ten high schools. Although local philanthropy and national office funds provided resources for start-up, district support was halting, and the program was never fully implemented. Kansas City had programs in two high schools, but only one was endorsed by the district. Local infighting followed, and the district eventually lost confidence in the program.

In Los Angeles, Push/Excel had the support of district administrators. First-year funding was adequate for the full complement of staff, but the second year coincided with the passage of Proposition 13, which resulted in a budget reduction of nearly 30 per cent. The program was finally terminated.

Despite difficulties and controversies at the older sites, there were high hopes for the future of the three new programs. Then, Jesse Jackson went to the Middle East.

Jackson's Trip to the Middle East

Days before the evaluation contract was signed, Jackson made front-page news when he was photographed arm in arm with PLO leader Yasir Arafat. The story sent shock waves reverberating through local Push/Excel communities. Jackson had intended to encourage links between third-world oil-exporting nations and black U.S. businesses, but his debut in international politics was unanimously censured by American public opinion and the press. Although his action was unrelated to Excel, it created serious problems for the program and for the evaluation. Support died in Memphis and wavered elsewhere, and the trip abruptly terminated Excel's prospects in Louisiana. Only in Chattanooga did the program survive essentially undamaged — in large part due to the efforts of Excel board member Ruth Homberg, publisher of the *Chattanooga Times* and an important part of the Chattanooga power structure.

Whatever the reasons for Jackson's trip, its consequences for the program were far-reaching. Local staff had not felt much support from the national office in their struggle to establish working relationships with school districts, and the estrangement deepened, setting the stage for a formal break. The AIR evaluation may also have been affected: The publicity — most of it negative — made Push/Excel and the evaluation highly visible and highly vulnerable.

Summary

As the AIR evaluation got under way, both it and Push/Excel faced several problems. First, Excel was less a program than a movement whose success depended on a charismatic leader. This was not the familiar terrain of evaluation studies. Second, the national staff lacked the inclination and skills needed to transform the movement into a structured school program. By failing to provide sufficient guidance to local programs already beset with political problems and weak management, they encouraged even greater program diversity. Third, Push/Excel was riddled with dissension. Although committed students and staff worked creatively together in many Excel schools, administrative conflict among national, district, and local levels was often the rule. Fourth, Jesse Jackson's credibility had been tarnished. His trip angered many and raised serious questions about his politics and judgment. This deflected energy and attention from program activities and increased local stakes in the evaluation's outcome.

Still another problem soon to confront Push/Excel was that the evaluators, in trying to provide constructive criticism to aid program development, in fact drew negative publicity that undermined the morale of the movement just as it faced a most difficult task: translating great potential into a sustained program at the grassroots level.

Evaluation Design

Preliminary Activities

AIR's proposal was for an 'incremental evaluation,' a new approach that AIR president Paul A. Schwarz had been working on. Schwarz (1980) noted that evaluations were commonly treated as scientific experiments, as a result of which they posed the question, Did *A* (the activities) result in *Y* (the outcome)? But, program outcomes could occur long after the activities that were supposed to produce them, and although these distal effects were considered valuable, they were hard to detect and to attribute to program activities; there were other possible explanations. Proximal effects, though less robust, were easier to demonstrate and provided better diagnostic information. Thus, according to Schwarz, the real question is, Given *Y*, does *A'* lead to *Y*?

Schwarz viewed the choice of outcomes as critical. Measuring more proximal effects would show whether the program was on track. If it was not, it could be modified piecemeal — a process Schwarz labeled *incremental*. These increments and their relationship were defined in terms of the program rationale: 'The blueprint for building solutions.' If the program had no rationale, the evaluator had to develop one.

Charles A. Murray and Saundra R. Murray (no relation), AIR's proposed principal investigator and project director respectively, drafted the evaluation proposal in that spirit. Noting that 'the core of [the] evaluation . . . is to establish causality: to document the impact of Excel,' they rejected the classical experimental design, proposing instead to 'split the causality question into a number of . . . components,' in each of which 'The problem of controls and extraneous effects can be managed adequately' (Murray and others, 1978). Over thirty-two months, the proposal states, '*it is possible to trace presumed linkages contemporaneously.*'

In agreement with Excel's assertion that student achievement was not the basic program objective, AIR proposed to measure Excel's effectiveness by examining change in student and community behavior ('investment behavior') as a precondition of the desired effects, which included improved achievement. These changes would be broken down into increments, each leading to the next and ultimately to the outcome. Some incremental objectives would be identified at the outset to obtain a data base for assessing change; others would be identified along the way. Since the interpretation of Excel would vary across sites, this implied that the data bases could be site specific. It was an ambitious plan.

The four-month design phase involved several tasks. One was to develop a program rationale. Another concerned the role of stakeholders in the study. AIR defined stakeholders as program staff and national users of the evaluation for program planning and decision making. But, where

NIE had envisioned stakeholders as active participants in the evaluation, the role that AIR conceived was limited to one of providing details about program operations and reacting to AIR's list of plausible outcomes. Also, AIR refused to convene the national users, whose hidden agendas might affect the developing program. Although stakeholders were to participate to some degree, no serious attention was given to making the evaluation useful to them.

Thus, the emphasis shifted from summative assessments for decision-making stakeholders to diagnostic appraisal. The shift was due both to AIR's skepticism about involving stakeholders and to its eagerness to test the incremental approach, which would provide local sites with feedback for formative purposes — a particular strength with Excel, where the evaluation could help to shape an ill-defined program. For AIR, this formative function outweighed the evaluation's increased usefulness to stakeholders that NIE had hoped for. Although Jesse Jackson's crusade was a movement, to allow incremental evaluation, it had to be treated as a program that had identifiable proximate steps. Thus, a major task of the evaluation would be to help Excel to develop into a program.

Stakeholder Participation

The principal parties to the evaluation met over a soul food dinner at Jesse Jackson's home in March 1979 to arrange for AIR-Excel staff briefings and visits to the three prototype sites, so that program descriptions could be developed and stakeholder needs assessed. After the site visits, panels were convened in Chicago and Kansas City. (The Los Angeles meeting was canceled by the site director.) AIR asked the twenty-five stakeholder groups — program and district staff, funding agencies, parents, clergy, and business and community organizations — to rank-order five evaluation questions and their preferred ways of receiving evaluation information. Interestingly, the top-ranked question in both cities was, 'What political considerations affect program success or failure?' Low on the list was whether the Push/Excel concept of total involvement had the desired effects. As ways of presenting information, Kansas City chose press releases, newsletters, and annual reports, while Chicago chose information briefings. AIR noted that 'the diversity in expectation reflects the many interpretations . . . of Push/Excel. We are confident that we have engaged our users for future interactions and increased the likelihood that evaluation products will be used' (American Institute for Research, 1979, p. 17).

Charles Murray had a less sanguine reaction (personal interview, December 1980): 'The program people [believed] that there were certain things they had to say: "We are going to raise grades, we are going to improve test scores." . . . I said, "Well, . . . this is not what you're really trying to do!" ... And [they replied], "We don't think we are either, but we have to [say that] in order to make ourselves plausible." ... [I said], "We want you to help us design this evaluation, ... to hear your priorities and adapt the evaluation to that ...." The [subsequent] discussions were generally very forced, very artificial.'

Norman Gold recalled much squabbling about role definitions, while AIR's proposed indicators were not discussed (personal interview, October 1980). All in all, the stakeholders contributed little to the evaluation design or to the plan for disseminating findings. For its part, AIR discussed methods and what the evaluation could and could not accomplish and pointed out why local information needs were implausible or impracticable. According to Gold, the meetings helped people to understand the evaluation but largely failed to elicit what people wanted to know or when. The final design was not the result of joint planning by AIR and Excel, and neither NIE nor AIR was pleased. Norman Gold's view was that the stakeholder notion was not well used, and Charles Murray shared Gold's dissatisfaction (personal interview, December 1980): 'We don't really have it right yet ... You do want people who are going to make decisions about a program to be involved in the evaluation ... but too much of the way we were going about it ... is a charade. Now, the technical review panel for Cities-in-Schools said, ... 'You could have gotten these folks to talk about what they wanted [and] to contribute much more to your design." ... I don't think we [did] it better for Excel. And, it was not for lack of trying. It was because we didn't have much better ideas than we had the first time around.'

If the stakeholder meetings did not produce the collaboration that NIE had intended, one reason was stakeholder naiveté about what evaluations can accomplish. Program staff knew what they wanted to learn about Excel, such as its effect on test scores, but many stakeholders did not know about the attendant political and methodological problems or the limits of evaluation science for studying certain questions that AIR rejected as unresearchable. And, although stakeholders supported the program's laudable aims, they often knew little about its local operation and goals. They thought of Excel much as they thought of the poverty program or the civil rights movement. One day, Excel's success or failure would be self-evident, not because of the pronouncements of sponsored studies. But, collaboration also fell short because AIR was not squarely behind it. Stakeholders were concerned with political issues, which did not interest AIR, not with community involvement, which was the chief interest of AIR and NIE. Furthermore, the evaluators had preferred ways of reporting information, and when the stakeholders' ideas diverged they were rejected.

The inclusion of stakeholders' preferences was precisely what NIE had in mind in requesting a stakeholder-based study. The evaluation process was to be reformed by examining what stakeholders wanted to know, making the evaluation more useful and precluding arguments about program effects. But, the study was conceived and developed in the mainstream of applied science, and unorthodoxy was not taken seriously. In this context, where stakeholders lacked sophistication in evaluation research, program objectives were unclear, and the evaluator was luke-warm about stakeholder involvement, it is not surprising that AIR's preferences prevailed.

The Evaluation Design

In the design of the evaluation, Schwarz's incremental approach took pride of place. AIR's program rationale defined various proximal goals as preludes to achievement, the most distal outcome. Each of the proximal goals would be affected by student, parent, and community involvement. But, the evaluators cautioned, '[We] must recognize that Push/Excel has a route to impact that bypasses all of the usual trappings of a social action program: Impact can occur simply because someone has listened to the Reverend Jackson's speeches and has been motivated to act' (Murray and others, 1979, p. 8).

According to the program rationale developed by AIR, national and local efforts would lead to parent, school, and community involvement, which in turn would lead to student involvement. This would engender motivation, responsibility, atmosphere, and opportunity, which would lead to 'investments': the expenditure of time, effort, or money for a future return. AIR hoped to document results for each sequence of steps to an outcome. These 'knowledge modules' would be fed back to program developers for possible modification. Only when cause and effect had been established would resources be devoted to the next link.

Most outcome measures would be collected through interviews. Other information, such as attendance, could be gleaned from school records and from Push/Excel activities. Program personnel would be interviewed three times a year, and students and parents would be interviewed twice. At six sites, 100 tenth graders from each of twelve schools would be interviewed. Detailed two-year case histories would be constructed for half. Not until page fifty-nine of the *Evaluation Design* was the stakeholder notion discussed: Stakeholders would be assembled to review the evaluation design (Murray and others, 1979).

Reactions of National and Federal Stakeholders

A draft evaluation design was ready by the annual Push/Excel national convention in Cleveland in May 1979, when Saundra Murray reviewed it with Excel personnel. But, it was not distributed until two days later.

Because the oral briefing took place first, AIR expected no specific suggestions for revision (American Institute for Research, 1979). However, program staff raised two questions: What had AIR meant by being 'helpful' to the program, and how did it propose to ensure 'the independence of the evaluation from external influence'? In response to the second issue, Norman Gold noted that program staff would pass on the 'fairness and validity' of the evaluation and that AIR's independence would be protected.

A month later, Charles Warfield, Excel's director of operations and management, met with the AIR team to express two concerns: First, because Excel was a social action program whose impact could occur independent of local activities, AIR should study movement effects. Second, the evaluation should take political issues into account, since they affected implementation.

In mid July, NIE met with AIR and three members of a technical advisory group hired by NIE: Peter H. Rossi, director of the Social and Demographic Research Institute at the University of Massachusetts; Paul M. Wortman, codirector of the methodology and evaluation research group in the psychology department at Northwestern University; and Edgar Epps of the University of Chicago. The agenda centered on NIE's concern that AIR was concentrating on only two sites in a supposedly national evaluation, that the student sample was too small, and that 'hard measures of achievement are more important... than AIR's design acknowledged' (American Institutes for Research, 1979, p. 15).

Two days of discussion ensued. The first two points were rather easily settled. As for the third, some people at NIE felt strongly that achievement test scores were the ultimate program test in an impact study. According to one of them, 'I don't care what the social scientists say; the farmer in Iowa wants to know if kids read any better as a result of all the money that's being spent' (personal interview with Norman Gold, October 1980). After lengthy discussion among AIR, NIE, and the three-member technical advisory group, the orthodox view prevailed. AIR reports: '[It was agreed that] achievement data would be collected ... *and be fully analyzed as part of the evaluation*' (American Institute for Research, 1979, p. 15).

More fundamental concerns about the evaluation were expressed in writing by members of the technical advisory group. From Paul Wortman: 'In all candor, my first reaction is that it is impossible and unfeasible to evaluate [Push/Excel] at this time. Quite simply, there is no program yet evident ... This has left the evaluation staff groping about looking for something to grab on to. They have finally come up with four goals, which may be best described as states of mind, [and these] still must be translated into concrete program activity. The formative evaluation presents more problems .... [Local sites will modify] [Push/Excel] programs to their specific needs. The question facing the evaluators then is: Can all the elements of the program be evaluated? Despite the brave vigor of the AIR staff, it seems unlikely that they will have the energy or the funds to chase the program all over the map. If this is indeed the case, then a procedure for targeting program components for focused formative evaluation will be necessary.'

Peter Rossi's reaction was in a similar vein: 'Apparently, the [program] goals will be reached by a combination of social movement experiences ... and specific activities. The latter are yet to emerge ... [Thus], most of the effort ... should be spent on implementation monitoring.' Acknowledging Jackson's charisma, Rossi added, 'Charisma is a necessary but embarrassing concept in sociology. [Push/Excel] is amateurish and lacking in technical expertise; whether the charisma ... can overcome the hit-and-miss improvization is a serious question.'

The evaluation design received qualified approval from national program staff, federal staff, and the technical advisory group. The NIE liked AIR's emphasis on implementation documentation because of its interest in evaluation utility. NIE staff agreed that Excel was fragmented by most program standards but concluded that it was still in its early stages, although it had been operating for more than two years. It needed technical feedback to develop further, and AIR's approach seemed particularly well suited for this purpose. At the same time, NIE staff agreed to include achievement testing, which suggested that Excel was a program whose impact could be measured. Although the technical advisory group was more cautious about the nature of Excel, its members recommended implementation monitoring and various evaluation design improvements.

Unable to characterize Excel, the experts were thus at a loss to suggest how to evaluate something that was not already a program and that might never become one. This may help to explain why Warfield's radical suggestion that Jackson's movement might have effects independent of local activity fell on deaf ears. Those concerned knew how to evaluate programs and how to do so for formative purposes. They therefore agreed that Excel was a program manqué and that AIR's incremental approach would provide the information and guidance that it needed. Moreover, the evaluation would give NIE another chance to test its stakeholder approach while overseeing the federal investment in Push/Excel, while AIR would get its first real chance to test Schwarz's incremental model — with possible stunning effects for professional careers. The central and problematic assumption was that, in fostering Excel's development, the evaluation would help to turn a movement into a program.

Implementation

During 1980, 1981, and 1982, AIR collected data and issued four evaluation reports, all with the same theme: Push/Excel had no program. As each report was released, news media across the country publicized the findings and suggested that Jackson had taken the federal funds without producing anything. Push/Excel was already having severe organizational difficulties in the national office, and the negative publicity handicapped it still further. AIR and NIE both insisted that the evaluation was to help the program, but the actual effect was to portray it as a failure.

Technical Report No. 1, March 1980

AIR's first technical report (Murray and others, 1980a) presented one-page overviews of program structure and funding at the six sites and described involvement activities by school for parents, community, school staff, and students. Involvement activities were extensive and differed a good deal across sites, but AIR did not think that they constituted proper development: 'There should be activities for each element: parents, communities, schools, and the students. By that standard, none of the sites is fully implemented at the school level .... A coherent program of total involvement has not evolved' (p. 40).

This theme was to continue throughout the evaluation: Push/Excel had no coordinated activities tied to measurable outcomes, no step-by-step description, no how-to-do-it manual. The activities listed were one-time events, and there was little follow-up or guidance from the national office. There were no directives, no internal evaluation, no central monitoring. By AIR's definition, Push/Excel had no coherent program.

The press was particularly interested in AIR's first technical report. For months before its publication, Spencer Rich, staff writer for the *Washington Post,* had tried to obtain a copy. When it finally became available, Rich wrote a front-page story that appeared in the 22 April, 1980 issue under the headline 'US Study Faults Jesse Jackson's School Program': 'Despite $2 million in federal appropriations voted so far and an additional $1 million likely, the Reverend Jesse Jackson has failed to convert the high ideals and inspirational message of his Push/Excel movement into a systematic, workable, public school program, according to a new government report.' The story portrayed a charismatic leader who was long on rhetoric to promote his program but short on skills to make it work. In making its judgment that there was no 'coherent program,' AIR was applying specific technical criteria; in the context of the *Post* article, however, the AIR judgment implied incompetence or even malfeasance.

A major confrontation between the Excel national stakeholders and Saundra Murray occurred that summer at the annual convention of Operation Push and Push/Excel. There, she gave a talk on the uses of evaluation — a talk that AIR vice-president Vic Rouse called 'cruel.'

Murray told us (personal interview, October 1980): 'A lot of flashy activities do not amount to a product. A lot of the people running these programs are amateurs ... For the first three years, ... they got away with hell. The funders didn't shoot straight about what was going on, and they didn't force the [program] people to shape up. They need honest feedback, and I plan to give it to them.'

Murray was to participate in a plenary session to discuss the Bakke case. After her talk and only hours before the plenary session, the topic was switched to 'Push/Excel: Success or Failure.' The plenary session had been billed as a major conference event, and the hall was filled. According to Murray, 'all the people who mattered were there.' Criticism of the evaluation was severe. Afterwards, Murray was told that the panel was 'a setup' designed to embarrass AIR and discredit the evaluation. She did not think that the ploy had succeeded, but it left her in considerable conflict about the evaluation work.

Technical Report No. 2, September 1980

The second technical report, somewhat more positive than the first, noted (Murray and others, 1980b, p. 37) that the 'sites are building systematically' and that there was now an *implementation* guide for them. The evaluators applauded these facts: 'For each outcome, there is at least one site with an activity that could plausibly lead to an expected end' (p. 48). Less positively, they noted that most of the activities were still in the initial phase, not in the second phase. The sites were urged to get on track with the new program model. The evaluation could document implementation progress, but it could do no more until the sites produced 'inputs' whose outcomes AIR could assess. Push/Excel still did not constitute a program; activities were too unsettled, and development was spasmodic.

This time NIE anticipated problems with the press. When the *Washington Post* reporter telephoned NIE to ask for a copy of the report, there was some reluctant talk at HEW of forcing the *Post* to invoke the Freedom of Information Act, but Jesse Jackson requested that the report be released. Three days later, Spencer Rich published an article in the *Post* under the headline 'US Study Faults Jackson's Push School Plan.' On the day the report was released, Norman Gold recommended to the deputy director of NIE that fewer sites should be evaluated and that further data collection should be deferred until the program was evaluable. This recommendation disappeared without a trace, presumably because repercussions would be too explosive.

Unofficially, AIR was forced to abandon its incremental approach. According to Saundra Murray (personal interview, January 1982): 'That decision wasn't ever really made, about how much adjusting we should do, and in fact we did make some adjustment. We didn't continue that incremental thing ... We just couldn't do it. I think [NIE] would have been willing to go along with ... a tailored design for all the sites. We couldn't do the same thing across sites. That was always one of the problems.' Thus, use of Schwarz's incremental evaluation model foundered on Excel's lack of program structure and systematic implementation. AIR had assumed that Excel could be translated into objectives and activities so uniform across sites that common instrumentation could be used for formative and, ultimately, for summative purposes. But, by the time a blueprint for Excel had been developed, the three sites of the original six that remained had developed their own Excel models.

When this became evident, AIR was already well launched on data collection, with tools, blessed by FIDAC, that represented considerable financial and intellectual investment. Short of scuttling the project — or shelving it temporarily, which had been proposed to NIE — AIR had little choice but to continue.

Technical Report No. 3, April 1981

The third technical report (Murray and others, 1980c) reported on local and national Push/Excel activities during the preceding six months. AIR still saw Push/Excel activities as lacking much effort or commitment, as uncoordinated, and as having no explicit involvement strategy. In the baseline data, AIR noted that some scores were quite high and questioned Push/Excel's assumption that students had low expectations.

The above-mentioned first three published assessments by AIR of Push/Excel faulted the program for not being something that it had not set out to be. It blamed this on Jackson and the national office staff, who described themselves as 'catalysts' and as 'sowers of seeds' to be nurtured locally. AIR acknowledged that Excel's inspirational message might have some impact independent of the usual trappings of social action programs, but AIR focused on the trappings. Unable to find a program with an overarching organization, a fundamental rationality, structure, plans, and procedures, AIR announced the Excel was a failure. At best, Excel was in the early stages of program development, a process that it had vigorously to pursue in order to succeed.

The press magnified these gloomy findings into major news stories, thereby shaping public opinion about the program. While the media had been a strong force in rallying support for Jackson's movement, they now announced that Excel had not lived up to its promise. The theme of no program was converted into program failure and implications of irresponsibility on the part of Push/Excel staff. Saundra Murray, the chief evaluator, said that the media misunderstood the reports, but to no avail. And, although Push/Excel countered with its own media message, it was never able to escape this judgment.

The Final Report

The *Final Report* (Murray and others, 1982) was published in a sociopolit-ical climate very different from that in which the study had been launched thirty-six months earlier. The Democratic administration, which had supported Push/Excel so vigorously, was replaced in 1980 by a Re-publican administration, which tried to cut Excel's HEW funds prema-turely and opened investigations into Excel's alleged misuse of Depart-ment of Labor funding. Local districts, as well as national and local Excel staff, saw the handwriting on the wall; federal support would end in February 1982, and survival would depend on local political and fund-raising skill. In fall 1981, Jackson informed the national office staff that henceforth they would have to generate their own funds; by spring, only a few of the local programs remained.

The final report received scant attention when it appeared. Part of the reason was that resources were exhausted at AIR and NIE, so that very few copies were printed or circulated. One copy went to the Push/Excel national office, one copy each to Chattanooga and Denver, ten copies to NIE, and one to the Department of Education. The report was never distributed to the more than 300 stakeholders. Local stakeholders, including Excel program staff, received copies at the discretion and expense of their districts.

In the *Final Report* (Murray and others, 1982), AIR assessed Push/Excel's effect on students in Chattanooga and Denver. The in-dicators of impact were ranged under the labels *atmosphere and opportun-ity, motivation, responsibility, investment,* and *achievement,* drawn from the program rationale. The evaluators concluded that the average student's contact with Push/Excel activities was so low that these 'did not add up to an interaction that could be expected to produce measurable effects' (Murray and others, 1982, p. 72).

The attrition between the spring 1980 sample of students and the spring 1981 sample was tremendous. AIR attributed this primarily to parents' refusal to have their children interviewed. In Chattanooga, two of the three schools were not represented by the sample. In Denver and Chattanooga, AIR obtained only 276 interviews from 1,615 attempts — about 17 per cent, a very poor response; at one school in Chattanooga, the response rate for questionnaires was 9 per cent.

The most questionable aspect of the impact evaluation, however, was the data analysis. The evaluators used the spring 1980 data as predata and the spring 1981 data as postdata; differences between the data were regarded as the effects of the Push/Excel programs. But, the programs had already operated for most of the academic year before the predata were collected. The mass rallies led by Jackson, the pledging of students, and all the kickoff activities had already taken place. In their own reports, the evaluators listed dozens of Push/Excel activities that preceded data collection. (See Murray and others, 1980a, pp. 27, 30, 35 and 37; and Murray and others, 1982, Appendixes A and B.) While many of these events may have been insignificant, many others may have improved students' attitudes. The indicators used to assess impact made sense within the rationale that AIR had developed, but AIR's analyses of these indicators did not.

In the evaluators' views, since there was no Push/Excel program, the collection of data at midpoint made no difference. This response prejudges the question of whether the program had impact. The evaluators seem to have been so captured by their convictions that they allowed no other possibilities. In their summary of the entire evaluation, they conclude: 'Push/Excel as a program never constituted a "cause" large enough to plausibly produce an "effect"' (Murray and others, 1982, p. 182). There is no question that Push/Excel had many difficulties during its years of federal involvement. Unfortunately, the impact evaluation was so flawed that it did not document whether there were any program effects.

Conclusions

Despite Califano's good intentions, it seems obvious that Jesse Jackson and Push/Excel would have been better off without federal funding. The *Washington Star's* editorial ('A Shove Comes to Push,' 1978) warning against government intrusion proved to be painfully prescient as Jackson's movement became tangled in a web of bureaucratic and political decisions and met unflagging belief in the images and categories of social science.

Even without intervention, Push/Excel might not have succeeded in the long run. Except perhaps in Chattanooga, its programs generally failed to penetrate the school bureaucracy to any substantial degree. Schools, particularly large city schools, have effective ways of insulating themselves from community interference, and Push/Excel was no exception. Every local program was caught in a losing struggle for control with the schools, and at many sites the struggle became a raging political issue. Things happened differently in Chattanooga because the city had a single, stable power structure and Push/Excel was consonant with Southern culture. The program was able to harness church and community authority to carry its message, and such authority is still strong in many Southern towns. And, once the program was firmly endorsed locally, the schools complied and even seemed to welcome Excel programs. Yet, even here, school staff argued that the achievements claimed by Excel might as easily have been due to their own efforts to improve students' performance.

The government's involvement in Push/Excel need not have exacerbated these internal problems. Although an evaluation was required, greater care at several federal levels might have prevented much of the ensuing damage. HEW's top-down decision to fund Push/Excel despite reservations at lower levels in the agency ensured a poor start if not eventual failure. Joseph Califano and Mary Berry asked NIE to undertake the evaluation, but top NIE administrators were unenthusiastic and uninterested in Excel, and the study was delegated to those lower down. In addition, the Department of Education failed to provide the technical assistance promised to Jackson, and funding delays persisted throughout the life of the HEW grant. These problems were not inevitable; they were largely the result of inattention and inadequate supervision. But, they sapped Push/Excel's program morale and set the stage for consistently negative reports on its implementation.

These difficulties were compounded by the interactions of government, press, and evaluators, which were critical in shaping public perception of Push/Excel. The government commissioned the evaluation knowing that it would be politically sensitive, but the design and reporting schedule made it a magnet for press attention. And, since the program had been initiated by a controversial and highly visible public figure, the uncomplimentary evaluation reports were tailor-made for the press. It responded characteristically, exaggerating and oversimplifying the findings. The government reacted by trying (unsuccessfully) to withhold the next report (and subsequently canceling one), but it would not permit AIR to revise the study, fearing charges of political intrusion and more adverse publicity. Determined to avoid political tangles the government paid the price of proceeding with an unsuitable evaluation. In fact, press and public opinion may have been influenced more by Jackson's Middle East trip than by the evaluation, but to local programs seeking funding as federal support ran out, the evaluation was of primary importance. Hence, program staff in Chattanooga believed that the evaluation had killed the program.

Negative publicity aside, the form of the evaluation was not appropriate to its object. The federal intention had been to reform the evaluation process by drawing stakeholders into it, but scant attention was given to stakeholders' needs. Instead, the evaluation was conceived in terms of the contractor's incremental notion, with the usual tools of social science. But, to be amenable to that approach, Push/Excel would have had to be a highly structured, coherent program, which it was not. The evaluators' eagerness to use this approach may have prevented them from forming a more accurate picture of Push/Excel and from evaluating it accordingly.

As it was, the evaluators' conception of program differed considerably from the Push/Excel concept of diverse, loosely coordinated, locally determined activities. For the evaluators, who were technically trained as social scientists and who were experienced as program evaluators, a social program had an explicit, coordinated structure and measurable objectives not apparent in the Push/Excel operation. Lacking both, Excel was either flawed or seriously underdeveloped. Operating from this angle of vision, the evaluators tried to help Push/Excel to become a program. This program was to be based on their program rationale, which had evolved from their reading of Jackson's speeches and national office promotion material. But, because each local program had developed its own distinctive characteristics and because each local program had different goals and priorities, the evaluators' plans met resistance and claims that their concept was not consonant with local goals. Even when the goals were identical, the evaluation findings on progress toward attaining them did not help local staff to make improvements. The evaluation helped to identify shortcomings but not to rectify them. Although AIR offered suggestions, they were more in the nature of guesses or hunches than prescriptions based on experience. The evaluators, after all, were not program developers.

Another consequence of the evaluators' definition of program was that the student impact study was very poorly designed. The Push/Excel operation started in Denver and Chattanooga in fall 1979, but the predata on students, parents, and teachers were not collected until the following spring, well into the second half of the program's first operating year. A great number of Push/Excel activities had occurred much earlier. Data were collected months after the initial rallies, Jackson's speeches, and student-parent pledging. Perhaps these events did not affect student and parent attitudes — an assumption apparently made by the evaluators. But, it is entirely plausible, even likely, that this public fanfare did have significant effects that were reflected in the preindicators of program impact, which were quite high. Since the evaluators believed that that there was no program, they ignored this possibility in comparing their pre and postdata. Combined with the extraordinarily low response rate from the student sample, this makes their conclusions about the program's impact highly suspect. Given the study design, even a program that met their specifications would have found it difficult to show student impact.

One lesson of the Push/Excel evaluation is that charisma and social science do not mix well. This point may be painfully obvious, but the lack of fit is greater than commonly believed. First, there is the bureaucratically imposed proposal writing, funding, scheduling, and reporting, which hampered the Push/Excel program from the outset. For example, a report was to appear every six months; yet even with great effort, the Push/Excel organization, hardly a smooth-running machine at best, could not remedy the deficiencies noted in one report before the next report was upon them. And, once having invested in a particular evaluation approach, the federal bureaucracy could not change course without admitting to miscalculation, which it was unwilling to do.

Perhaps even more damaging was the imposition of technical rationality on Push/Excel. AIR's incremental approach to evaluation was based upon activity-outcome, cause-effect, means-ends reasoning. Each outcome, effect, and end should be measurable. Once discovered and documented, these 'knowledge modules' could be transplanted from

Denver to Chattanooga or anywhere else. The notion of social technology underlying this approach was better suited to the manufacture of television sets or computers than to the development of a movement. And, it was not at all the way in which Jesse Jackson and his people thought of their role; their sense of mission could not be neatly systematized in this way.

A final point concerning the mismatch between charisma and social science involves the different notions of social change held by the two. The technocratic view of evaluators and bureaucrats suggests that change is — or should be — produced by incremental changes, which are facilitated by immediate feedback for correction, modification, reinforcement, and retrial. An extreme version of this view is stimulus-response theory, in which all change is trial and error modified by reinforcement. By contrast, the charismatic view of social change embodied in Push/Excel is that of change by conversion. Through a single event, one can commit oneself to a different course of behavior that will change one's life, and perhaps society, forever. This event can occur at a mass rally of the sort held by Push/Excel, which resembled the religious meeting at which a convert steps forward to pledge himself or herself to a life for Christ. Without such mass conversions, there would be no Christianity, no Russian revolution, no civil rights movement.

One of the embarrassments of social science is that it presumes to understand and explain social events in the way that the natural sciences explain physical events. In truth, social science is far more parochial than it claims; its concepts and viewpoints are narrow. In many instances of applied social research, a charismatic event has been viewed through a technocratic lens, and the results benefit no one. In the re-examination now under way of what social science is and what it can do, perhaps social scientists will keep this in mind.

Acknowledgements

This case study was supported in part by the National Institute of Education (NIE), but the study presents the views of the authors, for which the NIE is not responsible. This case reflects AIR's account of Push/Excel's early history. The authors are indebted to Maria Sachs and Stephen Raudenbush for proof that the story can be told at a fraction of its original length.

References

'A Shove Comes to Push', *Washington Star*, 8 January 1978.
American Institute for Research (1979) *Assessment of Stakeholders' Needs*, Washington, DC, American Institute for Research, July.

BRONSCOMBE, A. (1979) '"Sermon" by Jackson opens Push/Excel', *Denver Post*, 12 September.

CALIFANO, J.A. Jr. (1981) *Governing America*, New York, Simon and Schuster.

MURRAY, C. and others (1978) *Proposal to NIE*, Washington, DC, American Institute for Research, October.

MURRAY, C. and others (1979) *Evaluation Design*, Washington DC, American Institute for Research, July.

MURRAY, C. and others (1980a) *The Evolution of a Program*, Technical Report No. 1, March, Washington, DC, American Institute for Research.

MURRAY, C. and others (1980b) *Implementation Guide*, Technical Report No. 2, September, Washington, DC, American Institute for Research.

MURRAY, C. and others (1980c) *The Program, the School, and the Students*, Technical Report No. 3, April, Washington DC, American Institute for Research.

MURRAY, C. and others (1982) *Final Report*, Washington, DC, American Institute for Research, March.

National Institute of Education (1978) 'Evaluation of project Excel', FRP-NIE-R-78-0026, Washington, DC, National Institute of Education, 5 September.

Push for Excellence (nd) *Push for Excellence: The Developing Process of Implementation*, Chicago, Push for Excellence Inc.

RICH, S. (1980a) 'US study faults Jesse Jackson's school program', *Washington Post*, 22 April, p. 1.

RICH, S. (1980b) 'US study faults Jackson's Push school plan', *Washington Post*, 5 October, p. 5.

ROSSI, P.H. (1979) Personal communication to Norman Gold, National Institute of Education, 23 July.

SCHWARZ, P.A. (1980) 'Program devaluation: can the experiment reform?' in LOVE LAND, E (Ed.) *Measuring the Hard-to-Measure*, New Directions for Program Evaluation, No. 6, San Francisco, Jossey-Bass.

WORTMAN, P.M. (nd) Memo to Norman Gold, National Institute of Education 'Comments on the AIR draft evaluation design of the Push for Excellence program'.

Toward the Future of Stakeholder Approaches in Evaluation

Carol H. Weiss,
Harvard Graduate
School of Education

Given the very special situation in the Cities-in-Schools (CIS) and Push/Excel (Excel) programs, the stakeholder approach to evaluation has hardly received a fair test. In fact, some people argue that it was implemented with such a minimalist interpretation of its scope that its potential benefits inevitably went unrealized. So many other difficulties beset the evaluation — primarily as a result of the attempt to apply formal quantitative assessment to shifting (and, in the case of Push/Excel, inchoate) programs — that the stakeholder approach did not have much chance to affect the course of events. On the positive side, perhaps it engaged the attention of actors who might otherwise have ignored it entirely, particularly people at the local sites. On the negative side, it probably diverted a fair amount of evaluators' time from strictly evaluative functions. But the turbulent nature of the programs and the mismatch with standard outcome evaluation procedures were probably the critical elements in both cases.

The inability to attain the expected benefits in these cases may have been the result of extraneous factors (incomplete implementation of the stakeholder concept, inappropriate evaluation strategies, fluidity of programs, and so on). Is it possible that stakeholder-oriented evaluation would work in other, more congenial settings? Or are there basic flaws in its underlying assumptions that inevitably limit its capacity to deliver what it promises?

Conversations with colleagues on this project — Robert Stake, Ernest House, Eleanor Farrar, Anthony Bryk, and David Cohen — have encouraged me to see the intentions of stakeholder-oriented evaluation as fundamentally threefold: first, to increase the use of evaluation results in decision making; second, to empower a wider assortment of groups to determine evaluation priorities; and third, to shift governance of evaluation from sole control by NIE to shared control, thereby reducing NIE's responsibility. Partisans of the approach may have had other expectations, such as providing greater legitimacy for evaluations in general, for NIE's evaluations in particular, and for NIE as the evaluation agency. But the three aims listed here appear to represent the nub of the stakeholder argument.

I interpret the term *stakeholders* to mean either the members of groups that are palpably affected by the program and who therefore will conceivably be affected by evaluative conclusions about the program or the members of groups that make decisions about the future of the program, such as decisions to continue or discontinue funding or to alter modes of program operation. These are quite distinct categories of people, although there is some overlap. I include them both as stakeholders, because that is my reading of NIE's intent.

Perhaps it would be useful to maintain and elaborate the distinctions. Analytically, stakeholders can be divided into four categories, depending on the kinds of information that are likely to be valuable to them (Figure 1).

Assumptions

With these prefatory remarks, let us try to disentangle the expectations inherent in the stakeholder notion. As developed at NIE, the approach makes a series of assumptions about the involvement of stakeholders in the evaluation process.

1. Stakeholder groups can be identified in advance of the start of evaluation.
    (a) The sponsor, the evaluator, or both can figure out whose interests are at stake.
    (b) The sponsor and/or the evaluator will select a representative set of groups to participate in the evaluation.
2. Stakeholders want an evaluation of the program with which they are associated.
    (a) They want to have evaluative information available about the program.
    (b) They are willing to participate in the evaluation process.
3. They want specific kinds of information to help them make plans and choices.
    (a) They can identify their information needs in advance.
    (b) The kinds of information they want are the kinds that evaluation studies produce.
    (c) The kinds of information that different stakeholder groups want can be reconciled with one another.
4. Evaluators will respond to stakeholder requests for information.
    (a) They have the requisite time, resources, interest, and commitment to the process.

    (b) They have the interpersonal skills to solicit realistic information requests from groups, even from those for whom evaluative information is not salient.

    (c) They have the political skills to negotiate accommodations in priorities among competing stakeholder groups.

    (d) They have the technical proficiency to design and conduct a study that produces valid data to satisfy diverse information requests.

    (e) They will report back promptly, responsively, using forms of presentation that are appropriate to various audiences.

5 Stakeholders who have participated in an evaluation will develop pride of ownership in the conclusions.

    (a) They will accept them as true.

    (b) They will take them seriously.

6 Stakeholders who have decisions to make (mainly federal policy makers, school-district administrators, outside philanthropists, and program directors) will use evaluation results as a basis for decision making.

    (a) Information in and of itself is a decisive component in decision making.

    (b) The stakeholder approach makes a wide assortment of information available.

    (c) The information is relevant to the situation that exists when decisions are being made. If circumstances have changed since the study was planned, the information collected remains appropriate to changed conditions and sufficient to answer current questions.

    (d) Stakeholders who do not have program-wide decisions to make (principals, teachers, students, parents, community organizations) know that at least their criteria and concerns were taken into account in the evaluation and that information of importance to them was considered in decision making. They will therefore, perhaps, accord the decisions greater legitimacy.

7 (A revisionist assumption) Even if evaluation results do not sway specific decisions, they will enrich discussions about future programming and illuminate undertakings of program actors.

Analyzing the Assumptions

A number of these assumptions look perfectly reasonable — at least under reasonable conditions. Of course, if we push any one of them too far, we

Figure 1.   Categories of Stakeholders

Category	Types of Decisions to be Made	Types of Evaluation Results That Are Relevant
Policy maker (the Congress, the secretary of the Department of Education, local philanthropists, school board members)	Shall we continue to fund the program? Is it achieving the desired results? Shall we expand it or reduce it?	Outcomes of program for participants, causally linked to the intervention.
Program manager (national program staff, program directors in cities, program designers)	How can we improve the program? Should we recruit different staff, serve different kids, use different techniques?	Differential outcomes for different types of students, by types of service received, by type of staff, and so forth. Qualitative information on what is going well and poorly during implementation.
Practitioner	What shall I do to help Joan and Pedro? How can I get Elsie to try harder?	Usually not much, except perhaps for some overview of how the whole project is going. Practitioner's own knowledge and experience are more relevant and salient.
Clients and citizen organizations (students, parents, community groups)	Shall we keep attending the program (assuming we have the choice) and supporting it?	Not much. Outcomes of the program for previous participants should be relevant, but often the evaluation has not gone on long enough to provide such data. In any event, clients' own experiences are more salient.

can find situations under which it will break down. Let us see which assumptions seem generally viable and which depend on images of orderliness and rationality that rarely prevail in the program world.

The first assumption, that stakeholder groups can be identified in advance, looks feasible. The CIS and Excel evaluations seemed to have encountered little difficulty on this score. We could ask whether the groups that AIR identified and assembled were truly representative of all important stakeholder interests. For example, how actively represented were teacher, student, and parent concerns? How long did representatives of these groups continue to participate? There is also a perennial question about the representation of potential users of program information. Groups that are not actively associated with the program now can have a real stake in the information that evaluators will produce, such as school districts that would want to adopt the program if it proved successful. No procedural mechanisms appear capable of identifying, let alone representing, the entire set of potential users of evaluation results or the questions that they will raise. But in the normal course of events, adequate representation of stakeholders seems feasible.

The second assumption, that people want evaluations and that they will participate in them, probably holds good for some groups some of the time. Given a choice, however, it seems likely that many groups would forgo evaluation entirely. These groups have learned over past decades that evaluations are more likely to be the bearers of bad tidings than good. When results are circulated, they often pose a threat to the program rather than support and guidance. Information is a minor benefit compared to the questions and criticisms that it can provoke. Only when federal beneficence is contingent upon evaluation do many groups accept it as inevitable and come on board.

The third assumption, that people can specify their information needs in advance, has the same 'maybe/maybe not' quality, although it lists toward 'maybe not.' As cognitive psychologists have demonstrated and as decision theorists have learned to their regret, people do not always know in advance what they will need to know in order to make a decision (Slovic, Fischhoff, and Lichtenstein, 1977; Slovic and Lichtenstein, 1971). Unless situations are routine and repetitive, the human cognitive apparatus is not always up to the task of foreseeing which information will be critical. Moreover, the assumption that evaluation requests can be defined early in the study relies on a vision of an orderly and predictable environment. It assumes that organizations can schedule their choices and calculate their information needs with confidence that things will go as planned. In fact, neither the political environment nor the organizational milieu is stable. Program decision making is beset by unexpected occurrences from inside and outside the organization. Long experience with the development of management information systems and with managers' inability to specify their needs correctly is instructive here (AAACMIS, 1974; Ackoff, 1967; Grudnitski, 1981).

The capacity to define information needs far ahead of time is limited by individual, organizational, and political constraints. Many people will make an effort to tell what they need to know, but much of what they say is a learned, stereotypical response. People in schools, for example, almost always say that they want to know test scores. Whether or not test scores are relevant to the program or useful in decision making, people have been indoctrinated to the notion that achievement is the central mission of schools and that neglect of test scores would therefore be unprofessional conduct.

Not uncommonly, people do not actually want to know anything. If you define these people as stakeholders and ask them to describe their information needs, they will generally give an answer. In today's information society, saying that they do not need data is tantamount to branding themselves as illiterates. So, lacking any clear need, they can take the opportunity to ask for information that they know will cast the program in a good light, such as data on the number of hours of service provided or on parents' satisfaction with the program. Another strategy is to ask for something, without regard for exactly what it is, because information is a scarce resource and therefore worth fighting for. If stakeholders are competitive groups in a competitive environment and if information is the counter in the game, then information is what groups play for — almost regardless of its content.

Thus, the assumption that stakeholders are reliable sources of information priorities is not a very good one if specification is required far in advance, as in most pre-post designs. It is much more plausible if the evaluation is a qualitative, illuminative investigation of program operation. In most qualitative evaluations, evaluators have ample opportunity to shift direction and to follow new questions as they emerge. They are not locked in to a set of measures that can prove to be irrelevant when the 'post' time rolls around.

The fourth assumption, that evaluators will respond to stakeholder requests for information, needs to confront the fact that it takes a variety of skills and considerable dedication to be responsive. Under some circumstances, responsiveness might prove to be impossible. If stakeholders press demands for a great deal of information or if their demands are incompatible, the evaluators may be battered in the effort to satisfy all parties. Later or sooner, they may give up the effort to be responsive and assume unilateral control. The CIS and Excel evaluations demonstrate that being a responsive evaluator is an arduous task. Both evaluations also suggest, I think, that the task can be managed under favorable conditions.

The fifth assumption, that stakeholders who participate in a stakeholder-oriented evaluation develop a sense of ownership in the study, is open to considerable question. There is a good deal of experience with this particular strategy, since involvement of potential users in evaluations has long been a staple prescription (Eidell and Kitchel, 1968; Flanagan, 1961; Havelock, 1969; Joly, 1967). Many efforts have been made in the past to conduct evaluations in this style. Some have been successful in giving prospective users a stake in the findings, particularly when users are few in number and when there is relative agreement on most significant issues (Conway and others, 1976; Rothman, 1980). But even under these favorable conditions, many well-intentioned researchers have been unable to secure acceptance of the validity and usability of study results (Berg and others, 1978; Lazarsfeld and others, 1967; Rich, 1977).

It is when disagreement is rife that user involvement is expected to be especially important for winning the allegiance of discordant groups. If each group believes that it has had a say in designing the evaluation, and if each group believes that it has gotten the information that it wants, then presumably all groups will have common commitment to consideration of findings. But when disagreement is rife, the evaluators are caught in a bind. They have to resolve discrepant requests and conflicting advice, and it seems inevitable that they will disappoint one or another of the parties. Groups whose requests are disregarded will lose interest in the study and its findings; on occasion they may become overtly hostile.

Another concomitant of involving users in the planning and conduct of studies is that it gives users an inside look at how the study is done. A close view can engender disenchantment as well as commitment. Insiders know the weaknesses as well as the strengths of the research — the shortcuts, unreliabilities, missing data, contradictions in sources. Some develop considerable skepticism about the worth of the final report (Berg and others, 1978), and they have less allegiance to it than outsiders who were not privy to the compromises in data and method that were made.

Some stakeholders are likely to be happy with evaluation results and to feel a sense of pride, but their happiness can derive more from the support that the evaluation gives to their stake than from the part they played in the study. Groups that find their positions threatened by evaluation results can revoke their support if they see their crucial interests endangered, even if they did participate in the evaluation process.

In sum, experience suggests that participation in a study can increase support for the study, but only if certain conditions are met: One's advice has to be given due attention, one has to see the study as being appropriately and reputably conducted, and results must not threaten significant personal or organizational interests.

The sixth assumption, that people who take part in an evaluation will use the results as a basis for decisions, is constrained by the fact, noted earlier, that not all stakeholders have decisions to make — at least, decisions of the kind for which evaluation has much evidence to offer. But for those people who do make decisions, is it reasonable to expect that those who participate in the evaluation process will be more likely to base their decisions on evaluation results? On the positive side, it is safe to say that these people know more about the study than they would have if they had not taken part. In that sense, there is a better chance that they will absorb the information and use it. Not to use it takes a conscious decision. They can hardly remain oblivious.

The stakeholder approach also assumes that the results are relevant. Several factors already noted limit the generality of this assumption — for example, the common inability to predict information requests accurately, calls from different groups for inconsistent evaluation designs and information items, the possibility that one group's advice will be disregarded or overruled. Still, the notion that participation will improve relevance remains plausible. For example, when local groups take an active part in the evaluation, the study is much more likely to address the concerns that exercise them.

The rub comes at the point of applying results to a decision. The usual expectation is that decision makers will use evaluation results to choose between alternative A and alternative B. Unless A and B are minor matters, evaluation evidence is not likely to be the decisive element. Decision making about issues of import, such as whether to continue funding a project, is basically a political process. In making such a decision, people have to consider a wide range of factors — who supports the program and how much clout the supporters have, what alternatives there are that can serve clients if the program is terminated, whether alternative programs are likely to be more successful, whose jobs are in jeopardy if the program ends, how clients will feel and how they will fare without the program, what community reaction will be, what costs will be involved, and so on. Evaluation results provide evidence on only a small number of relevant issues. Thus, even if the evaluation is conducted with the broadly inclusive sweep anticipated for the stakeholder strategy, it never addresses all the issues that have to be considered. Nor does it settle the issues that it does address in a conclusive way. Therefore, evaluative evidence about program operations and outcomes goes into the hopper together with an array of other concerns, information, allegiances, ideological proclivities, and interests. Decision makers have to reach an accommodation that satisfies many people on many dimensions. While evidence of program effectiveness is important, it probably never will be the sole determinant — or even the most powerful determinant — of political choice.

If NIE or anyone else expects the stakeholder approach or any other reform in evaluation practice to make research information the major basis for decision making, they are destined for disappointment. Too many other factors must be considered, too many other conditions must be accommodated, for information to play such a stellar role (Lindbloom, 1968; March, 1982; Weiss, 1973).

The seventh, revisionist, assumption is that the stakeholder orientation can increase the use of evaluation for purposes of enlightenment (Caplan, 1977; Pelz, 1978; Weiss, 1977). Responsive, relevant, well-circulated evaluation results can provide information that keeps people well informed about a range of programmatic issues. Evaluation results can provide evidence about what works well and what does not, about the kinds of problems that arise, and about the reactions of staff and students. They can challenge prevailing assumptions about a program and the theories of behavior that underlie it. They can suggest reinterpretations of past experience and help to make retrospective sense about what the program has been doing. Without dictating specific decisions, they can permeate people's understanding of program potentials and limits. Over time, such understanding can have significant influence on the aims that people set, the alternatives that they consider, and the directions that they take in future programming (Weiss, 1980). Use in this sense seems to be a realistic goal for stakeholder-oriented evaluation.

In its early presentations, the stakeholder approach resembled many of the educational and social programs of the past generation. Its high-minded intentions were yoked to untested practices, and it promised too much. Its advocates expected a relatively minor reform to accomplish grand objectives. As evaluation of social programs have demonstrated time and again, changing behavior is not a simple task. More temperate expectations for stakeholder evaluation would put the idea in perspective.

A Tentative Balance Sheet

Our review of assumptions inherent in the stakeholder approach suggests that none of them is open-and-shut. There is leakage at every step along the way. The chances that any one step will be fully realized are less than one — often considerably less — and the cumulative chances of achieving expected benefits decline multiplicatively. Prospects for significant gains in evaluation utility do not seem especially bright unless collateral changes are made in the substance of evaluations and in the structure of the programs. Simply pasting the stakeholder process alongside current practice involves acceptance of many existing constraints.

Over all, the stakeholder approach seems to hold modest promise for achieving modest aims. It can improve the fairness of the evaluation process. It can probably make marginal improvements in the range of information collected and in the responsiveness of data to participant requests. It can counter the federal tilt of many previous evaluations and give more say to local groups. It can democratize access to evaluative information. If stakeholder groups take an active role, it can make them more knowledgeable about evaluation results and equalize whatever power knowledge provides. When many groups know the results of a study, the likelihood increases that the information will be absorbed and drawn upon in later deliberations.

However, the stakeholder approach will not ensure that appropriate information is collected. Stakeholders will not usually be able to specify the kinds of data that matter to them with much accuracy, and even when they can, program conditions and outside events will probably change before the data become available. By the time that stakeholders confront decisions, the evaluation will be able to provide evidence on only a fraction of the questions at current issue.

The stakeholder approach will probably not visibly increase the use of results in the making of specific decisions. For example, a philanthropist who sees a report of no success for a program that he supports may find that his participation in the evaluation process makes little difference to his decision about whether to continue support. He still has to think about the implications of his position on many dimensions. Nor will stakeholder evaluation bring harmony to contentious program arenas. It can elicit diverse views, but it cannot contain them. In fact, if differences are wide, the opportunity to stake out turf during the evaluation process can make people more aware of the conflicts that exist. Even if they can work out accommodations over evaluation priorities, accommodations over program issues will be no easier to arrange.

If the stakeholder approach has potential for improving evaluations, it also makes new demands. It increases the burden on evaluators, and it demands time and attention from groups associated with the program as policy makers, managers, planners, practitioners, and clients. Some of these groups — including, perhaps, evaluators — will find the experience illuminating and worthwhile, but it is likely that others will not. The approach will trade some people's heightened satisfaction of others' annoyance or frustration.

Questions for the Future

Some conditions of stakeholder participation can profit from further thinking. I nominate three issues for consideration: the definition of participation, the competing claims of a single study and several independent studies, and the mode of study design.

Participation

Which groups should be involved? Does it make sense to limit participation to groups that face decisions and care about information, such as funders, managers, and planners? Other groups have interests in the program that deserve consideration, but it is the program and its future that concern them, not information about the program. They want a voice in what happens, not in what data shall be collected. Evaluation planning is not necessarily the best forum to engage them. Participation with a more specifically programmatic focus could effectively attract their participation and profit from their perspectives.

The inclusion of multiple groups in the evaluation process is an attempt to redress the inequitable distribution of influence and authority. But evaluation planning is a strange avenue for such redress. The stakeholder approach could be construed as a way of deflecting stakeholder attention from decisions that more directly affect them. Indeed, it almost appears to be a substitute for involving stakeholders in the making of policy. A Machiavellian mind could conceive of the stakeholder approach as a way to mire stakeholder groups (particularly powerless groups) in the details of criteria definition and item wording, while the powers that be go blithely on with decisions as usual.

Of course, no such demonic scheme is at work. The reasons for involving stakeholders in evaluation is that NIE has control of evaluation, whereas it has little voice in program decision making. NIE is taking advantage of the opportunity to broaden representation in the one domain over which it has authority. The intent is high-minded. But the actuality is that participation takes place at some remove from the center circle of program decision making. Whether a reduction of inequities in the evaluation process results in net gains for all stakeholders is a matter that deserves attention.

One Study or Several

In the first two stakeholder-oriented evaluations a single contract was let. Placing the responsibility for an entire evaluation on a single team of evaluators lays a heavy burden on its members, particularly when they have to cope with all the extra demands that the stakeholder approach entails. It makes them the arbiter of the only game in town. It gives them the responsibility for adjudicating among rival interests (including their own interests) and for deciding the direction that the study shall follow.

There is nothing intrinsic to the stakeholder approach that requires the funding of a single study to accommodate the interests of all parties to the program. The single blockbuster study appears to be an unthinking carryover from previous evaluation practice. For some time, it was assumed that one large study was better than several smaller studies, because the large study would have larger sample sizes, use more consistent measures, and therefore produce more precise estimates of effect. The stakeholder approach was tacked on to existing contracting practice.

As recent critics have noted, the blockbuster study suffers from severe limitations. It provides only one set of readings on one set of indicators, and the results depend on the particular operationalization employed. Cronbach and his associates (1980) have advocated 'a fleet of studies' using different methods and different measures, done by different teams of investigators. If separate studies converge on results, the pattern of evidence is much more convincing than the results of a single study.

For the stakeholder approach, does it make more sense to fund several small studies? Each study could examine the program from the perspective of one set of stakeholders. The separate studies would be able to use the criteria of the separate groups and follow the issues that mattered to them. From the series of separate studies, a multidimensional view of reality would be more likely to emerge. The various pieces of evidence would illuminate the varied viewpoints.

It remains to be seen whether multiple studies would enrich understanding of the program, or whether they would create more conflict as each group pressed the evidence that supported its own case. It seems possible that multiple studies could do both. But they might enable interested groups of stakeholders to focus on issues that they defined as important without overloading traffic in a single study.

A sequence of studies could also explore diverse facets of programming. As new issues arose, new studies could pursue them. Since no one can foresee all contingencies in advance, sequential evaluations would be more likely to keep pace with shifting conditions. They could follow the variety of issues that a program encounters over the course of its life. Of course, there might be problems in maintaining continuity. A government funding agency like NIE would have to maintain its commitment to the exploration of a program's implementation and outcomes over a period of time. If early results proved disappointing, would the agency be under pressure to divert evaluation resources elsewhere, or could it continue to support study of the program, its problems, and its achievements?

Qualitative or Quantitative

What kinds of evaluation designs are compatible with the stakeholder approach? Does it fit best with qualitative, illuminative, ethnographic, process-oriented evaluation? The two case studies included in this volume seem to suggest so. Is that an idiosyncrasy of the particular programs, or is it inherent in the stakeholder idea? Can the approach ever be linked successfully with quantitative before-and-after evaluation? Could it work if the program under study had stabilized and settled down?

Are there ways that a stakeholder-oriented evaluation can serve both formative and summative purposes? Past experience suggests that studies that attempt the dual task tend either to scant one function or the other, or else they are swamped by floods of data, much of which usually goes unanalyzed. Can modifications in design overcome these problems, or should formative-qualitative and summative-quantitative studies routinely be separate undertakings?

As an attempt to cope with recognized shortcomings in evaluation practice, stakeholder-oriented evaluation retains modest promise. It has been tested with two particularly difficult programs, where its achievements were limited. Clearly, it cannot right all past wrongs or attain the nirvana that its advocates hoped for. At this point, I think it deserves further testing. As experience accumulates and if we conscientiously learn from that experience, we should be able to specify the conditions under which the stakeholder approach is likely to prove useful and to probe the realistic limits of its potential.

References

ACKOFF, R.L. (1967) 'Management misinformation systems', *Management Science*, B147–B156.

American Accounting Association Committee on Management Information Systems (AAACMIS) (1974) 'Current accounting issues in the area of management information systems', *The Accounting Review*, supplement.

BERG, M.R. and others (1978) *Factors Affecting Utilization of Technology Assessment Studies in Policy Making*, Ann Arbor, Mich, Center for Research on Utilization of Scientific Knowledge.

CAPLAN, N. (1977) 'A minimal set of conditions necessary for the utilization of social science knowledge in policy formulation at the national level' in WEISS, C. (Ed.) *Using Social Research in Public Policy Making*, Lexington, Mass, Lexington Books.

CONWAY, R. and others (1976) 'Promoting knowledge utilization through clinically oriented research: the benchmark program', *Policy Studies Journal*, 4, 3, pp. 264–9.

CRONBACH, L.J. and Associates (1980) *Toward Reform of Program Evaluation*, San Francisco, Jossey-Bass.

EIDELL, T.L. and KITCHELL, J.M. (Eds) (1968) (Eds) *Knowledge Production and Utilization in Educational Administration*, Eugene, Ore, Center for the Advanced Study of Educational Administration, University of Oregon.

FLANAGAN, J.C. (1961) 'Case studies on the utilization of behavioural science research' in *Case Studies in Bringing Behavioural Science into Use, Studies, in the Utilization of Behavioural Science*, Vol 1, Stanford, Calif., Institute for Communication Research.

GRUDNITSKI, G. (1981) 'A methodology for a listening information relevant to decision makers' in Ross, C.A. (Ed.) *Proceedings of the Second International Conference on Information Systems*, Cambridge, Mass, Second Internatonal Conference on Information Systems.

HAVELOCK, R.G. (1969) *Planning for Innovation Through Dissemination and Utilization of Knowledge*, Ann Arbor, Mich, Center for Research on Utilization of Scientific Knowledge.

JOLY, J.M. (1967) 'Research and innovation: two solitudes?', *Canadian Education and Research Digest*, 2, pp. 184–94.

LAZARSFIELD, P.F., SEWELL, W.H. and WILENSKY, H.L. (Eds) (1967) *The Uses of Sociology*, New York, Basic Books.

LINDBLOOM, C.E. (1986) *The Policy-Making Process*, Englewood Cliffs, NJ, Prentice Hall.

MARCH, J.G. (1982) 'Theories of choice and making decisions', *Society*, 20, 1, pp. 29–39.

PELZ, D.C. (1978) 'Some expanded perspectives on use of social science in public policy' in YINGER, J.M. and CUTLER, S.J. (Eds) *Major Social Issues*, New York, Free Press.

RICH, R.F. (1977) 'Uses of social science information by federal bureaucrats: Knowledge for action versus knowledge for understanding' in WEISS, C. (Ed.) *Using Social Research in Public Policy Making*, Lexington, Mass, Lexington Books.

ROTHMAN, J. (1980) *Social R & D: Research and Development in the Human Services*, Englewood Cliffs, NJ, Prentice Hall.

SLOVIC, P., FISCHHOFF, B. and LICHTENSTEIN, S. (1977) 'Behavioural decision theory', *Annual Review of Psychology*, 28, pp. 1–39.

SLOVIC, P. and LICHTENSTEIN, S. (1971) 'Comparison of bayesian and regression approaches to the study of information procession in judgement', *Organizational Behaviour and Human Performance*, 6, pp. 649–744.

WEISS, C.H. (1973) 'Where politics and evaluation meet', *Evaluation*, 1, 3, pp. 37–45.

WEISS, C.H. (Ed.) (1977) *Using Social Research in Public Policy Making*, Lexington, Mass, Lexington Books.

WEISS, C.H. with BUCUVALAS, M.J. (1980) *Social Science Research and Decision Making*, New York, Columbia University Press.

6
Teachers and Evaluation:
Learning to Labor

Introduction

One of the strongest current movements in the United States is the effort to evaluate teachers in various ways, presumably as a step towards improving the educational system. A number of teacher evaluation schemes have been proposed and most of them involve the testing of teachers directly or the testing of students and holding the teachers accountable for the student gains. Hence, various states and municipalities have employed tests to measure what prospective teachers know before they enter teacher training and tests to assess what they know after teacher training, often with a minimum test score the teacher must attain before being allowed to teach. Teacher evaluation is also linked to merit pay plans to differentially reward teachers for performance and to dismissal procedures for incompetent teachers. Needless to say, there is a lack of public confidence in teachers and the schools, a lack of confidence inspired and expressed by the highest political figures and the mass media.

In the chapter reprinted here Darling-Hammond and her colleagues have reviewed the current research literature on teacher evaluation and sorted it out according to fundamental perspective one holds about the nature of teaching itself. In their view one may conceive of teaching as labor, as craft, as profession, or as art. Teaching as labor conceives of teaching as a set of standard operating procedures rationally planned and programmed by administrators. Evaluation then consists of a direct inspection of the teacher's work by the supervisor to see if the work is being properly performed. This includes monitoring lesson plans, classroom performance, and performance results.

Teaching as craft means seeing teaching as requiring a repertoire of specialized techniques and rules for the application of those techniques. Evaluation does not require direct inspection but rather ascertaining whether the teachers possess the requisite skills. Teaching as profession requires not only specialized techniques and skills but also theoretical knowledge as well. Standards for performance are developed by peers. Finally, teaching as art requires personalized and creative problem-solving unique to each individual. Evaluation could involve self-assessment and perhaps critical assessment of one's work by others.

Most current reform activity in American education is based upon the notion of teaching as labor, or occasionally teaching as craft. Control is placed outside the teachers themselves, vested in tests and assessment procedures operated by administrators. The pressures are strong and we are likely to see intense conflicts over the issue of teacher evaluation in the next several years.

Teacher Evaluation in the Organizational Context: A Review of the Literature

Linda Darling-Hammond, Arthur E. Wise, and Sara R. Pease
The Rand Corporation

ABSTRACT. This article presents a conceptual framework for examining the design and implementation of teacher evaluation processes in school organizations. Research on teaching, organizational behavior, and policy implementation suggests that different educational and organizational theories underlie various teacher evaluation models. The conceptions of teaching work and of change processes reflected in teacher evaluation methods must be made explicit if educational goals, organizational needs, and evaluation purposes are to be consonant and well served.

Over the last decade teacher evaluation has assumed increasing importance. The demand for accountability in education has shifted from broad issues of finance and program management to specific concerns about the quality of classroom teaching and teachers. These concerns have led to a resurgence of interest in evaluating teachers and to the development of new systems for teacher evaluation.

As in other areas of education, the theory and practice of teacher evaluation diverge. In this chapter, we explore the reasons for this divergence by reviewing and integrating the findings of two distinct streams of research. The first is research on teaching effectiveness, its measurement, and development of models for teacher evaluation. The second area consists of organizational and implementation research. This literature treats organizational control and authority; management of internal and external demands for organizational maintenance and accountability; processes of decision-making, communication, and implementation in school organizations; and problems of achieving consensus among various actors in the organizational context.

There is a growing realization that the development of successful teacher evaluation systems requires attention to both these sets of issues (Knapp, 1982; Natriello, Hoag, Deal and Dornbusch, 1977). We suggest in this chapter that knowledge and practice can be advanced by making explicit the educational and organizational theories underlying different conceptions of teaching work and of teacher evaluation. We examine how external demands for accountability are at odds with internal organizational needs for stability and trust; how loosely coupled organizations like school systems handle these competing demands; and how teacher evaluation may affect organizational operations and teaching work. We synthesize educational and organizational theories about the nature and control of teaching work to examine the implications of teacher evaluation processes for organizational sorting functions, instructional improvement efforts, and maintenance of productive working relationships. Finally, we argue that successful teacher evaluation requires consistent and shared views of the teaching-learning process and of the organizational context in which teacher evaluation takes place.

This chapter develops a conceptual framework for understanding teacher evaluation in the organizational context. We do not present a detailed synopsis of all the literature that pertains to teacher evaluation techniques, methods, instruments, and processes. Some excellent compilations of this literature have been published recently (for example, Lewis, 1982; Millman, 1981a; Peterson and Kauchak, 1982; Stiggins and Bridgeford, 1982), and we refer readers to them for information on teacher evaluation practices. Instead we show how diverse areas of research on teaching and schools can be brought to bear on the question of designing and implementing successful teacher evaluation systems. We attempt to broaden the conceptual base for teacher evaluation research by adopting an organizational process framework for evaluating teacher evaluation.

Policy Context

The public has come to believe that the key to educational improvement lies in upgrading the quality of teachers rather than in changing school structure or curriculum. Improving teacher quality was the most frequent response to the 1979 Gallup poll's question on what public schools could do to earn an 'A' grade, beating by large margins such reforms as emphasizing the basics, improving school management, lowering class size, or updating the curriculum (Gallup, 1979). In response to these perceptions, states and local school districts have initiated a wide range of policy changes affecting the certification, evaluation, and tenure of both prospective and currently employed teachers (Gudridge, 1980; Vlaanderen, 1980).

Several states have adopted teacher competency tests, such as the National Teacher Examinations, for teacher certification; others are considering licensure, which would include statewide teacher examinations prior to certification along with the establishment of a professional standards and practices board (Lewis, 1979; McNeil, 1981; Southern

Regional Education Board, 1979; Vlaanderen, 1980). Some, like Oklahoma, are adopting comprehensive programs that include higher admission standards for colleges of education, competency tests for certification and recertification, evaluation of performance, and continuing teacher education (Kleine and Wisniewski, 1981). Most states have legislated requirements for teacher performance evaluation (Beckham, 1981), and some of the more recent statutes specify which testing instruments or evaluation procedures are acceptable.

Not surprisingly, teacher evaluation processes increasingly have become the subject of collective bargaining agreements. A Rand Corporation study found that between 1970 and 1975, the percentage of contracts examined that contained teacher evaluation provisions increased from 42 to 65 (McDonnell and Pascal, 1979). Contracts often specify methods of information gathering, frequency of observations and evaluation, processes for communicating evaluation criteria and results, opportunities for teacher response and remediation in the case of negative evaluations, and due process procedures (Strike and Bull, 1981).

Mitchell and Kerchner (1983) argue that because of collective bargaining, teacher evaluation has become an increasingly rule-based process, linked less to judgments of competence than to evidence about whether teachers have adhered to clearly specified minimum work standards. 'The objectification of evaluation standards,' they state, 'has had the effect of discoupling the relationship between teaching performance and the behaviors on which teachers are held subject to discipline and discharge' (pp. 19–20). Their observation reflects the difficulty in using teacher evaluation results for both formative (improvement-oriented) and summative (personnel decisionmaking) purposes.

Although a survey by the American Association of School Administrators (Lewis, 1982) found that few school districts were using evaluation results as the basis for layoff decisions, there is growing literature on the legal requirements for using evaluation results for dismissal (Beckham, 1981; Peterson and Kauchak, 1982; Strike and Bull, 1981). Courts have generally required that a school system strictly apply an established formal dismissal procedure with due process safeguards. Further, the school authorities must determine minimum acceptable teaching standards in advance, inform the staff of these standards, and, finally, document for the court how a teacher's performance violates these standards (Beckham, 1981). Beckham recommends that to withstand judicial scrutiny an evaluation policy must include: (a) a predetermined standard of teacher knowledge, competencies, and skills; (b) an evaluation system capable of detecting and preventing teacher incompetencies; and (c) a system for informing teachers of the required standards and according them an opportunity to correct teaching deficiencies.

Each of these criteria poses some problems for the design and implementation of a teacher evaluation system. There are particular difficulties in integrating the requirements of an evaluation policy geared toward job status decisions with those of a policy aimed at improving teaching. The most obvious problem is that developing a predetermined standard of teacher knowledge, competencies, or skills poses nontrivial controversies about the content and specificity of the standards. Furthermore, where standardized tests or performance assessments are used to make job status decisions, courts generally require that they have a demonstrable, direct relationship to effective job performance, that is, they must have proven validity. We explore the difficulties of such a demonstration in a later section of this chapter.

Detecting teacher incompetencies involves the development and careful application of reliable, generalizable measures of teaching knowledge or behavior. The state-of-the-art of measurement for teacher evaluation may not be adequate. *Preventing* incompetency implies the development of either a fool-proof approach to teacher training or a teacher-proof approach to instruction; we leave that to utopians. *Correcting* deficiencies seems a more approachable objective; however, this is the point at which research on teaching effectiveness leaves off and where summative and formative evaluation approaches collide.

It is one thing to define and measure teacher competence in a standardized fashion; it is quite another to change teacher performance. Research on individual and organizational behavior suggests that first-order solutions are unlikely to effect change, and, further, that successful approaches involve processes that may be inconsistent with those used to derive summative evaluation judgments. That is, the context-free generalization necessary for implementing a uniform evaluation system may counteract the context-specific processes needed to effect change in individual or organizational behaviors.

Policy Conflicts and Tensions

Many observers have pointed out that public pressures for summative evaluation affecting teacher job status — selection and promotion, dismissal, and reduction in force decisions — may make formative evaluation much more difficult (Knapp, 1982; Peterson and Kauchak, 1982; Feldvebel, 1980). Increasing the prescriptiveness and specificity of evaluation procedures, particularly the need for extensive documentation of all negative findings, generates anxiety among teachers and inhibits the principal's role as instructional leader or staff developer (Munnelly, 1979). Summative evaluation criteria must be more narrowly defined if they are to be applied uniformly, thus limiting their use for formative purposes. Furthermore, constraints on classroom behavior intended to weed out incompetent teachers may prevent good teachers from exercising their talents fully (Darling-Hammond and Wise, 1981). Knapp (1982) concludes

The net result of these pressures for more careful summative judgments of teachers is to put administrators under particular strain. Though 'better' performance evaluation may appear to make the issues explicit and decisions objective, it may also generate as much heat as light, particularly where the various constituents to the design of evaluation do not agree. The pressure to improve teaching performance may foster more elaborate evaluation systems, but with summative thrusts getting in the way of formative efforts. (p. 10)

This tension between evaluation goals is in part a reflection of the differences among evaluation constituencies. These stakeholders have divergent views on the primary purpose of teacher evaluation and, hence, of what constitutes a successful evaluation system. Knapp's (1982) articulation of various stakeholders' perspectives is useful. Teachers have a stake in maintaining their jobs, their self-respect, and their sense of efficacy. They want a teacher evaluation system that encourages self-improvement, appreciates the complexity of their work, and protects their rights. Principals have a stake in maintaining stability in their organizations, allowing them to respond to parental and bureaucratic concerns for accountability while keeping staff morale intact. They want an evaluation system that is objective, not overly time-consuming, and feasible in the organizational context. Parents and public officials have a stake in the 'bottom line' — the effects of teaching on student outcomes. They want an evaluation system that relates teacher performance to teacher effectiveness, and that guarantees appropriate treatment of children in classrooms.

These differing views make choices about teacher evaluation processes difficult. They also affect implementation, because even after a policy is adopted, its terms and emphases are renegotiated at every level in the implementation system (Berman and McLaughlin, 1973–1978; Elmore, 1979). This renegotiation may not occur in a formal way, but practices at the school district, school, and classroom levels will be a function of cross pressures that may alter the formal process in important ways.

All these factors argue for understanding teacher evaluation plans in the context of organizational behaviors and processes. In the succeeding sections of this chapter we examine the educational and organizational concepts underlying different views of teacher evaluation, we describe the teacher evaluation processes and models currently in use, and we discuss implementation of teacher evaluation in the organizational context.

Educational and Organizational Concepts

The newly emerging policy thrusts in the area of teacher evaluation reflect diverse perspectives on the role of teachers in the educational enterprise, the nature of teaching work, the organization and operations of schools, and even the purposes of schooling. Different theories of learning and of the operation of educational organizations are embodied in different models for teacher evaluation, and any attempt to identify the components of 'successful' evaluation procedures must explicitly recognize their underlying assumptions.

Perhaps most problematic is the definition of teacher knowledge, skills, and competencies in a fashion useful for a *policy system*. Policies rely on generalizations that can be uniformly applied and administered according to rules. The further away policy development occurs from the implementation level, the more uniformly applicable generalizations and prescriptions for practice must be. They must rely on context-free assumptions linking theory to results.

As Darling-Hammond and Wise (1981) point out, many current policies are 'rationalistic' — they seek to rationalize the actions of teachers by specifying curricular objectives, by prescribing instructional methods for attaining the objectives, and by evaluating the extent to which the objectives are attained. They assume a direct link between teacher behavior and student learning, as well as a close match between external goals and classroom activities.

Yet, other theories of education are possible. Various theories differ significantly in their explanations of the nature of teaching and learning, the processes of schooling, and the ways in which educational organizations operate. We cannot here develop a full exposition of the range of educational theories; a few examples must suffice. At the heart of the rationalistic theory stand the policymaker and the administrator who rationalize the operations of the school through deliberate decision-making and procedure-setting. In the spontaneous theory, the teacher is the central figure. 'The rest of the vast educational enterprise chiefly serves the purpose of permitting the teacher to give spontaneous expression to the educated man he finds within himself — and in so doing, to foster useful intellectual growth in his pupils' (Stephens, 1976, pp. 140–1). The individual child is the focal point for the humanistic theory, and the schooling system revolves around his needs and interests in providing an environment to facilitate his development.

The distinguishing elements of these and other theories of education include differences concerning how goals for education are set (and by whom), what the goals in fact are, how they are to be transmitted among and operationalized by the various actors in the schooling process. The actors are variously viewed as active or passive, deliberate and rational or spontaneous and instinctive. The components of the educational system are variously perceived as autonomous or interdependent, tightly or loosely couple, vertically or horizontally integrated, consensual or individualistic in their perceptions of values, norms, and objectives. De facto power may be perceived as centralized at various hierarchical levels or relatively decentralized.

Depending on which theory of education one subscribes to and which model of the educational process seems most aptly to describe what one observes, the appropriate roles and tasks of policymakers, school administrators, teachers, and students will appear quite different. Certainly if policymakers and practitioners view the reality of schooling in vastly different ways, policies and practices will be dissonant, and intended policy outcomes will be unlikely to occur. Furthermore, whether a particular evaluation approach meets its proximate and ultimate goals will depend on the specific organizational context in which it is used, as well as the implementation processes that take place at each level of the operating system — that is, how the procedures are carried out within the classroom, school district, and, where relevant, the state.

Much of the existing literature on teacher evaluation examines instruments and techniques for evaluation without reference to their theoretical underpinnings or to the organizational contexts in which they are to be used. Without such reference, potential users cannot easily assess whether a particular approach will be well suited to their aims, conceptions of education, or organizational characteristics. Nor can they evaluate the implementation processes necessary to successfully use a given instrument or technique. Our approach seeks to place existing teacher evaluation procedures within a conceptual framework that explicitly links the various types of procedures to the models of learning and school organization which they reflect and to the organizational contexts in which they can best be used.

Conceptions of Teaching Work

Evaluation involves collecting and using information to judge the worth of something. It is an activity that teachers themselves engage in, though often informally (Shavelson, 1976). As we will argue, different conceptions of teaching work imply different ways by which information is collected and judgments of worth are made. Implied in these different conceptions of teaching work are different notions of educational goals, teacher planning activities, interactive teaching behavior, and self or other evaluation activities. The evaluation of teaching — collecting and using information to judge worth — will vary depending on one's conception of teaching work.

One way to illuminate a complex subject is through comparison. Teachers have been compared to craftspersons and professionals (Broudy, 1956; Lortie, 1975), bureaucrats (Wise, 1979), managers (Berliner, 1982), laborers (Mitchell and Kerchner, 1983), and artists (Eisner, 1978). Here we will use four ways of looking at teaching work: labor, craft, profession, or art (Mitchell and Kerchner, 1983). These ways of viewing teaching work provide a theoretical framework for analyzing teacher evaluation, because they sharply reveal the assumptions that lie behind different techniques for evaluating teachers. In incorporating this typology into our conceptual framework, we describe 'pure' conceptions of teaching work, recognizing in reality that pure prototypes do not exist. Nevertheless, as a heuristic device, we will see that every technique implicitly rests on assumptions about teaching work and the relation of the teacher to the administrative structure of the school.

Every teacher evaluation system must embody a definition of the teaching task and a mechanism to evaluate the teacher. Under the conception of teaching as *labor*, teaching activities are 'rationally planned, programmatically organized, and routinized in the form of standard operating procedures' by administrators (Mitchell and Kerchner, 1983, p. 35). The teacher is responsible for implementing the instructional program in the prescribed manner and for adhering to the specified routines and procedures. The evaluation system involves direct inspection of the teachers' work — monitoring lesson plans, classroom performance, and performance results; the school administrator is seen as the teachers' *supervisor*. This view of teaching work assumes that effective practices can be determined and specified in concrete ways, and that adherence to these practices will be sufficient to produce the desired results.

Under the conception of teaching as *craft*, teaching is seen as requiring a repertoire of specialized techniques. Knowledge of these techniques also includes knowledge of generalized rules for their application. In this conception, once the teaching assignment has been made, the teacher is expected to carry it out without detailed instructions or close supervision. Evaluation is indirect and involves ascertaining that the teacher has the requisite skills. The school administrator is seen as a *manager* whose job is to hold teachers to general performance standards. This view of teaching work assumes that general rules for applying specific techniques can be developed, and that proper use of the rules combined with knowledge of the techniques will produce the desired outcomes.

Under the conception of teaching as *profession*, teaching is seen as not only requiring a repertoire of specialized techniques but also as requiring the exercise of judgment about when those techniques should be applied (Shavelson, 1976; Shavelson and Stern, 1981). To exercise sound professional judgment, the teacher is expected to master a body of theoretical knowledge as well as a range of techniques. Broudy (1956) makes the distinction between craft and profession in this way: 'We ask the professional to diagnose difficulties, appraise solutions, and to choose among them. We ask him to take total responsibility for both strategy and tactics . . . From the craftsman, by contrast, we expect a standard diagnosis, correct performance of procedures, and nothing else' (p. 182). Standards for evaluating professionals are developed by peers, and evaluation focuses on the degree to which teachers are competent at professional problem-solving; the school administrator is seen as an *administrator* whose task it is to ensure that teachers have the resources necessary to carry out their work. This view of teaching work assumes that standards of professional knowledge and practice can be developed and assessed, and that their enforcement will ensure competent teaching.

Under the conception of teaching as *art*, teaching techniques and their application may be novel, unconventional, or unpredictable. This is not to say that techniques or standards of practice are ignored, but that their form and use are personalized rather than standardized. As Gage (1978) explains, the teaching art involves 'a process that calls for intuition, creativity, improvisation, and expressiveness — a process that leaves room for departures from what is implied by rules, formulas, and algorithms' (p. 15). He argues that teaching *uses* science but cannot itself *be* a science because the teaching environment is not predictable. In this view, the teacher must draw upon not only a body of professional knowledge and skill, but also a set of personal resources that are uniquely defined and expressed by the personality of the teacher and his or her individual and collective interactions with students.

Because teaching viewed as an art encompasses elements of personal insight (as well as theoretically grounded professional insight), the teacher as artist is expected to exercise considerable autonomy in the performance of his or her work. Evaluation involves both self-assessment and critical assessment by others. Such evaluation would entail 'the study of holistic qualities rather than analytically derived quantities, the use of "inside" rather than externally objective points of view' (Gage, 1978, p. 15). It would rely on high-inference rather than low-inference variables, on observation of patterns of events rather than counts of specific, discrete behaviors (Eisner, 1978; Gage, 1978). In this view, the school administrator is seen as a *leader* whose work it is to encourage the teacher's efforts. The view assumes that teaching patterns (i.e., holistic qualities that pervade a teacher's approach) can be recognized and assessed by using both internal and external referents of validity.

Obviously, these four conceptions of teaching work are ideal types that will not be found in pure form in the real world. In fact, various components of teachers' work embody different ideal types (for example, motivating students, performing hall duty, presenting factual information, establishing and maintaining classroom relationships). Nonetheless, the conceptions of teaching work signal different definitions of success in a teacher evaluation system.

The disparity in implicit views cannot be ignored. McNeil and Popham (1973), for example, make a strong case for evaluating teachers by their contribution to the performance of students rather than by the use of teacher process criteria. Millman also argues that 'criteria and techniques for the fair use of student achievement in both the formative and summative roles of teacher evaluation can be devised' (Millman, 1981b). This view presupposes that students' learning as measured by their test performance is a direct function of teaching ability; it seeks to measure the worth of teachers by reference to the *product* or output of their work, thus it envisions teaching work as labor and the student as raw material. However, only 11 per cent of teachers believe that scores on standardized achievement tests are valid measures of teacher effectiveness (NEA, 1979). Implicit in the view of most teachers is the notion that other factors or dynamics of the teaching and learning process are at least as important in determining learning outcomes as the ability of the teacher. These other factors are a combination of those school conditions not under the teacher's control and the unpredictable elements inherent in human interaction that give rise to a conception of teaching work as profession or art.

Conceptions of Teaching in Teaching Research

Although the various conceptions of teaching work are distinct along several dimensions, they can be usefully viewed on a continuum that incorporates increasing ambiguity or complexity in the performance of teaching tasks as one moves from labor at one extreme to art at the other. The role of the teaching environment in determining teacher behavior also increases in importance as one moves along the continuum. The more variable or unpredictable one views the teaching environment as being, the more one is impelled toward a conception of teaching as a profession or art. Gage (1978) uses the distinction between teaching as science or art to describe how the elements of predictability and environmental control differentiate the two. A science of teaching is unattainable, he observes, because it 'implies that good teaching will some day be attainable by closely following rigorous laws that yield high predictability and control' (p. 17). Using science to achieve practical ends, he argues, requires artistry — the use of judgment, intuition, and insight in handling the unpredicted, knowledge of when to apply which laws and generalizations and when not to, the ability to make clinical assessments of how multiple variables affect the solution to a problem.

Research on teaching parallels these conceptions of teaching work in the degree to which predictability and environmental controls are assumed or even considered in the design and goals of the research. Some efforts to link specific teacher characteristics or teaching behaviors to student outcomes have sought context-free generalizations about what leads to or constitutes effective teaching. Although this line of research strongly suggests that what teachers do in the classroom does affect students, claims that discrete sets of behaviors consistently lead to increased student performance (for example, Medley, 1979; Rosenshine and Furst, 1971; Stallings, 1977) have been countered by inconsistent and often contradictory findings that undermine faith in the outcomes of simple process-product research (for example, Doyle, 1978; Dunkin and Biddle, 1974; Shavelson and Dempsey-Atwood, 1976). The most extensive process-product study of teacher effectiveness, the Beginning Teacher Evaluation Study, conducted for California's Commission for Teacher Preparation and Licensing, contributed to the discomforts associated with linking teacher behaviors to student learning. After that monumental effort, '[t]he researchers ... concluded that linking precise and specific teacher behavior to precise and specific learning of pupils (the original goal of the inquiry) is not possible at this time ... These findings suggest that the legal requirement for a license probably cannot be well stated in precise behavioral terms' (Bush, 1979, p. 15; see also McDonald and Elias, 1976).

At best, the teaching performances advanced as having consistently positive effects on student achievement are relatively broad constructs rather than discrete, specific actions of teachers. The Beginning Teacher Evaluation Study found little evidence that single teaching performance variables can be identified as essential for effective teaching, but found that differences in *patterns* of teaching performances contribute to learning. However, even these broader patterns are not uniformly applicable to all grade levels, subject areas, and teaching situations (McDonald and Elias, 1976). Similarly, the often cited variables identified by Rosenshine and Furst (1971) as consistently related to student achievement are best characterized as high-inference variables; that is, they do not readily break down into easily tabulated, discrete teaching actions. As Centra and Potter (1980) note, these variables — clarity, variability, enthusiasm, task-oriented or business-like behaviors, student opportunity to learn criterion material, use of student ideas and general indirectness, criticism, use of structuring comments, types of questions, probing, and instructional difficulty level — are undoubtedly important, 'but few of them could be usefully considered "basic teaching tasks"' (Centra and Potter, 1980, p. 282).

Furthermore, subsequent research on these variables, variously measured to be sure, has produced inconsistent findings that seem due to more than mere measurement differences. Rosenshine, for example, now finds that 'indirectness,' one of the effective teaching variables identified in his earlier review, is to be discouraged in classroom teaching as it detracts from student achievement (Rosenshine, 1979). The status of research on 'direct instruction' and its companion concept, 'academic learning time' bears special mention because of the eagerness with which it has been accepted as state-of-the-art knowledge by many researchers and practitioners concerned not only with the development of teacher evaluation systems but also with educational quality improvement more generally.

This line of research also highlights many of the dilemmas that confront those who must define criteria for effective teaching.

Direct instruction is generally proposed as the vehicle for increasing the amount of time students spend actively engaged in appropriate learning activities (see, for example, Berliner, 1977; Bruner, 1976; Rosenshine, 1977). Berliner (1977) defines academic learning time as 'on task or engaged time by students, interacting with materials or participating in activities of intermediate level difficulty that are academically focused' (p. 3). Following Wiley and Harnischfeger's (1974) not surprising finding that the amount of time students spend in school is related to their achievement, others have found that time spent on academic subjects is related to achievement in those subject areas (Fisher *et al.*, 1978; Stallings, 1977), although the strength and consistency of the relationship has been found to vary considerably (Gage, 1978, p. 75). Further refinements in the concept have sought to measure active student engagement in learning activities as related to achievement, but with equivocal success. McDonald and Elias (1976) reported mixed results for academic learning time as a predictor of achievement, and, surprisingly, found time allocated for instruction a generally better predictor than student engagement rate. McDonald (1976) also reported that more class-as-a-whole teaching, while leading to greater pupil attentiveness (i.e., engagement), had negative effects on achievement.

Assuming, nonetheless, that engaged time may positively affect achievement, what are the teaching behaviors that increase engaged time? The most common answer is direct instruction,[1] defined by Rosenshine (1979) as referring to,

> academically focused, teacher-directed classrooms using sequenced and structured materials. It refers to teaching activities where goals are clear to students, time allocated for instruction is sufficient and continuous, coverage of content is extensive, the performance of students is monitored, questions are at a low cognitive level ..., and feedback to students is immediate and academically oriented. In direct instruction, the teacher controls instructional goals, chooses materials appropriate for the student's ability, and paces the instructional episode. The goal is to move the students through a sequenced set of materials or tasks. Such materials are common across classrooms and have a relatively strong congruence with the tasks on achievement tests. (p. 38)[2]

In terms of teaching behaviors, Rosenshine's explication reveals that direct instruction is characterized by frequency of single-answer questions and drill, large-group instruction, and opportunities for 'controlled practice.' Teaching behaviors that are discouraged include the use of higher order, divergent, or open-ended questions, exploration of student's ideas, student-initiated discourse or choice of activities, conversation about personal experience or about subject matter tangential to the immediate objectives of the lesson at hand. In this sense, direct instruction contrasts with 'teacher indirectness' (Flanders, 1970) and with approaches generally ascribed to 'open' rather than 'traditional' instruction (Horwitz, 1979; Peterson, 1979).

Elements of the direct instructional approach have been investigated in several studies. Support for various elements of the approach in terms of effects on student achievement on standardized tests has been reported by Soar (1972); Evertson and Brophy (1973); Wright (1975); Bell, Sipursky, and Switzer (1976); Ward and Barcher (1975), especially for high-ability children; and Röhr (1976), especially for low-ability children. On the other hand, teacher *indirectness* has been found to have positive effects on student achievement in a review of research by Glass *et al.* (1977), especially for secondary school students, and in many of the studies reviewed by Dunkin and Biddle (1974) and Horwitz (1979). Thus, while we may concede that teachers ought to do something to engage their students in active learning, we are still left with serious questions about what that something is.

Some researchers have addressed the problem of inconsistent research findings by reference to interaction effects and attention to other situation-specific variables. This line of research finds that effective teaching behaviors vary for students of different socioeconomic, mental, and psychological characteristics (for example, Brophy and Evertson, 1974, 1977; Cronbach and Snow, 1977; Peterson, 1976) and for different grade levels and subject areas (Gage, 1978; McDonald and Elias, 1976). Nonetheless, given the particular teaching context, many infer from this research that appropriate behaviors can be specified to increase student achievement.

Problems have been identified even with this more limited approach to linking teaching behaviors with student outcomes. First, interaction effects that may be identified from teaching research are not confined to easily translatable two- or even three-way interactions. Thus, their generalizability for establishing rules of practice is severely constrained (Knapp, 1982; Shavelson, 1973). Cronbach (1975) questioned the application of the line of aptitude-treatment interaction (ATI) research that he helped initiate twenty years earlier when he observed:

> An ATI result can be taken as a general conclusion only if it is not in turn moderated by further variables ... Once we attend to interactions, we enter a hall of mirrors that extends to infinity. However far we carry our analysis — to third order or fifth order or any other — untested interactions of a still higher order can be envisioned. (p. 119)

With respect to teaching research, Cronbach has concluded that established empirical generalizations 'in a world in which most effects are interactive' might no longer be a fruitful strategy for research. Instead, he proposes that researchers pursue a course of short-run empiricism that is 'response sensitive,' one that takes exceptions as the rule, and that makes continual adjustments on the basis of individual, context-specific responses (pp. 121–2).

A related finding is that teaching behaviors that have sometimes been found to be effective often bear a distinctly curvilinear relation to achievement. That is, a behavior that is effective when used in moderation can produce significant and negative results when used too much (Peterson and Kauchak, 1982; Soar, 1972), or, as others have found, when applied in the wrong circumstances (see, for example, Coker, Medley and Soar, 1980; McDonald and Elias, 1976). This kind of finding also makes it difficult to develop rules for teaching behaviors that can be applied generally.

A more problematic finding is that the effectiveness of the two very distinct sets of teaching behaviors described above varies depending on the goals of instruction. Many of the behaviors that seem to result in increased achievement on standardized tests and factual examinations are dissimilar, indeed nearly opposite, from those that seem to increase complex cognitive learning, problem-solving ability, and creativity (McKeachie and Kulik, 1975; Peterson, 1979; Soar, 1977; Soar and Soar, 1976). As Centra and Potter (1980) observe,

> Higher order skills (for example, inferential reasoning) are not particularly likely to be acquired (and certainly will not be demonstrated) by students whose teachers ask only lower-order questions ... When the measure of student achievement is a multiple-choice, factually oriented test, it is not possible to assess the effects of teachers' higher-order questions, and no conclusions regarding the effectiveness of teacher questioning should be drawn from such studies. (p. 285)

Furthermore, some research suggests that desirable affective outcomes of education — independence, curiosity, and positive attitudes toward school, teacher, and self — seem to result from teaching behaviors that are different from those prescribed for increasing student achievement on standardized tests of cognitive skills (Horwitz, 1979; McKeachie and Kulik, 1975; Peterson, 1979; Traub *et al.*, 1973). To confound matters further, these effects also seem to vary by type of student (Peterson, 1979).

We say that this finding related to goals is 'problematic' because it raises more fundamental difficulties to agreement on effective teaching than does the identification of interaction effects or even the recognition of contextual factors. These variables complicate matters, but they do not entirely derail the effective teaching train. Attention to intervening variables can still, theoretically at least, lead to specifications of appropriate teaching behaviors. Goal specification, however, is not the province of educational researchers. If markedly different teaching behaviors lead to divergent results that can be deemed equally desirable, there is no way to identify a single construct called effective teaching, much less delimit its component parts. One can, at best, pursue alternative models of effective teaching, making explicit the goals underlying each. This has yet to become part of the empirical research base on teaching effects, although educational philosophers and organizational theorists have treated the issues of goal specification in more explicit terms (see, for example, Eisner and Vallance, 1974; Weick, 1976; Fenstermacher, 1978). As Fenstermacher (1978) notes:

> The process-product research on teacher effectiveness lacks a normative theory of education; this research does not incorporate a conception or justification of what is ultimately worth knowing or doing, it includes no view or defense of right conduct or moral integrity, nor does it give consideration to or argument for the ethical obligations and reasonable expectations of persons who act in specific historical, social, political, and economic settings. The lack of such a theory is not necessarily a fault of this research, except when its results are converted from theorems to rules for teachers to follow. (p. 175)

Questions of educational goals are clearly critical for the design of teacher evaluation systems, but, as we have noted, not central to teaching effects research. Putting such questions aside for the moment, we observe that, as the various lines of research on teacher effectiveness ascribe different degrees of generalizability to effective teaching behaviors and different weights to context-specific variables, they embody different conceptions of teaching work. The more complex and variable the educational environment is seen as being, the more one must rely on teacher judgment or even insight to guide the activities of classroom life, and the less one relies on generalized rules for teacher behavior.

The conversion of teacher effects research findings to rules for teacher behavior is a cornerstone of many performance-based teacher evaluation models. These models implicitly assume that the rules are generalizable because student outcomes are determined primarily by particular uniform teaching behaviors. By implication, the models assume either that other contextual influences on student outcomes are relatively unimportant, or that these other influences do not call for different teaching behaviors for teaching to be effective. Research on nonteaching variables in the educational environment calls into question the view of teaching as technological in nature, or at the least limits the generalizability of this view. This line of research constrains the application of process-product approaches to teacher evaluation in two ways: (a) it indicates that many factors other than teaching behaviors have profound effects on student learning; and (b) it suggests that effective teaching must be responsive to a number of student, classroom, and school variables in ways that preclude the application of predetermined approaches to teaching.

In a review of research on school and teacher effects on student learning, Centra and Potter (1980) observed that 'student achievement is affected by a considerable number of variables, of which teacher behavior is but one' (p. 287). Although they reject the extreme view that teachers have no effect on student outcomes, they conclude that 'teacher effects are likely to be small when compared with the totality of the effects of the other variables affecting student achievement, [and] ... the effects of any one of the variables ... are likely to be small when compared with the combined interactive effect of all the other variables' (p. 287). Anderson's (1982) review of research on school climate also indicates that many organizational and social system variables interact to influence teacher performance, student behavior, and student learning, and that these dependent variables simultaneously influence each other. Factors like school size, program characteristics and resources, administrative organization, incentive structures, and others mediate teacher and pupil performance both by imposing constraints and by presenting divergent models for successful teaching (Joyce and Weil, 1972; Mckenna, 1981).

Researchers who adopt an ecological perspective for investigating teaching also point out that reciprocal causality, particularly with respect to teacher and student behaviors, limits the applicability of process-product research findings (Doyle, 1979). Research grounded in this perspective finds that what students do affects teachers' behaviors and that the complexity of classroom life calls for teaching strategies responsive to environmental demands. As Doyle (1979) notes,

> Traditionally, research on teaching has been viewed as a process of isolating a set of effective teaching practices to be used by individual teachers to improve student learning or by policy makers to design teacher education and teacher evaluation programs. The emphasis in this tradition has been on predicting which methods or teacher behaviors have the highest general success rate, and much of the controversy over the productivity of research on teaching has centered on the legitimacy of propositions derived from available studies ... [The ecological approach] would seem to call into question the very possibility of achieving a substantial number of highly generalizable statements about teaching effectiveness. (pp. 203–4)

Doyle contends that the process-product paradigm for research leads us to focus on behaviors that promise to be 'context-proof, teacher-proof, and even student-proof' even though they may not be the most important behaviors in bringing about learning (Doyle, 1978, p. 169). He proposes instead the use of a 'mediating process' paradigm that takes into account the students' responses and the psychological processes that govern learning. Ecological analysis of teaching, as Doyle describes it, encompasses three basic features that are consonant with the research strategy advocated by Cronbach (1975). They are (a) a vigorously naturalistic approach, (b) a direct focus on environment-behavior relationships, and (c) a concern for the functional value or adaptive significance of behaviors in an environment (Doyle, 1979, pp. 188–9).

This approach is consistent with the interactionist view of teaching neatly capsulized by Brophy and Evertson (1976):

> [E]ffective teaching requires the ability to implement a very large number of diagnostic, instructional, managerial, and therapeutic skills, tailoring behavior in specific contexts and situations to the specific needs of the moment. Effective teachers not only must be able to do a large number of things; they also must be able to recognize which of the many things they know how to do applies at a given moment and be able to follow through by performing the behavior effectively. (p. 139)

The approach is also consonant with an intentionalist thesis for studying teaching that examines teachers' *reasons* for adopting particular behaviors in different classroom situations rather than simply examining behaviors (Fenstermacher, 1978; Shavelson and Stern, 1981).

Research on the stability and generalizability of measures of teaching behaviors lends support to a context-specific view of teaching. Stability refers to the extent that a teacher's behavior as measured at one point in time correlates with measures taken at another point in time. Generalizability refers to the extent that such measures are stable across different teaching situations (for example, different subject areas, grade levels, student ability levels, etc.). The bottom-line question is, Does a given teacher exhibit the same kinds of behavior at different points in time and within different teaching contexts? In general, the answer is 'no', especially with regard to measures of specific, discrete teaching behaviors (Shavelson and Dempsey-Atwood, 1976).[3] While this finding may be due to poor measurement instruments, it may also be due to the fact that teachers adjust their behaviors to the changing needs of the teaching context.

Some have suggested that teaching process research ought to account for this possibility by examining the variability or flexibility of teaching acts. Research on teacher characteristics has found that, of teacher characteristic variables, measures of teacher flexibility, adaptability, or creativity exhibit the most consistent relationship with ratings of teacher performance and effectiveness (McDonald and Elias, 1976; Schalock, 1979.) The implications for teacher evaluation of this view of teaching work are markedly different from those inherent in a view of teaching behaviors as stable or a view of the teaching environment as largely unrelated to effective teaching acts.

We see the manifestations of these different points of view in teacher evaluation systems that are based on divergent premises. On one hand, many states are considering or beginning to implement systems of competency-based certification or recertification and performance-based evaluation (Vlaanderen, 1980). These systems assume the validity, stability, and generalizability of effective teaching behaviors. On the other hand, teacher evaluation systems that rely heavily on approaches like clinical supervision, self-assessment, and interactive evaluation processes have been developed on the premise that situation-specific elements and teacher intentionality must play a role in assessing teacher performance. In the next section, we explore how choices of teacher evaluation systems also depend on views of schooling processes and of schools as organizations.

Theories of Schools as Organizations

The four conceptions of teaching work we have discussed can be divided into those which presuppose a more rationalistic school organization — labor and craft — and those which presuppose less rationalistic school organizations — profession and art. Teacher evaluation processes must operate within a school system's organization. General beliefs about how schools as organizations operate may influence choices of evaluation procedures (for example, hierarchical procedures vs. more lateral processes like self-assessment or peer review). The implementation of those procedures will depend not only on policymakers' implicit theories, but also on the realities of the organizational context. For example, is the organization really closed to environmental influence? Can it really operate as a tightly coupled bureaucracy? Below we discuss two models of school organization that are ideal types representing dramatically different organizational theories. Many other models exist in theory and can be found, at least in hybrid form, in the real world. We discuss these two to illustrate how radically different assumptions can result in divergent approaches to teacher evaluation.

The rationalistic model of school organization. Those who apply a rationalistic approach to education assume that the processes of teaching and learning rest on an underlying order. In the most simplified terms, the assumption of predictability requires a view that students are essentially passive objects, hence each student of X, Y and Z characteristics will react in the same way when a given stimulus or treatment is applied by the teacher. Outcomes are predictable; all that remains for decisionmakers to devise is a correct specification of inputs or processes. Results are achieved by the deliberate application of rationally conceived practices. Students will learn in direct proportion to the amount and kind of deliberate effort exerted by the teacher.

A rationalistic view of teaching presumes that once the goals of education are decided upon by external authorities, administrators will define behavioral objectives and teachers will teach to those objectives. Teacher and pupil performance can be tested; these assessments will yield meaningful measures of the success of the educational enterprise. The tests will give a clear picture of student and, by implication, teacher competencies. Objectively measured student competencies can be linked to other objectively measured teacher competencies because the student is an empty organism to be shaped in deliberate ways by the teacher-trainer. The teacher is to deliver a product which fits the specifications described by the goals and objectives.

The schooling process in the rationalistic model is characteristic of bureaucracies. It entails (a) a functional division of labor; (b) the definition of staff roles as offices which are distinguished by functional specificity of performance and universalistic, affectively neutral interaction with clients; (c) the hierarchic ordering of offices; and (d) operation according to rules of procedure which set limits to the discretionary performance of officers by specifying both the aims and the modes of official action (Bidwell, 1965). By conceiving of the teacher as bureaucrat, laborer, or craftsperson, the model gives little play for variations in teacher or student temperament, interests, or styles. It also ignores the importance of organizational context — the fact that in different situations teachers and students will perform differently. Finally, it ignores intervening variables between teacher competencies and teacher effectiveness by assuming tight coupling throughout the system and existence of environmental controls. A belief in this model might lead a school system to choose teacher evaluation processes that emphasized evaluation by superordinate specialists, material rewards and sanctions, precise ordering of tasks and/or specification of outcomes, the specification of processes, adherence to rules, and hierarchical relationships (Fuller, Wood, Rapoport, and Dornbusch, 1982).

The natural systems model of school organization. A less rationalistic model of school organization is based on the idea that effective teaching does not depend on deliberate, rational planning by superordinates (Stephens, 1976). The teacher as professional or artist is to be given an environment in which his or her profession or art can be practiced. The organizational model underlying this view is the natural systems model employed by some social scientists to look at organizations. This model posits loose coupling of organizational elements. If one believes that schools function as natural systems, then one will not try to impose bureaucratic procedures inappropriately. Bureaucratic procedures may still be employed, but their limits will be acknowledged and attention will be paid to teacher- and context-specific variables. Thus, viewing the school as a natural system *may* be conducive to a professional structure for teaching work. Suppose, for example, that policymakers think of the school system as a bureaucracy but it really functions as a natural system. The model tells us that certain rationalistic procedures may not be successful. A belief in this model does not tell us that teachers will, in fact, be treated as professionals or artists. It does, however, allow for that possibility.

> In the natural systems model, organization 'policy' accumulates crescively and in an unplanned manner ... [T]he model implies that power is dispersed, partly because of 'slippage' that can occur between the levels at which policies are formulated and those at which they are implemented ... Also the hierarchy accentuates communication problems; the longer the hierarchy the more distortion that can take place at each successive lower level, due to misinterpretations as well as to conflicts of interest between subordinate and superordinate groups.(Corwin, 1974, pp. 255–6)

The assumptions of the natural systems model differ from those of the rationalistic model in important ways. The natural systems model assumes the following organizational characteristics:

1 Absence of consensus among the membership on values, norms, and objectives;
2 Functional autonomy of the parts of the organization;
3 Bargaining and compromise to decide the terms of the relationship in the absence of consensus;
4 De facto decentralization of power;
5 Incomplete information for making decisions; and
6 Lack of coordination in planning and policymaking.

Corwin (1974) reasons that this model most accurately describes organizations with long hierarchies where the higher levels are directly linked to the political system and the organization is susceptible to outside influences. In school organizations thus conceived, teachers will maintain their own values and pursue their own objectives despite edicts from higher authorities. Because they are functionally autonomous and de facto power is decentralized, and because planning and policymaking are not highly coordinated, teachers may not govern their routine actions with reference to the deliberate decisions made by others in the hierarchy (see also Weick, 1976). They may accede to some rationalistic procedures through a process of bargaining and compromise, but these will not completely override the teachers' own conceptions of teaching work.

This view of school organizations also allows for the notion that teacher autonomy may be desirable in order for teachers to serve their clients in the way they judge best, based on more intimate knowledge of specific client needs (Lipsky, 1980). Similarly, Lewin's (1938) efficacy model suggests that less bureaucratic forms of organization may enhance workers' motivation and self-efficacy (Fuller *et al.*, 1982). What Fuller calls the 'humanistic views' of organizations sees hierarchical control and routinization of work tasks as undermining workers' efficacy by limiting their responsibility and their participation in problem-solving (*cf.* Bacharach and Aiken, 1979; French and Raven, 1977; Lawler, 1973; Mobley, Griffeth, Hand, and Meglino, 1979). In this view, the routinization or standardization that a rational-bureaucratic model imposes on teaching work may be seen as counterproductive to the extent that it constrains teachers in using their professional or personal judgment.

The degree to which these educational and organizational theories are reflected in teacher evaluation processes is examined in the succeeding sections of this paper.

Approaches to Teacher Evaluation

The choice of a teacher evaluation process is, as we have observed, associated with views of teaching work and of the school as an organization, although quite often these associations are made only implicitly in evaluation decisionmaking. A more explicit choice factor is the use to which the evaluation results are to be put.

Purposes for Teacher Evaluation

As indicated in Figure I, teacher evaluation may serve four basic purposes. The figure's cells artificially represent these purposes and levels of decisionmaking as distinct. In fact, teacher evaluation may be directed at small or large groups of teachers (rather than simply individuals or whole schools), and may represent degrees of hybrid improvement and accountability concerns (as when promotion decisions are linked to improvement efforts).

Many teacher evaluation systems are nominally intended to accomplish all four of these purposes, but different processes and methods are better suited to one or another of these objectives. In particular, improvement and accountability may require different standards of adequacy and of evidence. Focusing on individual or organizational concerns also leads to different processes, for example, bottom-up or top-down approaches to change, unstandardized or standardized remedies for problems identified. Berliner and Fenstermacher illuminate these differences with respect to staff development (our improvement dimension), although their observations are applicable to accountability purposes as well. Their definition of staff development encompasses four scales along which approaches may differ:

Figure 1.   *Four basic purposes of teacher evaluation.*

Purpose/Level	Individual	Organizational
Improvement (formative information)	Individual staff development	School improvement
Accountability (summative information)	Individual personnel (job status) decisions	School status (for example, certification) decisions

Staff development activities may be [a] internally proposed or externally imposed, in order to [b] effect compliance, remediate deficiencies, or enrich the knowledge and skills of [c] individual teachers or groups of teachers, who [d] may or may not have a choice to participate in the activities. (Fenstermacher and Berliner, in press, p. 6)

They note that as more differentiation occurs between participant roles and organizational levels, the profile of a staff development activity tends to shift from internal to external initiation, from an enrichment to a compliance focus, from participation by individuals or small groups to standardized programs for large groups, and from voluntary to involuntary participation. As the profile of a staff development activity shifts, so does its usefulness for a variety of purposes.

Staff development may be a vehicle for training teachers as technicians to implement policies devised by someone else (Floden and Feiman, 1981). Teacher evaluation in this case would focus on how faithfully the prescribed procedures or curricula are adhered to. This approach is most useful for organizational improvement or accountability purposes. Alternatively, staff development may be viewed as a means for helping teachers move from the acquisition of particular skills to applications of their judgment in order for them to play an analytic role in developing curricula and methods. Or staff development may be designed to help the teacher move to higher developmental stages in order to enable him or her to develop multiple perspectives about teaching and learning, to become more flexible, adaptive, and creative (Floden and Feiman, 1981). Teacher evaluation in these views would focus on teachers' personal stages of development and areas of confidence and would be most suited for individual improvement purposes.

In general, teacher evaluation processes most suited to accountability purposes must be capable of yielding fairly objective, standardized, and externally defensible information about teacher performance. Evaluation processes useful for improvement objectives must yield rich, descriptive information that illuminates sources of difficulty as well as viable courses for change. Teacher evaluation methods designed to inform organizational decisions must be hierarchically administered and controlled to ensure credibility and uniformity. Evaluation methods designed to assist decisionmaking about individuals must consider the context in which individual performance occurs to ensure appropriateness and sufficiency of data.

Although these purposes and the approaches most compatible with them are not necessarily mutually exclusive, an emphasis on one may tend to limit the pursuit of another. Similarly, while multiple methods for evaluating teachers can be used — and many argue, should be used — it is important to consider what purposes are best served by each if teacher evaluation goals and processes are to be consonant. Furthermore, some processes are distinctly inconsistent with others and with some purposes for evaluation. These disjunctures should be recognized before a teacher evaluation system is adopted and put in place.

Teacher Evaluation Processes and Methods

There have been several recent reviews of teacher evaluation processes in which the authors identified from six to twelve general approaches to teacher evaluation (Ellett, Capie and Johnson, 1980; Haefele, 1980; Lewis, 1982; Millman, 1981a; Peterson and Kauchak, 1982). They reveal that the approaches used to evaluate teachers seek to measure very different aspects of teaching and the teacher. They rely on different conceptions of what demontrates adequacy and on diverse notions of how to recognize or measure adequacy. Some seek to assess the quality of the *teacher* (teacher competence); others seek to assess the quality of *teaching* (teacher performance). Other approaches claim to assess the teacher or his or her teaching by reference to student outcomes (teacher effectiveness). Medley (1982) offers useful definitions of four terms often treated as synonyms:

- *Teacher competency*   refers to any single knowledge, skill, or professional value position, the possession of which is believed to be relevant to the successful practice of teaching. Competencies refer to specific things that teachers know, do, or believe but not to the effects of these attributes on others.
- *Teacher competence*   refers to the repertoire of competencies a teacher possesses. Overall competence is a matter of the degree to which a teacher has mastered a set of individual competencies, some of which are more critical to a judgment of overall competence than others.
- *Teacher performance*   refers to what the teacher *does* on the job rather than to what she or he *can* do (that is, how competent she or he is). Teacher performance is specific to the job situation; it depends on the competence of the teacher, the context in which the teacher works, and the teacher's ability to apply his or her competencies at any given point in time.
- *Teacher effectiveness*   refers to the effect that the teacher's performance has on pupils. Teacher effectiveness depends not only on com-

petence and performance, but also on the responses pupils make. Just as competence cannot predict performance under different situations, teacher performance cannot predict outcomes under different situations.

The tools and processes that are used to assess teacher competence, performance, or effectiveness are based on assumptions about how these qualities are linked to one another, how they may be measured, and how the measurements may be used to make decisions. There is substantial debate on all these questions. In this section, we will briefly describe the tools and processes currently used for evaluating school personnel and summarize the issues raised by each.

Teacher Interviews. Teacher interviews or conferences have been a prevalent evaluation method in the past and are a cornerstone of some of the more recent evaluation strategies. Haefele (1981, p. 49) has identified two uses for teacher interviews: for the purpose of hiring decisions and for communicating performance appraisals to a practicing teacher. Teacher selection interviews in the past have been generally informal and unstructured. One standardized interview method developed and used more recently is the Teacher Perceiver Interview. The instrument, which poses hypothetical questions or situations to the candidate, purportedly assesses noncognitive traits and reduces the possible interviewer bias of unstructured interviews. However, there is no empirical research regarding the ability of such instruments to predict the effectiveness of teachers.

In the past, the teacher appraisal interview and classroom observation represented the totality of the evaluation process. After the principal or evaluator observed a teacher's performance in the classroom, a conference was convened to communicate the evaluation results. In the conference, teaching performance standards were established, teaching performance was motivated, assessments were made, warnings were issued, guidance was given, and superior performance was recognized. Recently, however, the interview has been viewed as an important element of a broader evaluation procedure. In particular, a preobservation conference has been recognized as useful for the involvement of teachers in their own professional development and for a more regularized exchange of feedback from superiors (Garawski, 1980; Gudridge, 1980; Redfern, 1980). Hunter (in Gudridge, 1980, pp. 39–40) on the other hand, believes the preobservation conference, which determines what behaviors the evaluator is looking for, locks a teacher into those behaviors during the observation, inhibiting individual teaching styles.

Competency Tests. There is a strong trend toward the use of standardized tests for initial certification and hiring. This trend is based partly on the belief that teachers should be able to demonstrate cognitive competence as a prerequisite to a teaching position and partly on the public's suspicion about the effectiveness of teacher education and training (Harris, 1981). There is also a growing belief that such tests can be used for recertification and dismissal decisions.

By far the most widely used competency test is the National Teacher Examination (NTE). Harris estimated that 75,000 teacher candidates in 24 states and 311 school districts take the exam each year. In some states and school districts, passing the NTE is a condition of employment (Harris, 1981, pp. 63–4). The examination measures academic achievement and preparation in areas of general education, professional education, and specialized subject areas. The assumption is that test performance accurately reflects at least one determinant of successful teaching — cognitive competence. However, a review of studies that have examined the relationship between NTE scores and measures of teacher performance found no consistent relationships (Quirk, Witten and Weinberg, 1973).

There are also a number of state and locally developed teacher examinations. Most prominent in the literature is the Georgia Teacher Area Criterion Referenced Test,[4] which assesses a prospective teacher's knowledge of a specific curriculum area. Passing this exam is a precondition of certification throughout the state (Ellett *et al.*, 1980; Harris, 1981; Hathaway, 1980; Lewis, 1982). Similar tests have been developed in Florida, South Carolina, Dallas and Houston, Texas, and Montgomery County, Maryland.

Proponents of standardized teacher tests maintain that tests guarantee a minimum standard of knowledge on the part of prospective teachers, eliminate interviewer bias, and are legally defensible. However, critics claim that tests obviously cannot assess the classroom performance of a teacher (Haefele, 1980; Harris, 1981). Further, past studies (Coleman *et al.*, 1966; Guthrie, 1970) indicate that higher knowledge levels are not clearly translated into more effective teaching.

Indirect Measures. J.A. King (1981) has examined the possible use of indirect measures of teacher competence. She reviews the research literature on teacher personality and characteristics and concludes that 'no single set of skills, attitudes, interests, and abilities' has been found to discriminate between effective and ineffective teachers (p. 174; see also Gage, 1963). Despite this finding, she argues that indirect measures, especially professional commitment as expressed in extra-classroom activities, ought to be a supplementary source of evaluation data. Schalock (1979) identifies two promising lines of research on teacher characteristics. One finds relationships between teacher flexibility or adaptability and teacher effectiveness. The other finds that some teacher characteristics are more effective in some teaching contexts than in others. These findings have not yet found their way into the practice of teacher evaluation.

Traditionally, indirect measures such as training and experience are those linked to teacher salary and promotion opportunities and, implicitly, to teacher evaluation.

Classroom Observation. This method, usually coupled with teacher interviews or conferences, is the mainstay of most teacher evaluations. It involves direct observation of the teacher performing in the classroom. To the extent that observation can capture what the teacher knows and does in interaction with a class of students, it can result in measures of performance. Classroom observation reveals 'a view of the climate, rapport, interaction, and functioning of the classroom available from no other source' (Evertson and Holley, 1981, p. 90). Classroom observation techniques vary significantly in structure and methodology. Although the school principal acts as the observer in most cases, trained evaluators, school system administrators, other teachers, or students may observe and rate teachers. Increasingly, observations by supervisors are preceded by a preobservation conference (Garawski, 1980; Redfern, 1980). Frequency of observation and the length of each observation period vary according to time constraints and school board policies regarding evaluation. Finally, the observer may use a number of standardized observation instruments to guide him or her in the assessment.

This evaluation method has the advantages of seeing teachers in action and within the context of their schools. However, even proponents of classroom observation recognize its limitations. Observer bias, insufficient sampling of performance, and poor measurement instruments can threaten the reliability and validity of results (Evertson and Holley, 1981; Haefele, 1980; Lewis, 1982; Peterson and Kauchak, 1982). Supervisory ratings have generally been found to lack interrater reliability and validity (Medley, 1982; Peterson and Kauchak, 1982). Performance ratings have also shown limited stability and generalizability, particularly when low-inference measures of discrete teaching behaviors are used (Shavelson and Dempsey-Atwood, 1976).

Student Ratings. The potential use of student ratings for teachers has attracted a great deal of attention in the literature. Student ratings are another form of 'classroom observation' — they measure observed performance from the student's rather than the administrator's point of view. Although usually applied at the college level, several authors (Aleamoni, 1981; Haefele, 1980; McNeil and Popham, 1973; Peterson and Kauchak, 1982) believe that student ratings could be applied in secondary and, in some cases, elementary schools. The use of student ratings in evaluation assumes that: (a) the student knows when he has been motivated; (b) it is the student whose behavior is to be changed; (c) student rating is feedback to the teacher; and (d) student recognition may motivate good teaching. This method is inexpensive with a high degree of reliability, usually ranging from .8 to .9 and above (Peterson and Kauchak, 1982), with some studies finding a modest degree of correlation between student ratings of teachers and student achievement. On the other hand, questions about the validity and utility of student ratings limit their acceptance as primary policy instruments for teacher evaluation (Aleamoni, 1981; Haefele, 1980).

Peer Review. In this process, a committee of peers evaluates teaching through an examination of such documents as lesson plans, examinations, examples of graded examinations, and classroom observations. This process covers a broader spectrum of performance, encompassing not only performance in the classroom, but also intentionality (what the teacher intends to have happen) and other teaching behavior as exhibited by assignment and grading practices. Although seldom used in formal teaching evaluations, the literature identifies many potential advantages to peer evaluation. The assumption underlying this approach is that peers are in the best position to assess competence, thus it suggests a professional conception of teaching work. Also, evaluators who are familiar with the classroom experience, subject matter, and demands on a teacher can render specific and practical suggestions for improvement.

Peer evaluation in practice has received mixed reviews. Although a three year experiment including peer review was enthusiastically supported by the teaching staff in one district (Lewis, 1982), another school district found that teachers lacked respect for evaluations by their peers and that the evaluations resulted in staff tension (Lewis, 1982). Because the method is more open to divergent criteria for assessing performance and is not subject to direct administrative control, it is not generally recommended for use as the basis of personnel decisions (Haefele, 1980; Peterson and Kauchak, 1982; Thomas, 1979).

Student Achievement. In education, the ultimate concern is the student's learning. For some this means that student achievement is the only true indicator of teacher effectiveness. In an educational management system like teacher evaluation, student achievement must be measured in a manner consonant with the outcomes held to be important. Student achievement can be measured in many ways: comparing student test scores to a national norm; comparing test score gains with those of a comparable class; net gains over time, and so forth (Haefele, 1980). Such scores, while representing legitimate and understandable indicators for many audiences, nonetheless require that numerous assumptions be made to link them to teacher competence or even teacher performance.

Studies of the reliability of student test scores as a measure of teaching effectiveness consistently indicate that reliability is quite low, that is, that the same teacher produces markedly different results in different situations, calling into question the use of such teacher effectiveness scores as an indicator of teacher competence (Brophy, 1973; Rosenshine, 1970; Shavelson and Russo, 1977; Veldman and Brophy, 1974). Further, the use of tests to measure teaching performance may inhibit curriculum innovation since teachers will tend to teach to the test (Shine and Goldman, 1980), and may ignore or counteract the effects of teacher behaviors on other desirable outcomes (Centra and Potter, 1980; Peterson, 1979).

Some researchers recommend a variation of this method in which a teacher is assessed while teaching students a lesson in an unfamiliar subject. However, such teaching simulations are relatively time-consuming and very expensive evaluation methods. Moreover, samples of behavior in an artificial setting run the risk of simplifying the complexity of teaching work, thus rendering the method invalid (Medley, 1982).

Faculty Self-evaluations. Self-evaluation has recently joined other sources of assessment as a technique in teacher evaluation. The combination of self-evaluation and individual goal-setting may promote self-reflection and motivation toward change and growth. A teacher can use data derived form any technique — student or peer ratings, self-assessment measures of student achievement, and so forth, to make judgments about his or her own teaching. Externally developed 'objective' data may permit the teacher to assess his or her own strengths and weaknesses against both personal and organizational standards and reinforce a teacher's professionalism.

This process, less formal than the others, while obviously not suitable for accountability decisions, can be used for individual and collective staff development. In particular, both Redfern (1980) and Manatt (Lewis, 1982) consider self-evaluation an essential component of their cooperative evaluation models discussed below. Thus, self-evaluation should be regarded not as an evaluation process in itself, but as an important source of information and motivation in a broader evaluation program.

Conclusion. In the literature on evaluation processes and tools, some papers rely heavily on research for reaching their conclusions; others do not. It is safe to say that research has not identified a teacher evaluation method which is unvaryingly 'successful.' (A similar conclusion was reached by Ornstein and Levine, 1981.) This is not a surprising finding.

A judgment of success depends on the purposes for which a technique is used as well as its ability to measure what it purports to measure. Some of these approaches seek to measure competence while others, that rely on direct observation, seek to measure performance. Still others rely on student performance as a measure of teacher effectiveness, and by implication, teacher competence and performance. The generally low levels of reliability, generalizability, and validity attributed to teacher evaluation methods suggest that unidimensional approaches for assessing competence, performance, or effectiveness are unlikely to capture enough information about teaching attributes to completely satisfy any of the purposes for teacher evaluation.

Teacher evaluation methods are but one part of a broader process of goal-setting, standard-setting, assessment, and decision making that occurs within the organizational context. For any method, the criteria used for evaluation may vary, along with the instruments for assessing performance and the means for implementing the approach (for example, frequency of assessments, uses made of results). In the next section, we present some specific configurations of evaluation processes and methods that have been proposed as models for teacher evaluation.

Teacher Evaluation Models

Approaches to teacher evaluation and improvement vary depending on:

- What teacher attributes (for example, professional training, teaching competencies, etc.) are believed to be important for effective teaching;
- Which aspect of the instructional process the district hopes to affect (for example, assurance of teacher quality; improved teaching techniques; learning outcomes, etc.); and
- What will be the criteria for evaluating success (for example, demonstration by the teacher of desired behaviors or competencies, teacher or student test scores, etc.).

Because we cannot here provide a comprehensive list of teacher evaluation models, we will describe a few of the more widely reported models.

Two of the most widely discussed evaluation models[5] are Manatt's (Manatt, Palmer and Hidlebaugh, 1976) 'Mutual Benefit Evaluation' and Redfern's (1980) 'Management by Objectives Evaluation.' Both models have been implemented in a number of school districts,[6] and both models are characterized by (a) goal-setting; (b) teacher involvement in the evaluation process; and (c) centralized teaching standards and criteria. The major difference between them is the point at which a teacher is brought into the evaluation process.

Manatt describes his model as a system in which teachers, administrators, and the educational program itself may be objectively evaluated (Gudridge, 1980). Although Manatt insists that the model is designed primarily to improve teacher performance rather than to ferret out incompetent teachers, he nevertheless stresses points needed to withstand court scrutiny of resulting dismissals (for example, evaluation criteria must be 'legally' discriminating; must adhere to procedural due process).

There are four steps in the model:

1   The school board and administration (or whoever is responsible for evaluation development) must determine criteria for minimum

acceptable teaching standards. For example, Manatt suggests that these might include productive teaching techniques, positive interpersonal relations, organized class management, intellectual stimulation, and out-of-class behavior (Gudridge, 1980, pp. 36–8).

2   A diagnostic evaluation is performed to assess each teacher's present status *vis-à-vis* the standards. Although Manatt does not prescribe specific measurement instruments, he suggests that evaluation processes should include a preobservation conference with the teacher, a teacher self-evaluation, classroom observations, and postobservation conferences.

3   With the cooperation of the teacher, the evaluator sets job targets (three to five are recommended) for the teacher's performance improvement. Manatt suggests that the targets be specific and objectively measurable.

4   After a specified time, the teacher is reevaluated and new job targets are set.

Redfern borrowed the 'management-by-objectives' model from business and applied it to teacher evaluation. Like the Manatt model, a teacher's responsibilities and learning goals are set by the responsible school authority. However, before any evaluation takes place, the evaluator and teacher *jointly* establish individual objectives, an action plan, and measurable progress indicators (Haefele, 1980; Lewis, 1982; Redfern, 1980). The teacher's action plan is monitored through diagnostic rather than summative observations. The observation results are assessed by the evaluators who then meet with the teacher to discuss progress and to set additional objectives. Redfern does not prescribe monitoring or measurement processes because each action plan would call for different methods and tools (Redfern, 1980). The collegial nature of the model makes teacher self-evaluation essential (Iwanicki, 1981).

These models are intended to promote the professional growth of the individual teacher and the integration of individual performance objectives with school board policies. They also establish, with the teacher's participation, a structured set of evaluation goals intended to reduce uncertainties and misunderstandings between the teacher and evaluator. On the other hand, critics charge that the goal-setting models place too much emphasis on measurable objectives. Further, they argue, to be properly implemented the models may require large investments in time and money (Iwanicki, 1981).

Both models straddle the competency-based and outcomes-based evaluation philosophies. The models are 'results-oriented' but allow for various definitions of 'results.' In some cases, it would appear that results may be measurable increases in learning; in others, a positive result may be the demonstration of a new teaching competency. However, the

Redfern model seems to allow more input from the teacher, thus fostering the image of professionalism, while Manatt's model seems to delegate professional decisions to supervisors.

The evaluation program in Salt Lake City, Utah, also widely discussed, is more explicitly responsive to accountability demands. The school superintendent and principal establish building unit performance standards. In turn, the principal and teacher establish performance goals that support school board goals. Personal goals may also be set. Teacher performance is assessed annually using student test scores, classroom observation, and other means (Thomas, 1979). The remediation system is pivotal. A teacher may be 'placed on remediation' as the result of an annual evaluation or by a formal complaint lodged by a student, peer, or parent. If the complaint seems justified, a four-member, shared governance committee works with the teacher and, after five months, the teacher is dismissed or retained, based on the committee's recommendation. The Salt Lake approach may have survived in part because the local teacher organization is involved in the process — recommending two governance committee members — and the district has no mandatory tenure law (Thomas, 1979).

The Georgia evaluation system is also receiving considerable attention, especially among southern states. In essence, the Georgia system requires each teacher to possess professional knowledge and training and to demonstrate mastery of fourteen teaching competencies. Each prospective teacher must pass a criterion-referenced test as a precondition to receiving a three year non-renewable certificate. To receive recertification, sometime within three years a teacher must prepare a portfolio of lesson plans, test papers, and other teaching documents for a team of trained evaluators. In addition, he or she must pass a classroom assessment based on the Teacher Performance Assessment Instrument (TPAI). The instrument is used by three independent observers to rate the teacher's classroom performance in terms of demonstration of the specific competencies. If a teacher fails the evaluation, she or he may take it again. Georgia officials believe that the TPAI will withstand court challenges, in part, because the University of Georgia researchers believe they have found a connection between the TPAI's 14 teaching competencies and student learning gains (Ellett *et al.*, 1980; Lewis, 1982).

The program used in Salem, Oregon, is also based on the belief that certain teacher behaviors influence student learning; therefore, mastery of these behaviors by all teachers will result in more effective teaching. The slate of desired behaviors and competencies is determined by the administration. In fact, the administration presents the competency program to the teachers in a taped presentation to ensure standard communication of evaluation expectations and uniformity among schools. For those who fail to demonstrate mastery of all the competencies, retraining is provided by district 'master teachers' who have received fifteen to twenty hours of training in evaluation. The program calls for frequent classroom observation: four times annually for new teachers; three times for experienced teachers (DuBois, 1980; Lewis, 1982). The model is intended to 'reduc[e] the stress [and] trauma . . . of change . . . [by] controlling goals to assure a high rate of success' (Lewis, 1982, p. 55).

Finally, we cite two models that adhere to the belief that a teacher's professional needs vary over the course of his or her career and that each teacher is a professional even an artistic, individual (Lewis, 1982). The evaluation program used in Bedford, Ohio, is intended to evolve throughout a teacher's career. This model assures that criteria for evaluating an experienced teacher will be different from those used to make the original employment decision or for evaluating new teachers. This evolving model is unstructured and highly dependent on teacher self-evaluation and joint efforts between teacher and evaluator. Similarly, the New Hampton, Iowa, evaluation program is based on a belief that 'no single model [of instruction] will result in effective learning . . .' and that 'an evaluation system must respect the uniqueness of each individual staff member' (Lewis, 1982, p. 22).

An approach that seems consonant with flexible, multigoal models such as these is the clinical supervision approach, a process often compared to the Manatt and Redfern models (Lewis, 1982, p. 31). While the components are structurally similar, the clinical supervision approach is more informal in setting performance goals and generally involves more one-to-one interaction between the teacher and the evaluator. Ideally, areas of improvement and concern are mutually identified, and professional goals evolve during a systematic plan of classroom observations. As Manatt notes, without specific school board guidelines or evaluation criteria, 'supervisor and teacher are both assumed to be instructional experts, with the teacher identifying his concerns and the supervisor assisting . . .' (Lewis, 1982, p. 42). Clinical supervision is highly interactive and may promote professionalism and a sense of efficacy among teachers. However, it is also a time-consuming process, and the data gathered during the observations may be uninterpretable to those outside the supervisor-teacher relationship. Thus, clinical supervision approaches may prove to be of limited use for accountability purposes.

Application of the Models

Most of the above models can be characterized as having a decisionistic orientation (Floden and Weiner, 1978). They reflect a view of evaluation as an activity which functions to inform decisions about the pursuit of stable, consensual programmatic, and instructional goals. Other models of evaluation, such as the last two briefly described above, start from the premise that instructional goals are neither stable nor entirely consensual.

Such models include multiple goals for and functions of evaluation including, for example, conflict resolution and complacency reduction (Floden and Weiner, 1978; Chen and Rossi, 1980), as well as empowerment of the individual teacher.

The application of research-based teacher evaluation models to real-life settings must overcome the gap that exists between technically defensible specifications of criteria or methods and politically viable solutions to organizational problems. There is a growing recognition that any kind of evaluation activity involves value choices — and conflicts — at all levels of the operating system (Rein, 1976; Rossi, Freeman and Wright, 1979; Sroufe, 1977). Evaluation is political because it serves as a tool in a larger policymaking process and because it is inherently directed at making a judgment of worth about something. Any such judgment ultimately rearranges or reaffirms an existing constellation of stakes that individuals or groups have in what is being evaluated (Englert, Kean and Scribner, 1977). Furthermore, the *process* of evaluation must be understood as encompassing a continual process of bargaining and goal modification that occurs 'because the conditions and effective constituency surrounding goal setting are different from the conditions and effective constituency surrounding implementation' (Stone, 1980, pp. 23–24).

Knapp (1982) describes the divergence existing between many teacher evaluation models and actual practices in terms of the differing standards applied by researchers and practitioners to ultimately political value choices.

> Value choices are nowhere more clearly at issue than in decisions about the aspects of the teacher and teaching to be evaluated. Scholars have tended to make these value choices on scientific grounds: in effect, they are arguing that evaluation systems should be focused on whatever can be operationally defined and demonstrated to contribute to student learning ... A number of proposals for improved teacher appraisal systems have been advanced, but a 'better' system tends to be defined in terms of accuracy and links to an established base of teacher effects research. Such systems rest on an idealized image of school management, that ignores the powerful effects of organizational and contextual forces on management activity. (pp. 4–5)

In actual practice, he finds that schools follow 'the lines of least resistance,' evaluating aspects of teachers and teaching in more vague terms so as to simultaneously satisfy diverse constituencies. A defensible teacher evaluation process is one that allows them to balance several goals at once:

- Sorting teachers;

- Maintaining staff morale and collegiality;
- Maintaining organizational distance from environmental demands (for example, for accountability); and
- Devising improvements that require modest, incremental change.

This does not mean that research-based teacher evaluation models cannot succeed in the real world, only that adaptations to the organizational context must be explicitly considered and sought if the processes are to be implemented successfully.

Implementing Teacher Evaluation in the Organizational Context

The major findings of Rand's Change Agent Study (Berman and McLaughlin, 1978), which examined the local outcomes of federal program initiatives for innovation, are relevant to our discussion of teacher evaluation in the local context. The study found that

- Implementation dominated the outcome of planned change efforts.
- The process of implementation is shaped by local factors — rather than by adopting a particular technology, the availability of information, funding level, or particular type of program.
- Effective implementation is characterized by a process of mutual adaptation, in which both the project and participants change over time.

While the Change Agent Study concerned the implementation of selected federal programs, its findings are relevant since we are concerned with the implementation of teacher evaluation processes in specific schools and school systems. Numerous other studies have also established the importance of the local organizational context and its implementation processes in determining the outcomes of planned change efforts (see, for example, Lipsky, 1976; Milstein, 1980; Selznick, 1966; Stone, 1980). These studies have pointed to the importance of recognizing local participants in change efforts as purposive agents and to the need for adaptations of change strategies by those who actually implement them.

Research on individual and organizational change indicates that the degree of control and autonomy characterizing participants' roles in the implementation process is critical to success of a planned change effort. Although the literatures are distinct, their respective findings argue powerfully for an approach emphasizing 'transformation' rather than 'conversion' to new methods, techniques, or principles of behavior (Fenstermacher, 1978).

The transformation approach starts from the assumption that participants in any change process hold subjectively reasonable beliefs that direct their actions. The actions informed by these beliefs are unlikely to change substantially if change strategies are converted to rules for behavior without attention to transforming the belief structure underlying the existing behavior patterns. The objectively reasonable beliefs encompassed by a change proposal are offered as evidence for consideration by participants rather than as rules for them to follow (Fenstermacher, 1978). This evidence *empowers* people to change their own behaviors rather than forcing them to adhere superficially to rules that have no intrinsic meaning for them. A transformation approach allows for policy adaptation and for situation-specific responses where internal and external perspectives converge.

Changing Teacher Behavior

One of the primary goals of teacher evaluation is the improvement of individual and collective teaching performance in schools. Effectively changing the behavior of another person requires enlisting the cooperation and motivation of that person, in addition to providing guidance on the steps needed for improvement to occur. At the individual level, change relies on the development of two important conditions within the individual: knowledge that a course of action is the correct one and a sense of empowerment or efficacy, that is, a perception that pursuing a given course of action is both worthwhile and possible.

Most teacher evaluation processes attend to questions of how to identify effective teaching without addressing questions of how to bring about changes in teaching behavior, assuming that having discovered what ought to be done, implementation of recommended actions will naturally follow. Gage's (1978) translation of research findings into a series of 'teachers should' statements is representative of the externally oriented approach to effecting change. However, Fenstermacher (1978) argues that 'if our purpose and intent are to change the practices of those who teach, it is necessary to come to grips with the subjectively reasonable beliefs of teachers' (p. 174). This process entails the creation of internally verifiable knowledge rather than the imposition of rules for behavior. It incorporates an intentionalist thesis for observing and influencing teaching behaviors, one that gives full weight to teachers' beliefs and intentions in assessing what they do and in guiding them in the formation of alternative beliefs about useful courses of action.

The intentionalist view assumes (a) that teachers are rational professionals who make judgments and carry out decisions in an uncertain, complex environment; and (b) that teachers' behaviors are guided by their thoughts, judgments, and decisions (Shavelson and Stern, 1981). Thus behavior change requires transformation of belief structures and knowledge in a manner that allows for situation-specific applications.

Effective change requires knowledge control on the part of the teacher. Not only is information-processing reliant on the teachers' beliefs, but the ways in which new knowledge or transformed beliefs are applied must be under the teacher's control. Good and Power (1976) apply this notion to the effective use of teaching theory for changing teaching practice:

[A]t best, generalizations about teaching derived from research act as guides to assessing the likely consequences of alternative strategies in complex educational situations. Such generalizations must necessarily be indeterminate since they cannot predict precisely what will happen in a particular case. But this does not decrease their value for the teacher ... Theories can be of value in specifying those dimensions which are relevant to the understanding of classroom phenomena, can extend the range of hypotheses (alternative strategies) considered, and *sensitize* the teacher to the possible consequences of his actions. Indeed, ultimately, the validity and usefulness of theory may rest in the hands of teachers ... that is, whether it sensitizes them to the classroom context, helps them make more informed decisions, and to monitor their own behavior. (p. 58)

This concept entails the development of an internally verifiable knowledge base that empowers the teacher to apply internal against external referents of validity and to engage in appropriate self-assessment and self-improvement activities.

An understanding of how empowerment enables change is further informed by a substantial body of psychological research on self-efficacy. Perceptions of self-efficacy are an important element of the link between knowledge and behaviors. As Bandura (1982) notes:

Knowledge, transformational operations, and component skills are necessary but insufficient for accomplished performances. Indeed, people often do not behave optimally, even though they know full well what to do. This is because self-referent thought also mediates the relationship between knowledge and action ... Self-appraisals of operative capabilities function as one set of proximal determinants of how people behave, their thought patterns, and the emotional reactions they experience ... Social environments may place constraints on what people do or may aid them to behave optimally. Whether their endeavors are socially impeded or supported will depend, in part, on how efficacious they are perceived to be. (p. 122–3 and 131)

In this conception, self-perceptions of efficacy both affect performance and are affected by others' perceptions of a person's efficaciousness. Research on this topic indicates that perceived self-efficacy better predicts subsequent behavior than does actual performance attainment, and that it influences coping behaviors, self-regulation of refractory behaviors, perseverance, responses to failure experiences, growth of intrinsic interest and motivation, achievement strivings, and career pursuits (Bandura, 1982; Bandura and Schunk, 1981; Bandura, Adams, Hardy and Howells, 1980; Betz and Hackett, 1981; Brown and Inouye, 1978; Kazdin, 1979; Collins, 1982; DiClemente, 1981).

The relevance of teachers' self-perceptions of efficacy to their performance has been demonstrated in several studies. Berman and McLaughlin's study on implementation of innovative projects found that the teacher's sense of efficacy had stronger positive effects on the percent of project goals achieved, the amount of teacher change, and improved student performance than did teacher experience or verbal ability (Berman and McLaughlin, 1977, pp. 136–9). Armor (1976) found that teachers' self-perceptions of efficacy were strongly and positively related to students' reading achievement, unlike teacher education, experience, or other background characteristics. Other studies have reported similar positive relationships between teachers' sense of self-efficacy and student achievement (Brookover, 1977; Rutter *et al.*, 1979).

More important, substantial research also suggests that an individual's sense of efficacy can be influenced by interactions with others as well as by organizational factors. Individual perceptions of self-efficacy and motivation are influenced by the value of rewards and the expectancy of achieving objectives (Vroom, 1964). Self-efficacy is not an entirely internal construct; it requires a responsive environment that allows for and rewards performance attainment (Bandura, 1982, p. 140). However, the goals must be personally valued and must present a challenge to the individual, or the task performance will be devalued (Lewin, 1938; Lewin, Dembo, Festinger and Sears, 1944). Furthermore, role designations can enhance or underline self-efficacy.

> Situational factors that often accompany poor performance can in themselves instill a sense of incompetence that is unwarranted ...
> [W]hen people are cast in subordinate roles or are assigned inferior labels, implying limited competence, they perform activities at which they are skilled less well than when they do not bear the negative labels or the subordinate role designations. (Bandura, 1982 p. 142)

A review by Fuller, Wood, Rapoport and Dornbusch (1982) of the research on individual efficacy in the context of organizations suggests that increased performance and organizational efficacy for teachers will result from:

- Convergence between teachers and administrators in accepting the goals and means for task performance (Ouchi, 1980);

- Higher levels of personalized interaction and resource exchange between teachers and administrators (Talbert, 1980);
- Lower prescriptiveness of work tasks (Anderson, 1973);
- Teachers' perceptions that evaluation is soundly based and that evaluation is linked to rewards or sanctions; and
- Teacher input into evaluation criteria, along with diversity of evaluation criteria (Pfeffer, Salancik and Leblebici, 1976; Rosenholtz and Wilson, 1980).

These findings converge markedly with those of Natriello and Dornbusch (1980–81) on determinants of teachers' satisfaction with teacher evaluation systems. They found that teacher satisfaction is strongly related to (a) perceptions that all evaluators share the same criteria for evaluation; (b) more frequent samplings of teacher performance; (c) more frequent communication and feedback; and (d) teachers' ability to affect the criteria for evaluation. Furthermore, frequency of negative feedback did not cause dissatisfaction, but infrequency of evaluation did. Teacher satisfaction with evaluation, then, seems to be based on perceptions that evaluation is soundly based, that is, that the teacher has some control over both task performance and its assessment. These perceptions influence the teacher's sense of performance efficacy (Fuller *et al.*, 1982, p. 24).

Finally, opportunities for self-assessment and for reference to personal standards of performance strongly influence self-efficacy and motivation. As Bandura (1982) observes:

> In social learning theory an important cognitively based source of motivation operates through the intervening processes of goal setting and self-evaluative reactions. This form of self-motivation, which involves internal comparison processes, requires personal standards against which to evaluate performance.

The importance of self-assessment has begun to achieve recognition in the teacher evaluation literature (Bodine, 1973; Bushman, 1974; Riley and Schaffer, 1979), as has the importance of allowing teacher input into the determination of evaluation criteria and standards (Knapp, 1982).

Individual change relies on knowledge, self-referent thought, and motivation. These are, in turn, profoundly influenced by the signals and opportunities provided within the organizational environment. The transformatory character of individual change is equally applicable at the organizational level. Thus the success of change efforts is influenced by implementation processes that define opportunities for developing shared knowledge, diagnosing and designing strategies, and promoting collective efficacy.

Teacher Evaluation in the Organizational Context

The recent evolution of policy analysis and program evaluation has led to a recognition of the importance of including organizational considerations as an integral part of research that attempts to understand policy effects (Sabatier and Mazmanian, 1979; Sproull, 1979; Wildavsky, 1980). Formal policies and procedures, it has been found, may constrain, but do not construct, the final outcomes of any institutional endeavor. The local implementation process and organizational characteristics — such as institutional climate, organizational structures and incentives, local political processes, expertise, and leadership style — are critical elements in determining the ultimate success of a policy at achieving its intended effects (Berman and McLaughlin, 1978; Mann, 1978; Weatherley and Lipsky, 1977). Effective change requires a process of mutual adaptation in which change agents at all levels can shape policies to meet their needs — one in which both the participants and the policy are transformed by the convergence of internal and external reference points.

Implementation of any school policy, including a teacher evaluation policy, represents a continuous interplay among diverse policy goals, established rules and procedures (concerning both the policy in question and other aspects of the school's operations), intergroup bargaining and value choices, and the local institutional context. Teacher evaluation procedures, for example, will be influenced by the political climate that exists within a school system, by the relationship of the teachers' organization to district management, by the nature of other educational policies and operating programs in the district, and by the very size and structure of the system and its bureaucracy. These variables and others are equally potent at the school level.

Many organizational theorists have advanced the notion that school systems are loosely coupled. That is, they do not conform to the rational-bureaucratic model, which assumes consensus on organizational goals and technologies, tight links between vertical and horizontal functions and actors, frequent inspection of work tasks, and consistent and unambiguous lines of communication and authority (Deal, Meyer and Scott, 1974; March, 1976; Weick, 1976). Weick (1982) goes so far as to suggest that 'the task of educating is simply not the kind of task that can be performed in a tightly coupled system' (p. 674). He argues that it is wrong to treat evidence of loose coupling as the result of improper management or indecisiveness. Because of the nature of teaching work, the diversity of school constituencies, and the changing nature of demands on the educational system, tightly coupled, standardized responses to identified problems may reduce the organization's capability to respond to future needs or problems, and may set in motion actions that conflict with other educational and organizational goals.

This perception is supported by research on the effects of implementing performance-based teacher evaluation processes in local school systems. The results of four case studies of the implementation of performance-based staff layoff policies led Johnson (1980) to conclude that the existence of such policies does not guarantee automatic implementation. Furthermore, unintended consequences at the school site call into question the educational worth of top-down implementation processes, which 'compromise the autonomy of the local school; alter the role of the principal as protector, provider, and instructional leader; jeopardize the cooperative and collegial relations among staff; and diminish the effectiveness of teacher supervision' (p. 216). The inability of principals to adapt teacher evaluation practices to changing supervisory needs, combined with a decrease in the principal's overall autonomy in shaping school programs, seemed to diminish the principals' capacities to serve as advocates and leaders for their staff, programs, and schools. Ironically, the growing body of 'school effects' research suggests that strong leadership from principals is a key component in shaping successful schools (see for example Brookover, 1977). It appears possible that some kinds of tightly coupled teacher evaluation processes may jeopardize the effective functioning of the school organization to the extent that standardization from above inhibits the capacity of the principal for exerting school-level decision-making authority.

Meyer and Rowan (1978) reinforce this view of school operations by suggesting that school organizations must maintain a 'logic of confidence' to survive in a constantly changing, plural environment. They assert that the relative lack of direct inspection of teaching work is a sensible way of buffering the organization from conflicting external demands and from the uncertainties of teacher and pupil performance in educational settings. Standardized evaluation of teachers aimed at accountability purposes may undercut the logic of confidence that binds the school together and permits it to function. Among the propositions they advance to help understand educational organizations are the following:

- The more bureaucratically organized the educational system, the less actual control is exercised over instruction and the more the logic of confidence prevails. In such systems, more control is exercised over formal educational categories and definitions (for example, program definition, staff certification, pupil classification, etc.) than instructional processes.
- Loosely coupled educational organizations respond more effectively to environmental pressures. Instruction adapts more quickly to the informal pressures of parents and the desires of teachers. Programs adapt more quickly to institutional changes in environmental categories.
- Educational organizations respond to external institutional pressures with programmatic or categorical change ... They respond to local changes in teacher or parent preference with activity change ... Each part or level of the system responds relatively independently to its environment. Thus, the greatest part of organizationally planned change in instruction is never really implemented, and the greatest part of change in instruction is not organizationally planned.

If these observations are true, as the body of implementation research suggests they may be, we must ask what change strategies can be effective in such a seemingly confused and confusing milieu. Fortunately, organizational theorists do not stop short of suggesting some approaches that are plausible in loosely coupled, nonconsensual organizations like schools.

The first general area for attention concerns the nature and frequency of communications. Weick (1982) contends that one of the most important jobs of administrators in a loosely coupled system is 'symbol management'; that is, the articulation of general themes and directions 'with eloquence, persistence, and detail' (p. 675). He distinguishes symbols from goals: Symbols tell people what they are doing and why; goals tell people when and how well they are doing it. Because problems, hence goals, change constantly, symbols are the glue that holds the organization together.

> The administrator who manages symbols does not sit in his or her office mouthing clever slogans. Eloquence must be disseminated. And since channels are unpredictable, administrators must get out of the office and spend lots of time one on one — both to remind people of central visions and to assist them in applying these visions to their own activities. The administrator teaches people to interpret what they are doing in a common language. (Weick, 1982 p. 676)

Sproull's (1979) implementation research also directs our attention to the importance of communications and symbol management. The implementation processes that greatly affect policy outcomes include: (a) the processes by which the policy is made visible enough to capture the attention of the organization's members; (b) the processes by which it is made meaningful to the members, that is, how it is understood and interpreted at various levels of the operating system; (c) the processes by which response repertoires (standard operating procedures and practices) are invoked; and (d) the processes by which behavioral directives or guides for action are conveyed from the central office to school sites. Successful implementation processes rely on the existence of cognitive 'consistency-producing mechanisms' that relate the policy to interpretations of the organization's history and current work. Providing that mechanism is the province of the symbol manager.

The importance for teacher evaluation of frequent communication and shared understanding between administrators and teachers is supported in several empirical studies reported by Natriello and Dornbusch (1980–1981). Their findings, like those of other implementation researchers (for example, Cohen, 1976; Deal *et al.* 1974), reflect differences in perception between superordinates and subordinates regarding the frequency and substance of communications. Teachers report that they do not know what the criteria are for teacher evaluation, that they are rarely observed, and that evaluation feedback is scarce, while their principals report just the opposite.[7] More important, frequency of observation and feedback — even negative feedback — is strongly correlated with teacher satisfaction with the evaluation system. Furthermore, teachers are more satisfied with evaluation systems in which they can affect the criteria on which they are judged.

This brings us to the second area of concern: the development of a sense of efficacy among those at whom improvement efforts are directed. Earlier, we reviewed the psychological literature suggesting the importance of self-efficacy for change and the school effects literature suggesting that improved performance actually results from this quality. Theories on the exercise of authority in organizations also suggest that recognition of task complexity and preservation of some autonomy for personnel encourage a sense of self-efficacy (Dornbusch and Scott, 1975; Thompson, Dornbusch and Scott, 1975). In addition, motivation by intrinsic incentives through evaluations that allow self-assessment is more powerful than motivation that relies on external assessment and reward (Deci, 1976; Meyer, 1975).

Finally, the nature of decisionmaking and policy formulation processes, which are closely tied to communications and empowerment, is critical to successful implementation of a teacher evaluation system. These processes involve coalitions of stakeholders interacting to define problems and solutions under conditions of ambiguity (Cohen and March, 1974). Resolving ambiguity by attempts at tight coupling may not necessarily be as productive as indirect change efforts that preserve the ability of smaller units to adapt to local conditions (Deal and Celotti, 1980; March, 1976). As Knapp (1982) comments:

> The process of developing evaluation systems is an occasion for many things in an organization such as the interaction of constituencies, celebration of important values, and the joint recognition of problems. Whether or not performance objectives are met by a specified proportion of a school district's teachers, the *indirect* results of such efforts may have considerable impact on staff enthusiasm, beliefs, or behavior, with ultimate benefits for students. (p. 18)

These propositions lead us to hypothesize four minimal conditions for the successful operation of a teacher evaluation system:

- All actors in the system have a shared understanding of the criteria and processes for teacher evaluation;
- All actors understand how these criteria and processes relate to the dominant symbols of the organization, that is, there is a shared sense that they capture the most important aspects of teaching, that the evaluation system is consonant with educational goals and conceptions of teaching work;

- Teachers perceive that the evaluation procedure enables and motivates them to improve their performance; and principals perceive that the procedure enables them to provide instructional leadership;
- All actors in the system perceive that the evaluation procedure allows them to strike a balance 'between adaptation and adaptability, between stability to handle present demands and flexibility to handle unanticipated demands' (Weick, 1982, p. 674); that is, that the procedure achieves a balance between control and autonomy for the various actors in the system.

Conclusion

Teacher evaluation is an activity that must satisfy competing individual and organizational needs. The imperative of uniform treatment for personnel decisions may result in standardized definitions of acceptable teaching behavior. However, research on teacher performance and teaching effectiveness does not lead to a stable list of measurable teaching behaviors effective in all teaching contexts. Moreover, research on individual and organizational behavior indicates the need for context-specific strategies for improving teaching rather than systemwide hierarchical efforts. If teacher evaluation is to be a useful tool for teacher improvement, the process must strike a careful balance between standardized, centrally administered performance expectations and teacher-specific approaches to evaluation and professional development.

Acknowledgements

This review was prepared as part of a study of teacher evaluation practices sponsored by the National Institute of Education (Contract No. 400–82–0007). The empirical phase and the project will be completed in late 1983.

The authors wish to acknowledge the intellectual fuel and insightful criticism supplied by Milbrey McLaughlin and Rich Shavelson of the Rand Corporation at early stages of the chapter's development. The project is advised by a Stakeholder's Panel whose members contributed useful comments on the first draft. However, the chapter does not necessarily reflect the views of the panel, the National Institute of Education, or the Rand Corporation.

Notes

1 Direct instruction as we discuss it here is by no means the only way to increase academic learning time. Other school policies (for example, longer school days,

fewer interruptions, different curriculum and program requirements) and teaching practices are equally plausible means for pursuing this objective. However, the literature generally treats these two as companion concepts, and so we treat them here, though we observe that their marriage in the literature may be the result of the researchers' focus on teacher behavior, rather than on the total context of the classroom.

2 The congruence between what is taught and what is tested may, of course, contribute to the apparent success of direct instruction.

3 However, high-inference, global ratings that rely on patterns of overall teacher behavior are somewhat more stable than other measures (Shavelson and Dempsey-Atwood, 1976).

4 This test should not be confused with Georgia's Teacher Performance Assessment Instrument, which assesses actual teaching performance of a teacher and is necessary for recertification.

5 We use the word 'model' here because it is widely used in the field; we do not use it either in a judgmental sense or in the social science sense of a theoretically based exposition of interrelated assumptions.

6 Gudridge reported that the Manatt model has been used in five districts in Iowa and Illinois (Gudridge, 1980, p. 42). Between 1975 and 1980, Redfern assisted sixteen school districts across the country to develop an 'MBO' program (Redfern, 1980, pp. 159–61).

7 A principal may engage in evaluation behavior a great deal of the time; that behavior will be visible to a given teacher only a fraction of the time.

References

ALEAMONI, L.M. (1981) 'Student ratings of instruction' in MILLMAN, J. (Ed.) *Handbook of Teacher Evaluation*, Beverly Hills, Calif., Sage.

ANDERSON, B.D. (1973) 'School bureaucratization and alienation from high school', *Sociology of Education*, 46, 2, pp. 315–34.

ANDERSON, C.S. (1982) 'The search for school climate: A review of the research', *Review of Educational Research*, 52, 3, pp. 368–420.

ARMOR, D., CONRY-OSEGUERA, P., COX, M., KING, N., McDONNELL, L., PASCAL, A., PAULY, E. and ZELLMAN, G., (1976) *Analysis of the School Preferred Reading Program in Selected Los Angeles Minority Schools*, R-2007-LAUSD, Santa Monica, Calif., The Rand Corporation.

BACHARACH, S. and AIKEN, M. (1979) 'The impact of alienation, meaninglessness, and meritocracy on supervisor and subordinate satisfaction, *Social Forces*, 57, pp. 853–71.

BANDURA, A. (1982) 'Self-efficacy mechanism in human agency', *American Psychologist*, 37, 2, pp. 122–47.

BANDURA, A. and SCHUNK, D.H. (1981) 'Cultivating competence, self-efficacy, and intrinsic interest through proximal self-motivation', *Journal of Personality and Social Psychology*, 41, pp. 586–98.

BANDURA, A., ADAMS, N.E., HARDY, A.B. and HOWELLS, G.N. (1980) 'Tests of the generality of self-efficacy theory', *Cognitive Therapy and Research*, 4, pp. 39–66.

BEKHAM, J.C. (1981) *Legal Aspects of Teacher Evaluation*, Topeka, Kans, National Organization on Legal Problems of Education.

BELL, A.E., SIPURSKY, M.A. and SWITZER, F. (1976) 'Informal or open-area education in relation to achievement and personality', *British Journal of Educational Psychology*, 46, pp. 235–43.

BERLINER, D.C. (1982) 'The Executive Functions of Teaching', paper presented at the Annual Meeting of the American Educational Research Association, New York, March.

BERLINER, D.C. (1977) *Instructional Time in Research on Research on Teaching*, San Francisco, Far West Laboratory for Educational Research and Development.

BERMAN, P. and McLAUGHLIN, M.W. (1973–78) *Federal Programs Supporting Educational Change*, R-1589-HEW, Santa Monica, Calif., The Rand Corporation.

BERMAN, P. and McLAUGHLIN, M.W. (1977) *Federal Programs Supporting Educational Change, Vol. 7: Factors affecting implementation and continuation*, Santa Monica, Calif., The Rand Corporation.

BETZ, N.E. and HACKETT, G. (1981) 'The relationships of career-related self-efficacy expectations to perceived career options in college women and men, *Journal of Counseling Psychology*, 28, pp. 399–410.

BIDWELL, C.E. (1965) 'The school as a formal organization' in MARCH, J.G. (Ed.) *Handbook of Organizations*, Chicago, Rand McNally.

BODINE, R. (1973) 'Teachers' self-assessment' in HOUSE, E.R. (Ed.) *School Evaluation*, Berkeley, Calif., McCutchan.

BROOKOVER, W. (1977) *Schools Can Make a Difference*, East Lansing, College of Urban Development, Michigan State University.

BROPHY, J.E. (1973) 'Stability of teacher effectiveness', *American Educational Research Journal*, 10, pp. 245–52.

BROPHY, J.E. and EVERTSON, C.M. (1976) *Learning from Teaching: A Developmental Perspective*, Boston, Allyn and Bacon.

BROPHY, J.E. and EVERTSON, C. (1974) *Process-product Correlations in the Texas Teacher Effectiveness Study: Final Report*, Austin, Texas, Research and Development Center for Teacher Education.

BROPHY, J.E. and EVERTSON, C.M. (1977) 'Teacher behavior and student learning in second and third grades', in BORICH, G.D. (Ed.) *The Appraisal of Teaching: Concepts and Process*, Reading, Mass, Addison-Wesley.

BROUDY, H.S. (1956) 'Teaching — craft or profession?', *The Educational Forum*, January pp. 175–84.

BROWN, I.Jr. and INOUYE, D.K. (1978) 'Learned helplessness through modeling: The role of perceived similarity in competence', *Journal of Personality and Social Psychology*, 36, pp. 900–8.

BRUNER, J.S. (1976) 'Foreword' in BENNETT, N., JORDAN, J., LONG, G. and WADE, B. (Eds) *Teaching Styles and Pupil Progress*, Cambridge, Mass, Harvard University Press.

BUSH, R.N. (1979) 'Implications of the BTES', *The Generator*, 9, 1, pp. 13–15.

BUSHMAN, J.H. (1974) 'Are teachers playing "statue' in the classroom?" *NASSP Bulletin*, 58, p. 386.

CENTRA, J.A. and POTTER, D.A. (1980) 'School and teacher effects: An interrelational model', *Review of Educational Research*, 50, 2, pp. 273–91.

CHEN, H. and ROSSI, P.H. (1980) 'The multi-goal, theory-driven approach to evaluation: A model linking basic and applied social sciences', *Social Forces*, 59, 1, pp. 106–22.

COHEN, E. (1976) *Organization and Instruction in Elementary Schools*, Stanford, Calif., Stanford Center for Research and Development in Teaching.

COHEN, M. and MARCH, J. (1974) *Leadership and Ambiguity: The American College President*, New York, McGraw Hill.

COKER, H., MEDLEY, D. and SOAR, R. (1980) 'How valid are expert opinions about effective teaching?', *Phi Delta Kappan*, 62, 2, pp. 131–4 and 149.

COLEMAN, J., CAMPBELL, E.A., HOBSON, C.J., McPARTLAND, J., MOOD, A., WEINFELD, F.D. and YORK, R.L. (1966) *Equality of Education Opportunity*, Washington, DC, US Government Printing Office.

COLLINS, J. (1982) *Self-efficacy and Ability in Achievement Behavior*, unpublished doctoral dissertation, Stanford University.

CORWIN, R.G. (1974) 'Models of educational organizations' in KERLINGER, F.N. *Review of Research in Education Vol. 2*, Itasca, Ill., F.E. PEACOCK.

CRONBACH, L.J. 'Beyond the two disciplines of scientific psychology', *American Psychologist*, 30, pp. 116–27.

CRONBACH, L.J. and SNOW, R.E. (1977) *Aptitudes and Instructional Methods: A Handbook for Research on Interactions*, New York, Irvington.

DARLING-HAMMOND, L. and WISE, A.E. (1981) *A Conceptual Framework for Examining Teachers' Views of Teaching and Educational Policies*, N-1668-FF, Santa Monica, Calif., The Rand Corporation.

DEAL, T.E. and CELOTTI, L.D. (1980) 'How much influence do (and can) educational administration have on classrooms?', *Phi Delta Kappan*, 61, 7, pp. 471–3.

DEAL, T., MEYER, J. and SCOTT, R. (1974) 'Organizational support for innovative instructional programs: district and school levels', paper presented at the Annual Meeting of the American Educational Research Association, Chicago, April.

DECI, E.L. (1976) 'The hidden costs of rewards', *Organizational Dynamics*, 4, 3, pp. 61–72.

DiCLEMENTE, C.C. (1981) 'Self-efficacy and smoking cessation maintenance: A preliminary report', *Cognitive Therapy and Research*, 5, pp. 175–87.

DORNBUSCH, S.M. and SCOTT, W.R. (1975) *Evaluation and the Exercise of Authority*, San Francisco, Jossey-Bass.

DOYLE, W. (1978) 'Paradigms for research on teacher effectiveness' in SHULMAN, L.S. (Ed.) *Review of Research in Education*, Vol. 5, Itasca, Ill., F.E. PEACOCK.

DOYLE, W. (1979) 'Classroom tasks and students' abilities' in PETERSON, P.L. and WALBERG, H.J. (Eds) *Research on Teaching*, Berkeley, Calif., McCutchan.

DuBOIS, D.W. (1980) 'Teacher evaluation: the Salem public schools model', *OSSC Bulletin*, 24, 3.

DUNKIN, M.J. and BIDDLE, B.J. (1974) *The Study of Teaching*, New York, Holt, Rinehart and Winston.

EISNER, E.W. (1978) 'On the uses of educational connoisseurship and criticism for evaluating classroom life', *Teachers College Record*, 78, pp. 345–58.

EISNER, E.W. and VALLANCE, E. (1974) 'Five conceptions of curriculum: Their roots and implications for curriculum planning' in EISNER, E.W. and VALLANCE, E. (Eds) *Conflicting Conceptions of Curriculum*, Berkeley, Calif., McCutchan.

ELLETT, C.D., CAPIE, W. and JOHNSON, C.E. (1980) 'Assessing teaching performance', *Educational Leadership*, 38, 3, pp. 219–20.

ELMORE, R.T. (1979) *Complexity and Control: What Legislators and Administrators Can Do About Implementation*, Seattle, Wash, Institute of Governmental Research.

ENGLERT, R.M. KEAN, M.H. and SCRIBNER, J.D. (1977) 'Politics of program evaluation in large city school districts', *Education and Urban Society*, 9, pp. 425–50.

EVERTSON, C.M. and BROPHY, J.E. (1973) *High Inference Behavioral Ratings and Correlates of Teaching Effectiveness*, Austin, Tex, Research and Development Center for Teacher Education, University of Texas.

EVERTSON, C.M. and HOLLEY, F.M. (1981) 'Classroom observation' in MILLMAN, J. (Ed.) *Handbook of Teacher Evaluation*, Beverly Hills, Calif., Sage.

FELDVEBEL, A.M. (1980) 'Teacher evaluation: Ingredients of a credible model', *Clearing House*, 53, 9, pp. 415–20.

FENSTERMACHER, G.D. and BERLINER, D.C. (in press) *On Determining the Value of Staff Development*, Santa Monica, Calif., The Rand Corporation.

FENSTERMACHER, G.D. (1978) 'A philosophical consideration of recent research on teacher effectiveness' in SHULMAN, L.S. (Ed.) *Review of Research in Education*, Vol. 6, Itasca, Ill., F.E. Peacock.

FISHER, C.W., FILBY, N. MARLIAVE, R., CAHEN, L., DISHAW, M., MOORE, J. and BERLINER, D. (1978) *Teaching Behaviors, Academic Learning Time and Student Achievement: Final Report of Phase III-B, Beginning Teacher Evaluation Study*, San Francisco, Far West Laboratory for Educational Research and Development.

FLANDERS, N.A. (1970) *Analyzing Teacher Behavior*, Reading, Mass, Addison-Wesley.

FLODEN, R.E. and FEIMAN, S. (1981) *A Consumer's Guide to Teacher Development*, East Lansing, Mich., Institute for Research on Teaching, Michigan State University.

FLODEN, R.E. and WINER, S.S. (1978) 'Rationality to ritual: The multiple roles of evaluation in governmental process', *Policy Sciences*, 9, pp. 9–18.

FRENCH, J.JR. and RAVEN, B. (1977) 'The bases of social power' in STRAW, B. (Ed.) *Psychological Foundations of Organizational Behavior*, Santa Monica, Calif., Goodyear.

FULLER, B., WOOD, K., RAPOPORT, T. and DORNBUSCH, S.M. (1982) 'The organizational context of individual efficacy', *Review of Educational Research*, 52, 1, pp. 7–30.

GAGE, N.L. (1963) 'Paradigms for research on teaching' in GAGE, N.L. (Ed.) *Handbook for Research on Teaching*, Chicago, Rand McNally.

GAGE, N.L. (1978) *The Scientific Basis of the Art of Teaching*, New York, Teachers College Press.

GALLUP, G.H. (1979) 'The eleventh annual Gallup poll of the public's attitudes toward the public schools', *Phi Delta Kappan*, 60, pp. 33–45.

GARAWSKI, R.A. (1980) 'The eleventh annual Gallup poll of the public's attitudes toward the public schools', *Phi Delta Kappan*, 60, pp. 33–45.

GLASS, G.V., COULTER, D., HARTLEY, S., HEAROLD, S., KAHL, S., KALK, J. and SHERRETZ, L. (1977) *Teacher 'Indirectness' and Pupil Achievement: An Integration of Findings*, Boulder, Col, Laboratory of Educational Research, University of Colorado.

GOOD, T.L. and POWER, C.N. (1976) 'Designing successful classroom environments for different types of students', *Journal of Curriculum Studies*, 8, 1, pp. 45–60.

GUDRIDGE, B.M. (1980) *Teacher Competency: Problems and Solutions*, Arlington, Va, American Association of School Administrators.

GUTHRIE, J. (1970) 'Survey of school effectiveness studies', in MOOD, A. (Ed.) *Do Teachers Make a Difference?*, Washington DC, US Government Printing Office.

HAEFELE, D.L. (1980) 'How to evaluate thee, teacher — let me count the ways', *Phi Delta Kappan*, 61, 5, pp. 349–52.

HAEFELE, D.L. (1981) 'Teacher Interviews' in MILLMAN, J. (Ed.) *Handbook of Teacher Evaluations*, Beverly Hills, Calif., Sage.

HARRIS, W.U. (1981) 'Teacher command of subject matter' in MILLMAN, J. (Ed.) *Handbook of Teacher Evaluations*, Beverly Hills, Calif., Sage.

HATHAWAY, W.E. (1980) 'Testing teachers', *Educational Leadership*, 38, 3, pp. 210–15.

HORWITZ, R.A. (1979) 'Effects of the "open classroom"' in WALBERG, H.J. (Ed.) *Educational Environments and Effects: Evaluation, Policy and Productivity*, Berkeley, Calif., McCutchan.

IWANICKI, E.F. (1981) 'Contract plans: A professional growth-oriented approach to evaluating teacher performance' in MILLMAN, J. (Ed.) *Handbook of Teacher Evaluation*, Beverly Hills, Calif., Sage.

JOHNSON, S.M. (1980) 'Performance-based staff layoffs in the public schools: Implementation and outcomes', *Harvard Educational Review*, 50, 2, pp. 214–33.

JOYCE, B.R. and WEIL, M. (1982) *Models of Teaching*, Englewood Cliffs, NJ, Prentice Hall.

KAZDIN, A.E. (1979) 'Imagery elaboration and self-efficacy in the covert modeling treatment of unassertive behavior', *Journal of Consulting and Clinical Psychology*, 47, pp. 725–33.

KING, J.A. (1981) 'Beyond classroom walls: Indirect measures of teacher competence' in MILLMAN, J. (Ed.) *Handbook of Teacher Evaluation*, Beverly Hills, Calif., Sage.

KLEINE, P.E. and WISNIEWSKI, R. (1981) 'Bill 1706: A forward step for Oklahoma', *Phi Delta Kappan*, 63, 2, pp. 115–17.

KNAPP, M.S. (1982) *Toward the Study of Teacher Evaluation as an Organizational Process: A Review of Current Research and Practice*, Menlo Park, Calif., Educational and Human Services Research Center, SRI International.

LAWLER, E. (1973) *Motivation in Work Organizations*, Monterey, Calif., Brooks-Cole.

LEWIN, K. (1938) *The Conceptual Representation and the Measurement of Psychological Forces*, Durham, N.C., Duke University Press.

LEWIN, K., DEMBO, T., FESTINGER, L. and SEARS, P. (1944) 'Level of aspiration' in HUNT, J. (Ed.) *Personality and Behavioral Disorders*, Vol. 2, New York, Ronald Press.

LEWIS, A. (1982) *Evaluating Educational Personnel*, Arlington, Va, American Association of School Administrators.

LEWIS, D.M. (1979) 'Certifying functional literacy: Competency testing and implications for due process and equal educational opportunity', *Journal of Law and Education*, 8, 2, p. 145.

LIPSKY, M. (1976) 'Toward a theory of street-level bureaucracy' in HAWLEY, W. and LIPSKY, M. (Eds) *Theoretical Perspectives on Urban Politics*, Englewood Cliffs, NJ, Prentice Hall.

LIPSKY, M. (1980) *Street-level Bureaucracy*, New York, Russell Sage.

LORTIE, D. (1975) *Schoolteacher*, Chicago, University of Chicago Press.

McDONALD, F.J. (1976) *Summary Report: Beginning Teacher Evaluation Study*, Phase II, Princeton, NJ, Educational Testing Service.

McDONALD, F.J. and ELIAS, P. (1976) *Executive Summary Report: Beginning Teacher Evaluation Study, Phase II*, Princeton, NJ, Educational Testing Service.

McDONNELL, L. and PASCAL, A. (1979) *Organized Teachers in American Schools*, R-2407-NIE, Santa Monica, Calif., The Rand Corporation.

McKEACHIE, W.J. and KULIK, J.A. (1975) 'Effective college teaching' in KERLINGER, F.N. (Ed.) *Review of Research in Education*, Vol. 3, Itasca, Ill., F.E. Peacock.

McKENNA (1981) 'Context/environment effects in teacher evaluation' in MILLMAN, J. (Ed.) *Handbook on Teacher Evaluation*, Beverly Hills, Calif., Sage.

McNEIL, J.D. (1981) 'The politics of teacher evaluation' in MILLMAN, J. (Ed.) *Handbook of Teacher Evaluation*, Beverly Hills, Calif., Sage.

McNEIL, J. and POPHAM, W. (1973) 'The assessment of teacher competence' in TRAVERS, R.M. (Ed.) *Second Handbook of Research on Teaching*, Chicago, Rand McNally.

MANATT, R.P., PALMER, K.L. and HIDLEBAUGH, E. (1976) 'Evaluating teacher performance with improved rating scales', *NASSP Bulletin*, 60, 401, pp. 21–3.

MANN, D. (Ed.) (1978) *Making Change Happen?*, New York, Teachers College Press.

MARCH, J.G. (1976) 'The technology of foolishness' in MARCH, J.G. and OLSEN, J.P. (Eds) *Ambiguity and Choice in Organizations*, Bergen, Norway, Universitetsforlaget.

MEDLEY, D.M. (1979) 'The effectiveness of teachers' in PETERSON, P.L. and WALBERG, H.J. (Eds) *Research on Teaching*, Berkeley, Calif, McCutchan.

MEDLEY, D.M. (1982) *Teacher Competency Testing and the Teacher Educator*, Charlottesville, Virginia, Association of Teacher Educators and the Bureau of Educational Research, University of Virginia.

MEYER, H.H. (1975) 'The pay-for-performance dillemma' *Organizational Dynamics*, 3, 3, pp. 39–50.

MEYER, J. and ROWAN, B. (1978) 'Structure of educational organizations', in MEYER, M.W. (Ed.) *Environments and Organizations*, San Francisco, Jossey-Bass.

MILLMAN, J. (Ed.) (1981a) *Handbook of Teacher Evaluation*, Beverly Hills, Calif., Sage.

MILLMAN, J. (1981b) 'Student achievement as a measure of teacher competence' in MILLMAN, J, (Eds) *Handbook of Teacher Evaluation*, Beverly Hills, Calif., Sage.

MILSTEIN, M.M. (Ed.) (1980) *Schools, Conflict and Change*, New York, Teachers College Press.

MITCHELL, D.E. and KERCHNER, C.T. (1983) 'Collective bargaining and teacher policy' in SHULMAN, L.S. and SYKES, G. (Eds) *Handbook of Teaching and Policy*, New York, Longman.

MOBLEY, W., GRIFFETH, W. HAND, H. and MEGLINO, B. (1979) 'Review and conceptual analysis of the employee turnover process', *Psychological Bulletin*, 86, 3, pp. 493–522.

MUNNELLY, R.J. (1979) 'Dealing with teacher incompetence: Supervision and evaluation in a due process framework', *Contemporary Education*, 50, 4, pp. 221–5.

National Education Association (1979) *Teacher Opinion Poll*, Washington, DC, National Education Association.

NATRIELLO, G. and DORNBUSCH, S.M. (1980–81) 'Pitfalls in the evaluation of teachers by principals', *Administrator's Notebook*, 29, 6.

NATRIELLO, G., HOAG., M., DEAL., T.E. and DORNBUSCH, S.M. (1977) *A Summary of the Recent Literature on the Evaluation of Principals, Teachers, and Students*, occasional paper no. 18, Stanford, Calif., Stanford Center for R & D in Teaching, Stanford University.

ORNSTEIN, A.C. and LEVINE, D.V. (1981) 'Teacher behavior research: Overview and outlook', *Phi Delta Kappan*, 62, 8, pp. 592–6.

OUCHI, W.G. (1980) 'Markets, bureaucracies, and clans', *Administrative Science Quarterly*, 25, 1, pp. 129–41.

PETERSON, K. and KAUCHAK, D. (1982) *Teacher Evaluation: Perspectives, Practices and Promises*, Salt Lake City, Utah, Center for Educational Practice, University of Utah.

PETERSON, P.L. (1976) *Interactive Effects of Student Anxiety, Achievement Orientation, and Teacher Behavior on Student Achievement and Attitude*, unpublished doctoral dissertation, Stanford University.

PETERSON, P.L. (1979) 'Direct instruction reconsidered' in PETERSON, P.L. and WALBERG, H.J. (Eds) *Research on Teaching*, Berkeley, Calif., McCutchan.

PFEFFER, J., SALANCIK, G. and LEBLEBICI, H. (1976) 'The effect of uncertainty on the use of social influence in organizational decision making', *Administrative Science Quarterly*, 21, 2, pp. 227–48.

QUIRK, T.J., WITTEN, B.J. and WEINBERG, S.F. (1973) 'Review of studies of the concurrent and predictive validity of the National Teacher Examination', *Review of Educational Research*, 43, pp. 89–114.

REDFERN, G.B. (1980) *Evaluating Teachers and Administrators: A Performance Objectives Approach*, Boulder, Colo, Westview Press.

REIN, M. (1976) *Social Science and Public Policy*, New York, Penguin Books.

RILEY, R.D. and SCHAFFER, E.C. (1979) 'Self-certification: Accounting to oneself', *Journal of Teacher Education*, 30, 2, pp. 23–6.

ROHR, G. (1976) 'Results on standardized achievement tests for students in grades 3 and 6: A comparative study of some open-plan schools and traditionally built schools in Malmo', *Didakometry and Sociometry*, 8, 1, p. 12.

ROSENHOLTZ, S.J. and WILSON, B. (1980) 'The effect of classroom structure on shared perceptions of ability', *American Educational Research Journal*, 17, pp. 75–82.

ROSENSHINE, B. (1970) 'The stability of teacher effects upon student achievement', *Review of Educational Research*, 40, pp. 647–62.

ROSENSHINE, B. (1977) 'Review of teaching variables and student achievement' in BORICH, G.D. (Ed.) *The Appraisal of Teaching: Concepts and Process*, Reading, Mass, Addison-Wesley.

ROSENSHINE, B.V. (1979) 'Content, time, and director instruction' in PETERSON, P.L.

and WALBERG, H.H. (Eds) *Research on Teaching*, Berkeley, Calif., McCutchan.

ROSENSHINE, B. and FURST, N. (1971) 'Research on teacher performance criteria' in SMITH, B.O. (Ed.) *Research in Teacher Education: A Symposium*, Englewood Cliffs, NJ, Prentice Hall.

ROSSI, P.H., FREEMAN, H.E. and WRIGHT, S.R. (1979) *Evaluation: A Systematic Approach*, Beverly Hills, Calif., Sage.

RUTTER, M., MAUGHAN, B., MORTIMORE, P., OUSTON, J., and SMITH, A. (1979) *Fifteen Thousand Hours: Secondary Schools and Their Effects on Children*, Cambridge, Mass, Harvard University Press.

SABATIER, P. and MAXMANIAN, D. (1979) *The Implementation of Regulatory Policy: A Framework of Analysis*, Davis, Calif., Institute of Governmental Affairs.

SCHALOCK, D. (1979) 'Research on teacher selection' in BERLINER, D.C. (Ed.) *Review of Research in Education*, Vol. 7, Washington, DC, American Educational Research Association.

SELZNICK, P. (1966) *TVA and the Grass Roots*, New York, Harper and Row.

SHAVELSON, R. (1973) 'What is the basic teaching skill?', *Journal of Teacher Education*, 14, pp. 144–51.

SHAVELSON, R. and DEMPSEY-ATWOOD, N. (1976) 'Generalizability of measures of teacher behavior', *Review of Educational Research*, 46, pp. 553–612.

SHAVELSON, R. and RUSSO, N.A. (1977) 'Generalizability of measures of teacher effectiveness', *Educational Research*, 19, 3, pp. 171–83.

SHAVELSON, R. and STERN, P. (1981) 'Research on teachers' pedagogical thoughts, judgments, decisions and behavior', *Review of Educational Research*, 51, 4, pp. 455–98.

SHINE, W.A. and GOLDMAN, N. (1980) reply to Fred G. Burke, *Educational Leadership*, 38, 3, p. 201.

SOAR, R.S. (1972) *Follow Through Classroom Process Measurement and Pupil Growth*, Gainesville, Flo, Institute for Development of Human Resources, University of Florida.

SOAR, R.S. (1977) 'An integration of findings from four studies on teacher effectiveness' in BORICH, G.D. (Ed.) *The Appraisal of Teaching: Concepts and Process*, Reading, Mass, Addison-Wesley.

SOAR, R.S. and SOAR, R.M. (1976) 'An attempt to identify measures of teacher effectiveness from four studies', *Journal of Teacher Education*, 27, pp. 261–7.

Southern Regional Education Board (1979) *Teacher Education and Certification: State Actions in the South*, Atlanta, Georgia, Southern Regional Education Board.

SPROULL, L.S. (1979) *Response to Regulation: An Organizational Process Framework*, Pittsburgh, Pa, Carnegie-Mellon University.

SROUFE, G.E. (1977) 'Evaluation and politics' in SCRIBNER, J. (Ed.) *The Politics of Education*, Chicago, University of Chicago Press.

STALLINGS, J.A. (1977) 'How instructional processes relate to child outcomes' in BORICH, G.D. (Ed.) *The Appraisal of Teaching: Concepts and Process*, Reading Mass, Addison-Wesley.

STEPHENS, J.M. (1976) *The Process of Schooling*, New York, Holt, Rinehart and Winston.

STIGGINS, R.J. and BRIDGEFORD, N.J. (1982) *Performance Assessment for Teacher Development*, Portland, Ore, Center for Performance Assessment.

STONE, C.N. (1980) 'The implementation of social programs: Two perspectives', *Journal of Social Issues*, 36, 4, pp. 13–34.

STRIKE, K. and BULL, B. (1981) 'Fairness and the legal context of teacher evaluation' in MILLMAN, J. (Ed.) *Handbook of Teacher Evaluation*, Beverly Hills, Calif., Sage.

TALBERT, J. (1980) *School Organization and Institutional Changes: Exchange and Power in Loosely-Coupled Systems*, Stanford, Calif., Institute for Research on Educational Finance and Governance, Stanford University.

THOMAS, M.D. (1979) *Evaluation of Educational Personnel*, Bloomington, Ill., Phi Delta Kappa Educational Foundation.

THOMPSON, J.E., DORNBUSCH, S.M. and SCOTT, W.R. (1975) *Failures of Communication in the Evaluation of Teachers by Principals*, no. 43, Stanford, Calif., Stanford Center for Research and Development in Teaching.

TRAUB, R., WEISS, J., FISHER, C., USELLA, D. and KHAN, S. (1973) *Openness in Schools: An Evaluation of the Wentworth County Roman Catholic School Board Schools*, Toronto, Ont., Educational Evaluation Center, Ontario Institute for Studies in Education.

VELDMAN, D.J. and BROPHY, J.E. (1974) 'Measuring teacher effects on pupil achievement', *Journal of Educational Psychology*, 66, pp. 319–24.

VLAANDEREN, R. (1980) *Trends in Competency-based Teacher Certification*, Denver, Colo, Education Commission of the States.

VROOM, V. (1964) *Work and Motivation*, New York, Wiley.

WARD, W.D. and BARCHER, P.R. (1975) 'Reading achievement and creativity as related to open classroom experience', *Journal of Educational Psychology*, 67, pp. 683–91.

WEATHERLEY, R. and LIPSKY, M. (1977) 'Street-level bureaucrats and institutional innovation: Implementating special education reform', *Harvard Educational Review*, 47, 2, pp.171–97.

WEICK, K.E. (1976) 'Educational organizations as loosely-coupled systems', *Adminstrative Science, Quarterly*, 21, pp. 1–19.

WEICK, K.E. (1982) 'Administering education in loosely coupled schools', *Phi Delta Kappan*, 63, 10, pp. 673–6.

WILDAVSKY, A. (1980) *Speaking Truth to Power: The Art and Craft of Policy Analysis*, Boston, Little, Brown and Company.

WILEY, D.E. and HARNISCHFEGER, A. (1974) 'Explosion of a myth: Quantity of schooling and exposure to instruction, major educational vehicles', *Educational Researcher*, 3, pp. 7–12.

WISE, A.E. (1979) *Legislated Learning*, Berkeley, University of California Press.

WRIGHT, R.J. (1975) 'The affective and cognitive consequences of an open education elementary school', *American Educational Research Journal*, 12, pp. 449–568.

Contributors

Linda Darling-Hammond is a social scientist with the Rand Corporation and specializes in educational policy analysis, law and governance of education and research into teaching.

Eleanor Farrar is Senior Research Associate at the Huron Research Institute and specializes in the study of the implementation of federal programs.

Ernest House is Professor of Administration, Higher and Continuing Education, and Educational Psychology in the Center for Instructional Research and Curriculum Evaluation at the University of Illinois at Urbana, USA.

Stephen Kemmis is Associate Professor of Curriculum Studies at Deakin University, Victoria, Australia. He specializes in educational research and evaluation methodology.

Gill Kirkup is a Lecturer at the Institute of Educational Technology at the Open University, UK, and specializes in course development and evaluation and particularly in women's studies.

David Nevo is a Senior Lecturer in the School of Education at Tel-Aviv University in Israel. He specializes in evaluation theory, educational measurement and research.

Sara Pease is a Research Assistant with the Rand Corporation specializing in domestic federal policy, legal and regulatory analysis.

Michael Scriven is Professor of Education at the University of Western Australia.

Robert Stake is Professor of Educational Psychology in the Center for Instructional Research and Curriculum Evaluation at the University of Illinois at Urbana, Illinois.

Rob Walker spent many years at the Centre for Applied Educational Research and the University of East Anglia, UK, and is now at Deakin University, Victoria, Australia. He specializes in evaluation studies.

Carol Weiss is Senior Lecturer at the Harvard Graduate School of Education and specializes in evaluation theory and practice. She was winner of the Evaluation Research Society's Myrdal Award for Science

Arthur Wise is a Senior Social Scientist with the Rand Corporation specializing in educational policy analysis, law and governance of education and research on teaching.

Index